MUIRHEAD LIBRARY OF PHILOSOPHY

An admirable statement of the aims of the Library of Philosophy
was provided by the first editor, the late Professor J. M. Muirhead,
in his description of the original programme printed in Erdmann's
History of Philosophy under the date 1890. This was slightly
modified in subsequent volumes to take the form of the following
statement:

'The Muirhead Library of Philosophy was designed as a contribution to the History of Modern Philosophy under the heads:
first of Different Schools of Thought—Sensationalist, Realist,
Idealist, Intuitivist; secondly of different Subjects—Psychology,
Ethics, Political Philosophy, Theology. While much had been
done in England in tracing the course of evolution in nature,
history, economics, morals and religion, little had been done in
tracing the development of thought on these subjects. Yet "the
evolution of opinion is part of the whole evolution".

'By the co-operation of different writers in carrying out this plan
it was hoped that a thoroughness and completeness of treatment,
otherwise unattainable, might be secured. It was believed also
that from writers mainly British and American fuller consideration
of English Philosophy than it had hitherto received might be
looked for. In the earlier series of books containing, among others,
Bosanquet's *History of Aesthetic*, Pfleiderer's *Rational Theology
since Kant*, Albee's *History of English Utilitarianism*, Bonar's
Philosophy and Political Economy, Brett's *History of Psychology*,
Ritchie's *Natural Rights*, these objects were to a large extent
effected.

'In the meantime original work of a high order was being produced both in England and America by such writers as Bradley,
Stout, Bertrand Russell, Baldwin, Urban, Montague, and others,
and a new interest in foreign works, German, French and Italian,
which had either become classical or were attracting public attention, had developed. The scope of the Library thus became extended into something more international, and it is entering on the
fifth decade of its existence in the hope that it may contribute to
the mutual understanding between countries which is so pressing
a need of the present time.'

The need which Professor Muirhead stressed is no less pressing
today, and few will deny that philosophy has much to do with
enabling us to meet it, although no one, least of all Muirhead

himself, would regard that as the sole, or even the main, object of philosophy. As Professor Muirhead continues to lend the distinction of his name to the Library of Philosophy it seemed not inappropriate to allow him to recall us to these aims in his own words. The emphasis on the history of thought also seemed to me very timely; and the number of important works promised for the Library in the very near future augur well for the continued fulfilment, in this and other ways, of the expectations of the original editor.

H. D. LEWIS

MUIRHEAD LIBRARY OF PHILOSOPHY

General Editor: H. D. Lewis

Professor of History and Philosophy of Religion in the University of London

Action by SIR MALCOLM KNOX
The Analysis of Mind by BERTRAND RUSSELL
Brett's History of Psychology edited by R. S. PETERS
Clarity is Not Enough by H. D. LEWIS
Coleride as a Philosopher by J. H. MUIRHEAD
The Commonplace Book of G. E. Moore edited by C. LEWY
Contempory American Philosophy edited by G. P. ADAMS and W. P. MONTAGUE
Contemporary British Philosophy first and second Series edited by J. H. MUIRHEAD
Contemporary British Philosophy third Series edited by H. D. LEWIS
Contemporary Indian Philosophy edited by RADHAKRISHNAN and J. H. MUIRHEAD 2nd edition
Contemporary Philosophy in Australia by ROBERT BROWN and C. D. ROLLINS
The Discipline of the Cave by J. N. FINDLAY
Doctrine and Argument in Indian Philosophy by NINIAN SMART
Essays in Analysis by ALICE AMBROSE
Ethics by NICOLAI HARTMANN translated by STANTON COIT 3 vols
The Foundations of Metaphysics in Science by ERROL E. HARRIS
Freedom and History by H. D. LEWIS
The Good Will: A Study in the Coherence Theory of Goodness by H. J. PATON
Hegel: A Re-examination by J. N. FINDLAY
Hegel's Science of Logic translated by W. H. JOHNSTON and L. G. STRUTHERS 2 vols
Hegel's Science of Logic translated by A. V. MILLER
History of Aesthetic by B. BOSANQUET 2nd edition
History of English Utilitarianism by E. ALBEE
History of Psychology by G. S. BRETT edited by R. S. PETERS abridged one volume edition 2nd edition
Human Knowledge by BERTRAND RUSSELL
A Hundred Years of British Philosophy by RUDOLF METZ translated by J. H. HARVEY, T. E. JESSOP, HENRY STURT
Ideas: A General Introduction to Pure Phenomenology by EDMUND HUSSERL translated by W. R. BOYCE GIBSON
Identity and Reality by EMILE MEYERSON
Imagination by E. J. FURLONG
Indian Philosophy by RADHAKRISHNAN 2 vols revised 2nd edition

Muirhead Library of Philosophy

EDITED BY H. D. LEWIS

ASCENT TO THE ABSOLUTE

ASCENT TO
THE ABSOLUTE

METAPHYSICAL PAPERS AND LECTURES

J. N. FINDLAY
M.A., PH.D., F.B.A.
Clark Professor of Metaphysics
Yale University

LONDON · GEORGE ALLEN & UNWIN LTD
NEW YORK · HUMANITIES PRESS

FIRST PUBLISHED IN 1970

© *George Allen and Unwin Ltd* 1970
BRITISH ISBN 004 111003 X
US SBN 391 00073 X

PRINTED IN GREAT BRITAIN BY
ALDEN & MOWBRAY LTD
AT THE ALDEN PRESS, OXFORD

TO MY WIFE

WHO

THOUGH NOT A NECESSARY BEING

REMAINS

NECESSARY TO ME

PREFACE

The lectures and papers in the present collection, of which some
have not been previously published, were all written over the last
decade. All are concerned, either with the nature of metaphysics
in general, or with the more special topic of 'Absolute-theory', by
which is meant the theory of an intrinsically necessary, all-
explanatory existent. From having (in 1948) constructed an
argument designed to disprove the existence of an Absolute
Being, I have moved to a position where, by a change of attitude
to a single premiss, the disproof has swung over into something
that may, if it betrays no inward, logical flaw, converge towards a
proof. An Absolute is the sort of thing that can be shown *not* to
exist (if it can be shown not to exist) on purely conceptual grounds,
but it is also the sort of thing whose existence depends on purely
conceptual considerations. What these considerations are is of
course not the easy question that some have taken it to be, and
it is not to be decided by invoking a *soi-disant* topic-neutral logic
which in fact rests on a hidden metaphysic. The sequence of
papers in the present volume will, however, show how, from
denying what may be loosely described as my Creator's existence,
I have come to be surpassingly interested in his logical properties.
The stages of my intellectual biography are, of course, of no
importance whatever, but there may be interest and importance
in the matters with which they were concerned. With one exception, the papers are chronologically arranged: I have, however,
put the three Matchette Lectures on Absolute-theory at the
beginning of the collection (though given in 1968), since they,
together with the final paper 'Towards a Neo-neo-Platonism',
provide the most systematic account of my present ideas.

I have to thank the International Institute of Philosophy for
permission to reprint 'The Teaching of Meaning', the Editor
of the Hartshorne Festschrift *Process and Divinity* for permission
to reprint 'Some Reflections on Necessary Existence', the Editor
of *The Monist* for permission to reprint 'Metaphysics and Affinity'
and 'Hegel's Use of Teleology', the Editor of *Philosophy East and
West* for permission to reprint 'The Diremptive Tendencies of
Western Philosophy', the Editor of *Religious Studies* for permission
to reprint 'The Logic of Mysticism', Quadrangle Books Inc. for
permission to reprint 'Essential Probabilities', the Editor of the

Journal of Philosophy for permission to reprint 'The Logic of Ultimates', and the permission of the University of Kansas to reprint 'The Systematic Unity of Value'.

J. N. FINDLAY

Yale University, July 1969

CONTENTS

LECTURE I

THE NOTION OF AN ABSOLUTE

I am about to give three lectures on the Absolute, or on Absolutes, or rather on candidates for Absolute-status. My first lecture will attempt to suggest what should be included in the notion of an Absolute, and will then go on to ask to what, if anything, such a notion could have application. My second lecture will put the Absolute to work, as it were, much as God was put to work by the philosophers of the seventeenth and eighteenth centuries, though he has remained idle and demanding ever since: I shall consider the solvent role of an Absolute in the various philosophical fields of difficulty, that problematic terrain whose various bunkers and hazards are so utterly familiar, though it has never been decided by what strategy one may best soar clear of them. In my third lecture I shall be very bold and quite shocking: I shall deal with those last, other-worldly things which modern theology and philosophy does its best utterly to hide and forget. I shall use the notion of an Absolute to map regions of experience that are rarely entered in this life, but to which the dissolution of this too, too solid flesh may very well give us better access. My programme is completely outrageous from the current empiricistic-cum-formal-logical point of view, but I prefer to warn you of its outrage from the beginning rather than to let it creep up upon you as I proceed.

To give lectures on the Absolute in 1968 on Anglo-Saxon soil is, of course, an immensely reactionary and anachronistic undertaking: on this side of the Atlantic it must be at least half a century since the name 'Absolute' was even mentionable in philosophical society. The Absolute flourished in the late nineteenth-century heyday of Anglo-Saxon commercial prosperity, but it was a curiously domesticated Absolute: it had lost the mystical *élan* of the Absolutes of the great Germanic idealists, and had become a curious hybrid of Berkeleyan subjectivism and scientific deter-

---

[1] Given as Matchette Lectures at Wesleyan University, Middletown, Connecticut, May 1–3, 1968.

minism. The world existed only in the mind, but it was also a
world in which everything was rigorously and lawfully connected
with everything else in a vast agglutinated system, so that the
ardent lecturer's thumping of a book on the table could be held
to alter the centre of gravity of Sirius. Exactly the same panto-
mime could take place in the materialistic professor of Physics'
classroom on the other side of the corridor. This Anglo-Saxon
Absolute was elaborately done to death in the early years of this
century: people ceased to believe in a mechanistically cemented
block-universe and they ceased to believe in the manufacture of
the universe by the mind. Personally I have no desire to revive
such an Absolute, and none of my treatments will owe anything
to Bradley or his equivalents on this side of the Atlantic. I believe,
however, that what I call Absolute-theory—I shall not give it the
question-begging title of theology—represents a fundamental
enterprise of philosophy, valuable not only for its intrinsic
illumination, but also valuable for the light it throws on the basic
obscurities of our most commonplace enterprises, and valuable
too for extending our thought towards ranges of experience
which are generally handed over to undisciplined thinkers. Our
approach in the present lectures is to have a predominantly
logical character: we are to develop the content and ways of working of certain typical absolutist notions in a manner that will be
distinctly dry and analytic. There may be mystical fires banked
in the background, but we shall not let them flare forth in the
course of our exposition. The effect that we desire is that certain
questions should be put back on the *tapis* of serious philosophy,
that they should be examined, discussed, treated tentatively in
various ways until we see what answers if any can be seriously
given to them. We live in a period when logic and analysis are
ceasing to be the restrictive, reductive force which banishes certain
questions to the ill-formed and unmeaning: they are coming to do
what Bertrand Russell falsely claimed that they were doing,
giving thought wings instead of binding it down by chains of the
most narrow, descriptive, extensional types of discourse. We are
coming to talk acceptably and not reductively of things changing
their status from futurity to pastness, of things intended privately
and internally, of things that ought to be the case, and so on.
Is it too much to ask that logic and analysis should provide us
with some sort of non-reductive restatement of the discourse
which concerns the mystically exciting but also logically very

interesting and special objects called Absolutes? It is to prepare the way for such treatment that I am giving the present lectures.

I now owe you some sort of a preliminary account as to how I propose to use the term 'Absolute' in the present lectures. I may say from the start that it represents not so much a clear notion as a definite notional direction, which has been followed with great differences of course and route in the past, and also with very different degrees of what I may call extremism. Some modes of pursuing Absolutes are quite certainly deplorable and destructive: they obliterate all divergences and differences in a great flood which, whether it be one of light or darkness, matters little. Certainly they put a stop to all further investigation. Others, on the other hand, have been inspirational, illuminating and regulative, and it is with these that I shall be concerned in the present lectures: Absolutes like other concepts must give light and leading or else they must be pitilessly discarded. The direction towards Absolutes is a direction towards what Kant called the termination of regressive synthesis, the coming to an end of the process in which we regard things as in some sense flowing from, consequential upon, explained by, grounded in something whose being is at once more intelligible *per se*, and also lends a derivative intelligibility to other existences, natures and circumstances. Absolutes are the limits of explanation, and as such they have been the main theme of traditional philosophy, whether we consider the Air of Anaximenes, which differentiates itself into everything possible by a simple act of rarefaction or condensation, or the Atoms and Void of Leucippus which generate the most varied things through their chance differences and meetings, or the Platonic Good which not only specifies itself in an ideal cosmos of ordered natures, but also lends half-being to a world of changeable instances which participate imperfectly in such natures. An Absolute as a bewildering but also satisfying limit of explanation is certainly seen in the Semitic Creator-God, whose hold on Western European thought has been almost as firm as his putative hold on the universe, and Absolutes are likewise seen in the unorthodox ultimates of scientific materialism, whether mechanistic or 'dialectical', in the 'logical space' of simple 'objects' and their boundless possible combinations posited by certain analysts, in the transcendental world-constituting Ego or Egos of Fichte and Husserl, or in the simple 'world', to be received with something between a sigh and a shrug, of the ordinary unreflective person.

In recent times there has indeed grown up a certain deliberate purblindness and piecemealness of thought which represents the antithetical policy to absolutism: men content themselves by using limited thought-techniques on limited issues, without attempting any comprehensive thought-strategy relating to things in general. To be content to do the immediate thought-task on hand, and to limit one's analysis of it to what is immediately part of it, may be said to be the intellectual policy of modern non-absolutism, I shall not call it anti-absolutism. It is certainly a defensible stance, and one that one will have to fall back on if all one's absolutist ventures prove abortive. But it is not clear that the modest, minimal stance in question is not ready to pass over into the most arrogant and self-destructive of absolutisms, into a belief that piecemealness is an intelligible and intellectually justifiable policy, which is deeply adjusted to the structure of a disconnected, randomly organized universe. There is in such piecemealness often a faith, sometimes messianically promulgated, in a pluralism of *disjecta membra*, thrown together in defiance of sense and order, in a flat disconnection of our hermeneutic demands and the material standing before us for interpretation, in an ill-ordered infinity of supposedly logical possibilities. All these doctrines are not humble confessions of ignorance and impotence to prove: they are arrogant assertions of knowledge and of boundless power to liquidate the efforts of constructive understanding. They are absolutist assertions which show their absolutist character by their unwillingness to be considered alongside of other better constructed, less self-destroying, more arguable absolutisms. Our thought and discourse operate on at least three distinct levels. There is the level of descriptive talk, only concerned to ask how things are and how they stand to other things: this is the kind of thought mainly explored by modern logic and analysis. There is the level of explanatory talk, which raises the question 'Why?' in regard to every matter of fact, and which is irreducibly pledged to find causes and forces and laws and natural kinds behind the surface welter of phenomena. This level of explanatory talk was much studied in the older logic of induction, but the stupefying effect of modern formalism has been to push it into the background. Finally we have the level of self-explanatory, absolutist talk, talk which sees isolated matters of fact in the framework of a single self-differentiating conceptual totality which demands no further explanation or reduction. It is arguable that the self-explanatory, absolutist levels of thought are as essential as its descriptive and explanatory levels, and that they permit of well-formed statement and coherent development as much as do the lower levels. And absolutism need not represent a violation of empiricism so much as the giving to empiricism of a framework and a background within which its inquiries can be fruitfully pursued. Nothing is more terrifying than the wild indiscipline of certain branches of modern science, broken loose from an old, hard-headed, naïve world-picture, and now ignorant of any distinction between facts and categories, between what can be learnt from experience or tested by it, and what is needed to make learning from experience and testing by experience possible at all. Confusions so frightful have overlaid the sciences with a strange amalgam of hard-headed and soft-brained nonsense, so barnacled with technicalities as to be quite uncaulkable by a mere philosopher. Arguably a careful and conscientious development of Absolute-theory will at least set limits to the burgeoning of this total nonsense.

Having indicated generally the direction in which Absolute-research is to go, I shall now try to sketch in a few salient traits in the profile of an Absolute. An Absolute is, first of all, an entity, an existent, something that is, in the very fullest and highest sense permitted by the ontology, the view of what is and can be, accepted by a given thinker or class of thinkers. Nothing that merely is there in some derivative or as-if or secondary manner, which pre-supposes and points to something that in a more full-blooded and unqualified sense is there, is an Absolute in the sense relevant to the Absolute-theory that I am here developing. On the ontology that most ordinary thinkers, and a majority of philosophers, espouse, what primarily exist are individual things, entities of the type of this man or that city or that flock of birds cruising together: characters, procedures, respects, positions, conscious stances, things done or undergone, absences, potencies and what not, are all taken to have being only in the sense that individuals are describable in terms of them, and not as having any absolute status of their own. On such an ontology an Absolute will have to be some sort of an individual or set of individuals: it would be absurd to regard something non-individual, however pure and underived and self-sufficient in its own category, as explanatory of the individuality it essentially presupposes. This is not to say that Absolute-research may not force us, as it forced Plato and

others, to change the basic pattern of our ontology, so that
individuality becomes parasitic upon entities or an entity belonging to some other category, and not vice versa. We shall, in fact,
find ourselves forced in the direction in question. But whatever
our ontology, an Absolute, if admitted, must be placed in the
supreme category of that ontology, and not in any reducible or
dependent segment. I may say here that I do not regard it as an
undeniable mark of prime-category status that something is the
value of a variable, nor that something is accorded the rank of a
grammatical subject. Most Absolutes have been spoken of by
means of nouns, often dignified with initial capitals, but such a
convention is not mandatory nor sacrosanct.

An Absolute is, further, the sort of entity which not only
occupies a prime ontic category, but also occupies it necessarily
and unconditionally: other prime-category entities could be
dislodged from their ontic rank, and leave gaps in their places,
but an Absolute is immune from such a possibility. Whatever
was or was the case, our Absolute or Absolutes would still be: their
being is ineliminable, presuppositional, a background or framework to whatever there is or could be. The notion of such ineliminable, presuppositional being is of course deeply suspect
and unfamiliar to many modern thinkers, to whom the being of
anything only makes sense, only has content, in contrast with a
corresponding non-being, and who automatically regard as
redundant, empty, anything we could say would be there *whatever* was the case. The trivialities of formal logic hold whatever
may be the case, and it is arguable that to believe in an Absolute is
to believe in something as ineliminably trivial as these all-per-
missive principles. The feeling that real being *does* involve a
contingent element, something that is but might have been different, certainly does reflect a profound insight: that nothing
that is can be wholly necessary in every respect. Some aspects or
features of it, at least, must fall among the things that could be
otherwise. There is a side of things that corresponds to what may
be called the side of specific empirical content, since it can only be
discovered by encounter with particular cases or instances, not
by any generalized reflection. This side must, moreover, be represented in *everything* fully real, whether in respect to what it incorporates by way of parts or aspects or in respect of what it has
relations towards. Even the absence of specific *positive* empirical
content represents a limiting case of empirical content: there is,

in a queer sense, empirical content in an Absolute Space that harbours no bodies, an Absolute Creator that creates no world, an Absolute Platonic Form without instances, and so on. Absolutes to be fully rounded beings, on which other beings can be founded, must therefore have faces looking in all directions where contingent being or truth is to be found. There must be something in them which 'takes care' of whatever is thus contingent, though this may not necessarily be the possession of such properties as contingent things possess.

But that genuine existence thus does always involve a decision between alternatives, either of which, but not both, could be true, does not prove that there may not be cases, or aspects of cases, of genuine existence which admit of *no* alternatives, which we recognize, in fact, by their *contrast* with what thus admits of alternatives. And these necessary cases and aspects will, further, necessarily be inseparable from all cases of specific empirical content, and so, in a sense, be part and parcel of the latter. The necessary features of Absolute Space, if Space be truly an Absolute, will be present in all cases of occupancy and non-occupancy, the creative will of God, if God be a true Absolute, in all cases of creaturely being or non-being, and so on. There is some difficulty of course in the question as to what is *excluded* by a postulation of necessary being, since an exclusion which excludes only an empty inconceivability is arguably void of content. The answer, however, lies in the stratified, regional character of modality, so that what is not excluded, and seems quite possible, at *one* level of abstraction, *is* excluded, and reveals itself as impossible, as soon as one thinks more concretely and more regionally. That there should be nothing which exists of necessity, though superficially self-contradictory, is, at one level of abstraction, a perfectly entertainable proposition: this does not exclude the possibility that, at another, more deeply engaged level, we may come to feel that it is not not really entertainable at all. The position of an Absolute, as an existent which cannot *not* exist, certainly has some odd features: if it may exist, it certainly does exist and exists of necessity, which suggests that we can infer its existence from its mere possibility. We can indeed do so, but we can equally infer its necessary non-existence from the mere possibility of its non-existence. That the possibility of its existence coincides with its necessary existence, means, in fact, that its existence is only possible if its existence represents the *only* possibility, and this obviously is a vastly harder thing to see, as one's mind roves over the seemingly infinite possibilities of things, than the possibility of an ordinary case of existence. The only way, in fact, to see its possibility is to see its necessity, and this excludes the tempting argumentative *coup de tonnerre* from its mere conceivability to its full reality. All we are saying can, in fact, only be an anticipatory flapping of wings in the void. An Absolute must be given an essential content, other than its mere necessity of existence, before we can determine whether it makes sense, and whether it alone makes sense, to conceive of *it* as necessarily existent. It would not make sense to put in this essential content any features falling on one side only of what may be called an empirical contrast: an Absolute could not be an Absolute in virtue of being loud or blue or situated in Connecticut, and *not* equally in virtue of their contraries. It remains to be seen whether anything contentful, anything positively meaningful, though not falling on one side alone of an empirical contrast, can be significantly attributed to an Absolute.

Before we get on to this, we are committed to saying that an Absolute is plainly such as to admit of *no* alternatives or substitutes. If there is an Absolute of a certain essential sort, then there cannot *not* be an Absolute of that essential sort, and it makes no sense to suppose that there might *instead* have been an Absolute of some other somewhat different nature or essence. There may be alternative Absolutes *for us*, with our imperfect insight into modality, but with perfect insight into modality all such alternativity would vanish. The mere fact, therefore, that we lose hope as to the possibility of deciding between what are, for us, alternative Absolutes, would mean that, for us too, *none* of the putative Absolutes before us can be genuine Absolutes: an Absolute can, as we have said, only exist possibly, if its existence represents the *only* possibility. But the impossibility of there being ultimate alternative Absolutes does not, however mean, *prima facie*, that there may not be quite a lot of Absolutes and that they may not be more or less externally related. They would, of course, all have to exist *together*, ineliminably and of necessity, but from the point of view of each there might none the less be something of a high-grade accident in their all being, as it were, thrown together in a common plight of necessary existence. I for long believed that such a bizarre conception could from the start be ruled out by some nice *a priori* argument, and perhaps there is one, though I have been unable to find it. But now it seems to me that our thought must necessarily play among a variety of candidates for absolute status, some close-knit and deeply unified, and others more or less dissolute and disunified, and that only a close examination of the candidates in question can decide what we are entitled and bound to accept. Here, however, pragmatic as well as ontic pressures enter the picture, and obviously we have an *interest* in postulating the existence of a close-knit Absolute, one in fact which, in all essential respects, carries close-knitness *to the limit*, rather than one more or less dissolute or loosely knit. For our cognitive *motive* in doing Absolute-research is our deep desire to increase explanation and mutual coherence, and to diminish independence and loose externality, and it is clear that we attain the aims of normative reason more completely the more deeply unified our Absolute is. We may, on deep consideration of what we see or imagine, be forced to retreat from this position, but we must not retreat from it lightly, nor without notional compulsion from the materials at hand. We are, in short, *in quest* of an Absolute having the highest conceivable degree of mutual requiredness among its essential members or features, so that the thought of each, trained only on each, inevitably pushes us to the thought of all the others. Such an Absolute cannot be an Absolute in which every aspect or element necessarily entails the *existence* of every other, as in the Spinozistically inspired Absolutes of the Anglo-Saxon idealists, for such an Absolute would have no contingent features whatever, and this, on our view, is not a truly meaningful and coherent conception, countless determinations of things being such that, neither alone, nor in company with any non-necessary complement, they exclude all possibilities of otherwiseness. Possible otherwiseness of some features is the necessary complement to what admits of no otherwiseness, and alone makes the latter meaningful: this is an irrefragable modal principle, if any can claim to be such. But we should wish to move as far in the direction of the Anglo-Saxon idealists as our ideal material allows, and we should never gratuitously suppose independence and relative contingency among the more rooted or pervasive features of the world.

We are therefore committed to a more or less profoundly unified Absolute, which need not, however, be *penitus simplex*, like the Absolute of scholastic theism. Our Absolute may be articulated into a number of members each of which requires, and so, after a fashion includes, all the others, like the persons of the Trinity: it may even be articulated into members belonging to different logical types, none of which has any absolute ontic preference over the others: the analogy of a λόγος, a meaningful sentence, in which subject, predicate and connectives all play an indispensable part, is a valuable model in Absolute-theory. It may well be that the only coherently constructible Absolute has many of the properties of a sentence. All this will be debated later. For the moment we may pass to a further general point, also involving pragmatic considerations, which we hope will ultimately dissolve in the perfection of modal insight. This is the demand that the Absolute—for the demand for close-knitness is tantamount to the demand for a *single* Absolute—should not only have no other Absolutes external to itself, but should also have no contingencies of existence or characterization or relation which are thus external, which are not in some sense *its own* determinations. From the standpoint of Absolute-theory, contingencies of existence or characterization or relation which the Absolute neither determines nor explains, are in a sense rival Absolutes alongside of itself. For though we may denominate such matters contingent, we also set them down as unexplained, and also as not requiring explanation, and this is in effect to turn them into rival Absolutes. Philosophers who believe in a boundless empirical contingency which neither admits of nor requires ultimate explanation, are in effect erecting such boundless empirical contingency into something absolute, something in which thought rests, and beyond which it need not seek to go. And, if we are venturing on Absolutes, it seems better to have Absolutes which guide and shed light rather than Absolutes which allow us to expect practically anything. Of course, as I have said, there is always the alternative of a radical piecemealism, of a refusal to look beyond the finite problem or method on hand, but such piecemealism is not what we are considering this evening.

But the demand that a true Absolute should determine all contingencies of existence and characterization strikes severe shoals on which it seems likely to be shipwrecked. For by 'explanation' is generally meant something that implies deduction: the nature of an agent, e.g., must be given as such and such, and from this it must follow either unconditionally, or in relation to certain conditions, that such and such will eventuate. To explain contingencies by deducing them from the nature of the Absolute would, however, be to destroy their contingency, much as contingency vanishes in Spinozism where all things are held to flow from the necessity of God's nature. Spinoza's attempt to retain something like contingency in his system by making the finite modes follow from the Divine Nature only *qua* modified by other finite modes, is radically unsatisfactory: modes thus conditionally necessary do not really flow from the necessity of God's nature at all. Absolute-theory, it is plain, requires that we make use of a type of explanation that ordinary thought does not disdain, but which is often thought of as not amounting to an explanation at all: it must make use of the notion of something freely self-determining, which can in some wide sense 'opt' or 'decide' for one alternative among others, can educe a categorical outcome from a disjunctive situation, without being decided to decide in this manner by anything other than its own essential power of decision. This is the 'power of opposites' held by Aristotle to be found in the rational potencies, but it is not necessary for us to limit this self-determining capacity to entities endowed with rationality, nor even to make it a matter of determination in time. The situation, in fact, is severely logical, and has nothing to do with temporal happenings: we work within a system, call it deductive or call it something else, in which particular stances permit of alternative consequences, *either* of which is entirely legitimated by the stances in question. Such systems have not been studied by ordinary logicians[1] because they have at best been concerned with the descriptive and explanatory categories, and never with the forms and categories of self-explanatory discourse. Hence to them the self-explained is the unexplained, and they demand reasons upon reasons, and conditions upon conditions, without end. The logic of the self-explanatory is, however, deeply different from that of the merely explanatory, and an Absolute must, of its own proper motion, we may say, *give* itself contingent specifications, if it is to count as viable at all. Arbitrary choice is merely a special case of the self-determination in question, and we may well be able to conceive of others if only we will ponder enough.

We are led on from all this to frame a final requirement: that a satisfactory Absolute should in some manner embody all intrinsic, all mandatory values, all that we consider to be good in themselves, and not merely preferred by ourselves or some other class of conscious beings, and that it should incarnate them in some supreme, in some unsurpassable form. It must be *id quo melius*

---

[1] Except, to some extent, by Mr Arthur Prior and the tense-logicians.

cogitari nequit if it is anything. This demand obtains because values are essentially absoluteness-claiming: to experience their appeal is to experience the appeal of something that would attract us (we feel) whoever we were and whoever we conceived ourselves as being, and which would attract us no matter what we happened to be personally interested in. They lie like an embracing framework within which our finite personal ends deploy themselves, and they are ends which (we are assured) hold as much for others as for ourselves. Happiness, freedom from pain, freedom from arbitrary inequality, understanding and love of others, contemplation and love of the well-formed, practical zeal devoted to these ends: all these, and many others, are among the mandatory ends of our existence, and it is not possible for us to construct an acceptable Absolute to which these are external. The trouble lies not in the unattractive character of such an Absolute, its frustration of human aspirations, but in the defectiveness of its absoluteness: it would, in effect, have another Absolute outside of itself. For, whatever we may philosophically opine, to experience value is to experience what cannot be otherwise construed, what nothing whatever can repudiate or be free from: it has all the marks of absoluteness and invariance, and no Absolute can be construed that does not incorporate it. This is why even those who have tried to construct value-free Absolutes, have generally failed in their endeavours: the laws and tendencies of their value-free Absolute have taken on a note of the august and the approvable, and true peace is seen in acquiescence in them. The scientific materialists and evolutionists of the last century all found something good, if a little hard, in the matter and chance that they postulated, or, if they did not do so, as in the case of Huxley, remained bitterly torn between rival Absolutes. An Absolute must, therefore, be taken as containing within itself the source of the absoluteness-claiming realm of values: it must be such as to embody all such values and to explain their detailed content. And if the Absoluteness-claiming-ness of values can be shown to rest on a confusion, then there are and can be no Absolutes. Necessities of existence which are indifferent to the demands of value are, for our purposes, too poorly explanatory to be considered in Absolute-research. They leave unused the notion of an immanent teleology which we shall see to be as much the key-notion in the realm of the self-explanatory, as substance and causality are in the realm of the merely explanatory.

I now go on to the main task of my paper: to give more definite content to the notion of an Absolute, whose formal structure we have sketched in the last half-hour. An Absolute is self-existent, of prime category, without alternatives, as closely knit as may be in respect of its essential features, intrinsically capable of displaying itself in alternative contingencies, whether of existence, characterization or relation, and in fact capable of displaying itself in *all* such contingencies, not confronted by rival Absolutes or by contingencies external to itself, and embodying in the highest conceivable perfection all the values that are intrinsic and mandatory. These requirements are all purely formal: they express what it is to be an Absolute, but they do not tell us how such requirements are to be met, what are the necessary determinables of which contingencies will be the specifications, and how they are to be incorporated in our Absolute. It is this more contentful phase of construction upon which we now must enter: we shall pursue it in a negative manner, by excluding certain candidates for Absolute-status which the history of philosophy and our own explanatory tendencies have given an initial prerogative.

We may begin by excluding that darling of common sense and ordinary thought: the cosmos or world in which we all have our place. The world is by no means an inconsiderable candidate for Absolute-status. It involves the thoroughgoing unity and continuity of space and time, with the causal interactions these make possible, and which also ensure the existence of routes of possible influence and communication, direct or indirect, and serially or interlacingly joined, between everything and everything else. It also makes no clear sense to suppose that the world might not have existed: it is the abiding framework by location in which reality alone seems to have meaning, and in possible application to which even ideal objectivity has content and status. Spirits display themselves to each other in it, and various *irrealia* have a place in the life of such spirits, and it is not clear what could otherwise be meant by a spiritual society than just this worldly, bodily communion. If it is not the Absolute, the natural world or cosmos seems to be a necessary node or phase in the Absolute, a word or phrase in that analogue of connected discourse that the Absolute may very well turn out to be. But the entire Absolute it cannot be, as has been felt by all those philosophers who have located transcendent or transcendental sources behind it. For it is not thought to be generative of its contents, whose thinkable absence would leave it no more than a doubtfully thinkable space-time framework, nor are its contents thought to be mutually determining in any profound manner, nor to have more, in many cases, than a quite casual relation to one another, no matter how much such casualness may be continued in causal concatenations. The casual is a form of contingency tolerable in Absolute-theory, but it must be a casualness springing from a free self-determination to a largely independent plurality, whose encounters might, as far as each is concerned, have been quite other: it is not the sort of ultimate, nor further explicable, casualness that the world is thought to offer. The world is, moreover, not given as subordinated to values: whatever providential dispensations watch over it are seen as mysterious and deeply hidden. What we have said of the world applies likewise to Matter in most of its conceptual trans-mogrifications. The world and Matter can no doubt, be conceptually modified so as to admit of many further Absolute-making features: the Absolute which results is, however, not rightly regarded as a mere cosmic, naturalistic Absolute. Its nature is linked to so much that surpasses mere nature as to count as merely natural no longer.

But the objections we have raised to a cosmic Absolute apply equally to a supercosmic Absolute, whether this takes the form of a Semitic Creator-God, able to create or not to create anything whatever, or the more misty shape of an Upanishadic Self, able through its *māyā* to entangle itself in the varied ignorance of an imaginary world, or the lack of shape of a Neoplatonic One unconcernedly emanating a world by what may be called a sort of nocturnal emission. All these Absolutes are defective, in that, claiming elevation *above* all the one-sided, finite things of this world, they in effect are just as finite and one-sided as these are, since they lie merely outside of them and are excluded by them, a point on which Hegel insists often. Pragmatically, too, they fail in giving their Absolute little or no explanatory work to do: the existence of the cosmos may depend on the Absolute, but the Absolute could equally well have given rise to no cosmos or a very different one, and so explains little of cosmic being or structure. We have conceded that a power of alternatives is part of the notion of an Absolute, but, pragmatically speaking, such a power must be exercised as 'far down' as possible: it must fill in the interstices of being, not provide its solid framework. If the whole cosmos might not have existed, or been wholly different

from what it is, the Absolute has, to put it mildly, little of importance to do. The irrelevance of a cosmos to the Absolute is also
such as to impoverish and attenuate the Absolute, to reduce it
in fact to mere negativity and notional emptiness. For the infinity
and majesty of what transcends the finite is an infinity and majesty
only in so far as there can be or actually is a finite and contingent
to transcend, and it is greater in the face of existent, than of
merely possible, finitude and contingency. It is clear, further,
that the whole range of impersonal values has its roots, on one
side at least, in finitude and contingency, however much it may
point to culminations which transcend the latter: the tragic, the
beautiful, the dedicated, the penetratingly knowing and almost
any other human value, presuppose contingency and finitude, however much they may aspire beyond these. If the Absolute in its
beyondness is not also such as in some manner to bend down and
gather up these human values into itself, to incorporate them as
well as help to evoke them in other beings, then it can be a source
of values only in some nugatory, originative sense. It will not
embody the values that in some sense perhaps have their source
in it, and so will have the teasing presence of a rival Absolute
beside it, an Absolute that for human purposes is far more worthy
of devotion. We may therefore hold that an Absolute to which a
cosmos of finite, contingent beings is in some sense necessary, is an
Absolute which, paradoxically, exhibits greater inclusiveness,
greater self-sufficiency, truer all- and self-explanatoriness, than
an Absolute of which this is not true: it is (to play with unsatisfactory phrases, only useful *for us*) *more* of an Absolute than the
other. Pragmatically, we must work towards an Absolute that is
not only the unsurpassably best but the unsurpassably explanatory, the latter being in fact a specification of the former, and,
though we have to settle for less, or opt for mere piecemealism,
it is not right to anticipate disaster.

We may now add to our catalogue of negations a refusal to
admit any purely spiritual, conscious Absolute. Conscious life
may have an essential part to play *in* the Absolute, but it cannot *be*
the Absolute in terms of which all matters are explained. Though
incarnating practically all of the higher values—the beauty,
strength, harmony, health, etc. of the inorganic and organic
excepted—conscious life has countless features that debar it from
being all that there is in the Absolute: its essential concern with
objects and materials which, at the bottom of the scale, cannot

be psychic, and which are required, at least in some cases, to be independently real; its essential approach to these and other objects in a one-sided, 'angled' manner which indefinite supplementation could not round out into perfect vision; its essentially developmental character, so that all consciousness means *further* penetration into some object and precludes anything terminal; its essential dispersion, further, among a set of separate conscious persons, able by their parallax to give a dimension of reality to whatever is consciously entertained, conscious persons whose number and content are contingent without being determined by any of their number or all together, who have, further, an essential need for bodies and the bodily in order to pin themselves down, and acquire content both for themselves and for others, and so on. We cannot here dwell on the metaphysical insufficiency of conscious being, or meet possible arguments against its catalogue of defects: it seems clear, despite many idealistic and spiritualistic philosophies, that no exhaustive explanation of all there is is possible in terms of the forms and categories of conscious being, and that attempts to arrive at this involves an introduction of strange surds of various sorts, strange subterranean activities whose very notion involves contradiction, or incredible limiting transformations that could not really be cases of consciousness at all. At the same time it seems clear that conscious being, with its embrace of all higher values, and with its reduction to interpenetrating understanding of the most diverse and dispersed cosmic contents, must undoubtedly enjoy some key-position and function in the Absolute, and that no purely unconscious or only peripherally conscious entity can be an acceptable candidate for Absolute-status. In the unifying vision and self-determining energy of the conscious Ego, post-Renaissance and Romantic philosophy has rightly seen a main element in the 'meaning of the world'.

Two further negations are necessary: we must reject, for obvious reasons, those would-be Platonic Absolutes from which individuality and individuation have been excised, which have become no more than a pure 'such', ramifying, in ideal fashion, in a whole family of specific 'suches', the blueprint for innumerable shadowy instantiations which are, however, external to, and one-sidedly dependent on, such 'suches'. This type of Absolute has the same, and worse, pragmatic objections as the extracosmic Absolutes considered earlier: that it does too little explanatory work, that it has contingencies external to itself that it fails to explain, that it represents an extraordinary hypostatization of the one-sided and incomplete. While we do not reject the possibility of giving ideal entities a place in our Absolute, this must be in some essential connection with instantiation and instances: so much seems the worthwhile deposit of the many confused arguments of nominalism. But even more strong than our repudiation of a purely Platonic Absolute, must be our repudiation of any view that makes the Absolute individual, an *instance* of certain exalted properties, even if, perchance, the only one. Instances and classes of instances permit neither of ontological nor of axiological perfection: they can manifest no character except at the cost of not manifesting others, they can manifest no character in a manner or degree that does not admit of being surpassed, and for them to manifest all characters and all degrees would be to fall into self-contradiction: they have not, we may say, the omnitude necessary to an Absolute. And even infinite things in infinite modes, to quote Spinoza, will never amount to *all* things falling under the infinite intellect, the notion of *all* possibilities being provably an illegitimate totality. Individuals are, moreover, as the classic criticisms have shown, essentially vanishing and unseizable things: while we may believe that we hold them here and now, all that they leave in our hands are memories and meanings that are general. If individuals are our supreme category, and a putative Absolute must consequently be an individual, then there is not and cannot be an Absolute. Many of the objections to an anthropomorphic God rest on a perception of this fact.

Plato has in fact shown the one direction where an Absolute can, with some qualification and modification, be located, in the direction of certain characters or perfections *themselves*, being in such 'selfhood' capable of being welded together into a single comprehensive ideal of perfection as is not possible in their instances. Our Absolute cannot be merely beautiful, but must in some sense be Beauty Itself, it cannot merely be active but must in some sense be Actuosity Itself, it cannot merely enjoy true insights but must in some sense be the True and the Insightful themselves, and so on for all possible characters and perfections. Only so can the Absolute infinitely surpass all conceivable instantiations, however exalted, and only so can it be conceived as to be in some sense the generative source of all good qualities in things, and only so can it hope to unite numerous perfections which in

c

their instances necessarily fall apart. The conceptual transformation here required means that we no longer operate with dead universals which, as we saw, never could yield us a viable Absolute, nor with the vanishing particulars or individuals which are equally unsatisfactory, but with universals bound together, *qua* universal, in a single unrealizable ideal of perfection, and credited further with a relation to particulars which may be described, following Hegel, as a self-instantiating power, a notion to which Plato was working in the later phases of his thought. But the ideal we are outlining certainly goes as far beyond a merely Platonic, as it goes beyond a merely individual Absolute. Some sort of transcendence and confluence of universality and instantiation is essential to Absolute-theory, a point felt in various positions of Thomism.

After all these negations, I shall conclude my lecture with a few positive suggestions as to the true shape of a viable Absolute, one which being free from internal discrepancies (which in this case entails being the *only* Absolute in this position) also exists certainly and exists of necessity. The magnitude of what I am daring to pronounce upon must not be taken as indicating ignorance of my extreme audacity in pronouncing upon it. There is no harm, however, in training one's sights on the most exalted of targets, and doing so without unnecessary prostrations: if one adds to the world's nonsense, that is after all no great matter. It seems plain, from the negations we have pronounced, that our Absolute must involve, in the first place, an ideal point of unity in which all values, all possibilities of achieving excellence, come into coincidence, and from which they radiate, and in which all possibilities of falling short of such perfection have some sort of interstitial being, parasitic upon the many-sided perfection that they presuppose. If our Absolute is to be highly unified, and is also to incorporate all mandatory values and to incorporate them supremely, and also to have no possibilities of contingent being external to itself, then all these factors must themselves be highly unified: the mandatory values must be so many sides of a single systematic ideal of perfection and the prime possibilities of being must simply specify these mandatory values, while secondary possibilities of evil simply specify the possibilities of departure from these values and their specifications. In saying that our Absolute must converge upon such an ideal of perfection, I am not erecting such an ideal into a separate, self-existent something:

if so, it would be the Absolute itself, which it is not. I am only saying that the understanding of things involves seeing everything in the light of such an ideal, that things must be taken to move obscurely towards such an ideal and so on, in a way that I shall elucidate in a moment.

This ontological-axiological point of unity will be more of a Platonic, subsistential character than of an instantial, existential character, since it is axiomatic that no system of existent things can instantiate all values or do so in a supreme form: all existence involves a choice among incompatible directions of value, and all only can carry excellence to a definite limit and no further. There is not, however, the incompatibility among the ideal specifications of value that there is among their instances: they can all be sides of a single ideal, of a single demanded goal, though it is impossible ever to carry them out together in the detail of existence and practice. The surpassingness of the Absolute lies in the fact that it permits of no instantial carrying out: all instantiation involves sacrifice and limitation of what it involves. To carry out into instantiation all that is involved in the Absolute's ideal point of unity must always be a self-contradictory exercise, a squaring, as it were, of the circle, which is just why it can be attempted to all eternity.

We must go further in a Platonic direction by making our point of unity in some sense 'causative' or 'generative', which need mean no more than that its ideal subsistence must require a realm of contingent instances to be imperfectly present in, and can make no sense without them. The use of the terms 'generation' or 'causation' must mean that there neither is nor need be an answer as to why there are contingent instances of various aspects of the Absolute's ideal point of perfection, instances which deviate from its perfection in various directions, nor as to why their contingency has taken the particular form that it has taken; all these things are presupposed by the necessity of instantiation which cannot be other than selective, optional among alternatives (in a wide sense of 'optional'). To look for a special factor which will enable one to deduce the detail of contingency is to seek to eliminate their contingency, and to deprive the Absolute of the necessary contingency it demands or, what is the same, to deprive it of its true self-determination. The Absolute in its universal ideality must, as Hegel says, be self-specifying and self-instantiating, which means in the last resort that contingent exemplification is a part of its life. In requiring one-sided instantiation, our Absolute must, however, also require the integration of these one-sided mutually exclusive instances into a unity which, after its own poor fashion, imitates the Absolute instantially: we have to have something like our spatio-temporal cosmos where mutual outsideness is merely the reverse side of continuity, and where apparent isolation and internal purity of manifestation are shown up as the rootless things they are, when manifestations move or change over into one another. Finally the Absolute requires imperfect instantiations of those perfections in which its own reduction of the greatest and most discrepant diversity is most supremely emphatic. In the medium of interior experience the most separated and even incompatible items or features can be contemplated in unity, and can be taken as out of a store to be deployed in the work of theory and practice. If the height of value lies always in such interior gatherings-together, and if the Absolute requires contingent instantiations of such gatherings-together as well as their notional blue-print, then it is plain that the Absolute must in some way include a spiritual society among its elements, a society which in number and diversity to some extent makes up for the finitude and one-sidedness of its members, and in which the variously dirempted instances of materiality are gathered up into varied foci of mentality, and these in their turn gathered up into that further unity of mutual recognition and respect by which a spiritual society is constituted. My sketchiness must be pardoned, but something like a unique point of ideal convergence, something like a cosmos of dispersed but continuously linked instances, and something finally of the character of a spiritual society, linked by community of object and of goal and by possibilities of mutual recognition, must plainly enter into the life of an Absolute that is to satisfy the exclusions that we have laid down.

To specify elements is not, however, sufficient: one must specify the manner and the category of their integration. Here I shall simply borrow some wisdom from Hegel and from some other thinkers, religious and philosophical, who are akin to him. The peculiar concept, no doubt infinitely inadequate, under which an Absolute is least senselessly categorized, is not that, we may hold, of an originative source, nor of an underlying material, nor of a set of basic elements, nor of a perfect blue-print or plan, but that of a Task, an Enterprise, or a Way. This concept is that of a structure whose diverse elements, differing radically and even categorially in type, are all embraced in a close unity of purpose, a mutual conspiracy, which is absolute in the sense that it involves nothing beyond itself, that it aims only at its own endless continuance. Such a self-aiming Absolute must necessarily aim at itself with a certain indirection, achieving its eternal, living balance only by, as it were, moving towards an ideally exhaustive perfection which is not, and cannot be, its actual aim. The place of the point of ideal value in the absolute is thereby justified: it is a necessary projection, and necessarily guides the Absolute Enterprise. The Absolute Enterprise must also plainly involve infinitely many imperfect instances which serve to maintain the living approximation to perfection which the Absolute is, and an endless living activity of generating such instances and passing beyond them to different and sometimes better ones, approaching its inspiration through countless distinct avenues, and showing its infinite transcendence by falling short of its infinity in countless different ways. It also necessarily involves the element of untowardness, of resistance, of evil without which the endless approximation to its ideal would be impossible. This evil will either take the natural form of the mutual interference of diverse finite things, or the moral form of an abuse of that self-determination which is of the essence of the Absolute, and which it must confer in some degree on all its members, and pre-eminently on such as are aware of alternatives. Plato was right in seeing in instantiation one half of the problem of evil and in free choice the other. The Absolute will of course further require the conscious centres in which its being and character will become plain to itself, and in which all the values comprehended in its limiting ideal will receive ever deeper and more living fulfilment.

If we return at this point to the analogy of the sentence which I used in an earlier part of this paper, we may look for a sentence which will best express the Enterprise which the Absolute is. I understand that the Indian sacred word AUM is by some supposed to have such a meaning: what it declares is that 'I—that Other—am not,' in which utterance the Absolute, both identifies itself with finite contingent being and also cancels the identification. As an alternative to this piece of Hindu mysticism, I propose, not quite seriously, a mystical sense to be put upon the words of consecration in the Latin Mass. Here we can conceive that what is first identified with a body, then becomes transfigured, taken up into the glory signified by the possessive adjective *meum*. My interpretation is semi-serious, but has the serious meaning that the Absolute Task is an act of consecration, the lifting up of finite, transitory, metaphysically defective things into that infinite and absolute undefectiveness which alone truly is.

I intend, however, to pass from mystical edification to detailed elaboration and justification. What the Absolute is can be shown only in what the Absolute does, and one of the things that it does and must do is to ease the stresses of our main philosophical difficulties. In seeing it in relation to various philosophical difficulties we also see what it is: its being consists, among other things, in their removal or solution, in their being taken up into itself. This will be the content of my second lecture. In my third lecture I shall use the Absolute in certain daring extrapolations which take us quite beyond our ordinary, this-world experience: these extrapolations, also, show us what the Absolute truly is.

THE ABSOLUTE AND
PHILOSOPHICAL PROBLEMS

Last time I was trying to give some definite content to the notion of an Absolute. I explained that an Absolute was, first of all, an existent given a position in the most accomplished and independent category permitted in our ontology: it had to be real in the most accomplished way that our ontology allowed for, and not in any sense tagging along as a mere qualification or an appendage of something authentically existent. In our official Aristotelian ontology, this would make an Absolute an individual existent, and not anything that individuals did or underwent or exemplified or manifested in some manner: we said, however, that we should have to revise this official Aristotelian ontology, and to give categorial primacy to an entity other than an individual if we were to find place for an Absolute in our ontology. An Absolute is, in the second place, a self-existent or self-explanatory existent: no external reason need be given for supposing it to be there, for it would not be possible, coherently supposable, that it should not be there. If this notion of a necessary existent is logically incoherent, as many have supposed it to be, then the existence of an Absolute is of course logically impossible. An Absolute that existed, but which might just as well not have existed, is no Absolute at all. This means, however, that if we *can* coherently suppose there to be something which exists of necessity, and which is a true Absolute, then this true Absolute *does* exist and exists of necessity: it permits, i.e. of an Anselmian inference from entertainability in thought to real existence. Its entertainability in thought is not, however, anything that can be hastily and superficially and generally decided: we must work out a specific account of what it is to be an Absolute, we must meditate on its full implications, including the impossibility of its seeming alternatives, before we can decide whether it is coherently entertainable or not. The entertainability or non-entertainability here in question are an entertainability or non-entertainability for a mind that has worked out accounts to the limit, and that has plumbed modality to its last depths, an achievement to which human reflection can only approximate, and which can arguably only be executed by the Absolute itself. *For us* many accounts of an Absolute seem at first entertainable, but we must be guided by the pragmatic refusal to accept as an Absolute not only anything that has alternatives—this, as we have seen, is an analytic consequence of Absoluteness—but also anything which has disconnectedly coexistent Absolutes alongside itself, or contingencies for which it is not entirely responsible. There can, we presume heuristically, only be a single maximally unified Absolute: it may involve a variety of members and aspects, but the being of each must be incomplete without the being of all the others, and everything that is the case contingently must likewise depend solely and entirely on our Absolute for its being the case. The nature of this contingent side of an Absolute was not without its peculiar difficulty. That there must be such a contingent side was asserted, but that it was contingent meant that it must *depend* upon, although it did not *follow* from, the nature of the Absolute. This meant, we saw, that we must posit in the Absolute a power to resolve disjunctions, to bring them to a categorical outcome, without the presence of external resolving factors. The logical difficulty of such a power of alternatives rests more on a limited view of logic than on the nature of the conception: a branching system of reasoning, capable of complete explanation along alternative avenues, is at best unfamiliar.

We then went on to hold that an Absolute necessarily involves a synthesis of all values, and in a form transcending all finite embodiments: to hold otherwise, and to seek to build up a value-free Absolute, is in effect to set up a rival Absolute outside of one's Absolute. Whether or not we have a theory which explains how there can be absolute, mandatory values, the fact remains that values are given as being so: to deprive them of absoluteness is to destroy them, and to extrude them from our Absolute is to destroy that Absolute. Either there is no Absolute, or the Absolute in some manner carries away the palm for utter goodness, evil being in some way necessarily parasitic upon the good from which it falls short or positively deviates. Should there be irremovable contradiction in this notion, then there are irremovable contradictions in the notion of an Absolute.

From all this we went on to rule out various defective, unsuitably formed notions of an Absolute. Long ago we had ruled out *soi-disant* Absolutes such as Absolute Space which are mere substrates, rather than explanatory sources, for their contingent fillings; all ordinary materialisms fall under such a ban. But we were equally unwilling to accept spiritual or conscious Absolutes, in view of the essential self-transcendence and perspectival one-sidedness native to consciousness. Conscious life may play an essential role in the Absolute, but it cannot, in any transformation, be the Absolute itself. At the same time we ruled against both purely abstract and purely instantial Absolutes, the former for failing to explain instantiation, the latter for failing to cover the infinite richness of an Absolute's values, which cannot be exhausted by any array of one-sided instances, however varied or prolonged. We were likewise unable to find appeasement in any cosmic Absolute, in view of the randomness and defective unity and lack of common derivation involved in the notion of a cosmos or world, but we were as unable to find appeasement in any merely supercosmic Absolute, which made no true, necessary entry into the detail of the world. By and large, we were driven towards the notion of an Absolute having some sort of a multi-functional unity like a sentence or task, a sentence or task having its whole meaning and purpose in itself alone. What the Absolute plausibly was, was an eternal endeavour to assert singleness, unity over against plurality, infinite richness over against one-sidedness and limitation, value over against distortions and departures from value, an endeavour which went as far as might be away *from* its goal only in order to turn back towards it, thereby making its goal a goal, and giving it the richness, the poignancy and the transcendence that it could not otherwise have. And since the movement away *from* its goal was essential to the movement *towards* it, it became in a sense part and parcel of the latter, and there came to be something illusory, misleading, deceptive about the whole phase of retreat. And since the whole goal could not be held apart from what can be called the phase of retreat and the phase of advance, it became in fact totally explanatory, the source of all things done and suffered, manifest and unmanifest, in the whole make-up, content and history of the world. Such was the tentative Absolute that we sketched, with acknowledgements to Hegel and Proclus and certain medieval mystics, and this is the sort of Absolute that we must now examine in some detail to see whether we have any reason for preferring it to rival candidates for Absoluteness, or to the mere purblind piecemealism of thought and action which is the true rival of Absolutism.

To construct an Absolute without apparent inner flaw is not, however, to establish its true flawlessness: to do this we must put our Absolute to work, we must show that it in fact does the all-explanatory work that it has been constructed to do and that nothing else ought to be conceived as doing. The world we inhabit is beset with those deep unclearnesses, those profound paradoxes, those unbridgeable schisms, those seeming contradictions that have always engaged the attention of philosophers, and that constitute in effect the sole agreed subject-matter of philosophy. We may try to solve them in different ways, and we may differ profoundly in our choice of notional discomforts, but that there are persistent problems called 'philosophical', which appear and reappear in our best-adjusted schemes of thought and language, and appear in beautifully conceived schemes of exorcism or notional therapy, is a point on which there is a comparative consensus. If having an Absolute represents an important step in thought, then the Absolute must do something towards blunting the edge of such philosophical difficulties: if it merely adds to them, it is indeed superfluous. In talking like this, we appear to be buttressing the idea of an Absolute externally: having given the idea an initial plausibility, we now seem to be raising its acceptability by using it as an hypothesis which allows us to deduce certain otherwise strange and unaccountable features of the world. An Absolute, on this view, is like some entity postulated in a scientific theory, which we accept because it allows us to predict empirical details which would otherwise have been anything but predictable. The resemblance of our procedure to scientific confirmation is, however, illusory: there is nothing external in trying to use the notion of an Absolute to resolve or lessen our philosophical difficulties. For it is part and parcel of our notion of an Absolute that it should be in the highest degree explanatory, and even the possibility of wide territories of fact that it, in one way or another, fails to cover explanatorily, or that could be just as well covered by some other conception, shows it not to be a coherently conceived Absolute, one that can have the slightest internal recommendation for our thought. An Absolute that fails to do its explanatory work in all possible fields of conception is, in fact, no Absolute at all: it suffers from an internal as well as an external flaw. It can have no formal flawlessness which breaks down in the face of untoward facts or possibilities. What thus breaks down was always internally discrepant, was not the Absolute that we deluded ourselves into thinking that we had. Our procedure in putting our Absolute to work in the field of philosophical difficulties continues, moreover, a long philosophical tradition: God, or a personally pictured, conscious Absolute, has always been an incredibly hard-worked notion in philosophy. In antiquity and the Middle Ages He proved a repository for the eternal truths and the pure notions that we all acknowledge in our thought, and true thinking, on all matters that transcend change and contingency, could be only our participation in the eternal thought of God. Among post-Renaissance philosophers God has been the comprehensive guarantor of all our rational certainties, of the light and teaching of Nature, of the linkage of cause and effect, of the correspondence of different people's experiences, of the accommodation of the real to the good, and of destiny to desert. Belief in God became little more, in the pleasant noon of the enlightenment, than the feasibility of the main rational enterprises. The nineteenth century brought darker Absolutes into the picture, not only useless or detrimental, but in perilous health. They were kept alive by our own vague feelings of dependence or of ultimate concern: they teased instead of explaining, and they might even demand the surrender of our reason and our morals. For these perverse, latter-day Absolutes, we too, like the eighteenth century have little beyond impatience. They are, in fact, malign counter-Absolutes, distinguished by their exclusion and non-justification rather than by inclusion and illumination.

What, however, are the philosophical problems on which the notion of an Absolute can be used to cast light? And what account shall we give of a philosophical problem? Philosophical problems are issues, obviously differing vastly from case to case, where there is an inherent unsureness in our wielding of some concept, evinced either in the interchange of such a concept with others, or in its application to what we encounter in experience. This conceptual uneasiness shows itself in two directions. Either we carry on our notion further, and are then smitten with doubts as to the why or the how, the justification or the explanation of our procedure, or we break off in discouragement, and then feel disagreeably and incomprehensibly halted in our natural progression. The material on hand adds to the difficulty and obscurity, sometimes luring us on to excesses of confidence, when we would like to draw back and hesitate, sometimes bringing our procedure to a rude halt, when all is in train for a smooth continuation. There is, we feel, an unaccountable air of collusion and conspiracy among things we thought had nothing to do with one another, and there is, likewise, an unaccountable thwarting of our expectations, just at a time when all seemed set for smoothness. Neither disjointed items separated by gulfs, nor smoothly fitting accommodations, seem to have the unique preference in thought and experience: either seems the rational thing at one moment and the unwarranted thing at the next, and either confronts us in experience when we least expect it. All this is, however, to be expected on the view of the Absolute that we have put forward. For the Absolute is precisely the procedure of pushing disjoined independence nearly to its limit only to recoil to an equally strong assertion of intimate interdependence, and this is precisely the appearance that confronts us on every hand. What we are saying will, however, require documentation over a wide range of philosophical issues.

We may begin by considering the philosophical difficulties which arise in connection with Space and Time, those essential frameworks of a possible world. Space and Time obviously have many of the marks of an Absolute: we seem very well, as Kant rightly observes in the *Aesthetic*, to be able to conceive them void of contents, but we feel with our bones (whatever sophisticated arguments we may adopt with our brains) that they would not be annihilated or reduced thereby. Whatever is removable or variable, *they* are not: they are either the Absolute or some aspect of the Absolute. They have further the integrity, the unbounded wholeness, on which Kant also commented: they are not composed out of the stretches and lapses they contain, but the latter are, as it were, arbitrarily carved out of them. They cannot, however, be more than sides of an articulated Absolute, for, while they seem presupposed by their contents, and not merely, as has often been contended, a mere web of relations among these latter, which would not even yield us the all-pervasive, all-containing media of our deep background experience, they yet reveal themselves, on profound reflection, as presupposing the contents that occupy them, or at least *some* contents that will suffice to bring out the peculiar savour of their unbounded, structured emptiness. So much relativity there undoubtedly is in our notions of Space and Time, that they seem as little able to stand on their own legs without contents to diversify them, and to *realize* their structure, as their contents can stand on their own legs without filling a place in the two great media. Yet it is foreign to our view of the matter, to the notional 'phenomena', to conceive of the media as entirely responsible for their own occupation, as somehow fixing what shall be found in them. Shape things they strangely may by the oddities of their geometrical structure, but, within the limits of this structure, they remain permissive rather than prescriptive: free permissiveness of motion, change, duration and occupation are in fact part of what we understand by spatiality and temporality. If occupation perhaps goes with anomalies in spatial structure, as on some modern views it does, it still requires an additional qualitative element which is no part of the spatial and temporal as such, and in default of which the latter could exhibit no differentiations of motion, rest, emptiness, occupation or even of basic space-time structure. Space and Time, on the one hand, and their contents, on the other, seem mutually presupposing, and it is as little satisfactory to conceive of the two media as fixing the existence and character of their contents, as of their contents fixing the existence and character of the media. Both, it would seem, must play interconnected roles in the Absolute, buttressing and sustaining one another, and in neither case being solely fundamental. And if we meditate long enough on the matter, we come to see how both media and contents fit into the Absolute, and how their respective queernesses cancel each other out in the process.

Space and Time arguably go as far, in the first place, towards segregated instantial plurality, as it is possible to go without rending every form of togetherness, so as to make even classification and comparison, even set-membership, quite unmeaning. Space involves the possibility of setting an instance *outside* of another instance, while at the same time setting it *side by side* with it, while the continuous flux of time enables us to identify instances seen on many occasions and in various contexts. Instantial separateness would be impossible without something resembling the two media, and the separation that some have tried to effect in a world of non-spatial entities, e.g. pure tones, is arguably parasitic upon spatial separateness. The possibility of many alike, even to the point of repetitious indiscernibility, is part and parcel of what we understand by instantiation, and is arguably unrealizable except in the two orders of time and space. Minds appear to be sheerly diverse, but can arguably only be so in so far as they also have the mutual connection which depends on their bodily location in a common space. All forms of apartness, remoteness, independence, segregation, diversity have their foundation, immediate or distant, in the spatial and the temporal, and cannot well be conceived without it: the compatibility and incompatibility of abstracted characteristics has a relation to the regions and lapses in which they might be embodied. And it is not merely that *we* cannot be aware of instantial separateness apart from these media, but that it makes no sense to suppose that there *is* or could be such instantial separateness. Things cannot be separate unless there is a *field* in whose pervasive togetherness their distinctness first becomes possible.

But at the same time the two media involve throughout the impossibility of the total severance of one thing from another which is part of what we mean by an Absolute. Everywhere Space and Time reveal a continuity, a holding together, which is wholly understandable to babes and sucklings, even if it quite eludes the modern analyst of the continuum, brilliant and ingenious as his one-sided fictions may be. There are no true elements in the continuum, only parts that melt into one another and have essentially shifting boundaries: particularly in time is it the case that to reach a boundary is to transcend it. The most remote regions of space and time are linked by continuous transitions whose true parts are likewise continuous transitions, into which pointlike 'positions' are only introduced by a sort of fiction. All this is highly familiar, but the logic it involves, though involving no true contradiction, is yet felt to be disreputably mystical. Comfort arises only when punctiform elements are brought back, and punctiformity remains even when points and instants are reduced to infinite classes of less exact situations. Classes, sets, disjoined pluralities, represent the limiting abstractions from which all notional cement has been removed: taken by themselves, without cement presupposed, they represent only the quite impossible, what is not and cannot be. Despite their persistent use by Russell, they can explain nothing, since they are themselves infinitely needful of explanation: only as products of deliberate notional blinking can they be tolerated at all. If it be argued against the transitional character of all in time and space, that everything after all is what it is and not another thing, the answer is that this is indeed the case: everything is the one total spatio-temporal continuum adverbially shaded in all its varied ways. It is not that the parts only can exist in the whole, but that one can never really deal with anything but the whole, which may be said to exist, whole and entire, in each of the partial shadings that we miscall parts. The fact that we ourselves, as transitional shadings in this continuum, can 'pick out' shadings more or less transitional, gives neither ourselves nor them any true notional separateness. That what we are saying abuses ordinary language, and that ordinary language has its sense and its use, does not mean that we are not now being 'truer' to the world and our experience of it than we ever are in ordinary speech.

Understandable too, perhaps, in the light of a unitive, absolutist logic are those queer cases of finitude manifesting the properties of infinity with which modern physical theory has made us so familiar. Infinity has its place in the Absolute, but only in the firm bounds of measured diversity; the unlimited burgeoning of cases and possibilities in which all rational argumentation becomes nugatory is a nightmare springing from the rejection of Absolutes: it too is what is not and cannot be. Hence we see the open unboundedness of Euclidean spatiality being 'bent round', in Hegelian fashion, into an order finite though unbounded, in which a truer placing of objects is possible. In the same manner, in the as yet imperfectly interpreted 'critical velocity' of light, we have a strange combination of the properties of an attainable finitude, which yet has the unattainable transcendence of infinity, which packs, if I understand it, the long-drawn successiveness of events into an order having some of the features of the instantaneous, but at the same time specifies itself in all the local times which in concentrated unity it holds together. If the *punctum stans* of the schoolmen is to have physical representation, it has that representation in the limiting behaviour of light.

I must apologize for the unsatisfactory character of this part of my exposition. I am trying to do what Hegel admirably did in his *Philosophy of Nature*, one of the great unread masterpieces of philosophy, essential to the understanding of Hegel and I think of the universe, which I am happy to say will not be too long appearing in an English translation. Hegel sees the whole of Nature as manifesting the Absolute in a state of self-alienation. It is the realm of the *Aussereinander*, of things set apart from other things in illusory independence. It is also the realm of *die seiende Abstraktion*, the region where aspects that cannot really exist apart make a brave show of being independent existences. This *Aussereinander* exhibits characteristics most remote from the

Absolute, where all is translucent and total, and where everything *is* the whole seen in varied nuances and emphases, yet it is necessary that there should be this diremption, this *Entaüsserung*, this resultant *Aussereinander*, in order that the Absolute should act as the unity which holds it all together, which steadily reduces it to itself, and which enacts the truth that what it thus reduces has no independent truth at all.

Let us turn from the problems of Space and Time to the problems which specially concern the objects that we find in them, the natural substances and kinds of natural substance of an older tradition, and the causality which links them, and which is an instance of causal law. Here innumerable puzzles arise if we do not realize what I may call the two sides of the Absolute, the need to be and appear separated, dirempted, torn apart, and the need also to compensate for its schisms and sunderings, to show them up as mere presuppositions of an ever deepening union. We may be led, like Hume, to take the mere bright show of descriptive surface-separateness, with all its appeal to perception and imagination, as the last truth of the matter, and to build it into a logic which never rises above the surface, and which certifies as 'possible', non-self-contradictory, whatever can be perceived, imagined or described. But feeling with our minds the connective tissue in which descriptively separate items are embedded, we become at a loss to connect this deep tissue with the surface: we wonder how the one gives rise to the other, how it burgeons into such surface diversity, what indeed is to be understood by that deep substratum which can have no diversity in it. It is having an Absolute without dialectical movement, without a growing, unitary sense that articulates itself in and through diverse aspects and positions, that lies at the root of our difficulties; we will have matters one way or another, and not in one way as leading to another, and as having no sense apart from that other to which it leads, and of leading to it. The classical problem of substance is a characteristic case of what happens if one has no Absolute or the wrong sort of Absolute. The need for a relative sundering of items becomes exaggerated into a sundering of all items imaginatively or even cogitatively distinct; these become the true Absolutes, the ultimate, independent, all-explanatory substances, while their being brought together becomes either their common stuckfastness in a metaphysical quagmire, or a gay 'accompaniment' which has all the mystery of a flight of birds. The truth lies in the meaninglessness of the sheerly disjoined and the sheerly undifferentiated, in the truth that the smallest, and likewise the largest, unit of thought and being must exhibit an articulation of articulations never ending in anything inarticulate, and itself fitting into similar articulations of articulations without end. At the same time, at each level, the manifold items in each articulation have their own genuine loose-ness and incomplete fittingness: otherwise the articulation would not be a genuine articulation, and its unity a vain and empty thing. Those particular nodes of the world that we call natural things have obviously a central metaphysical role: an Absolute is essen-tially present in all things, operative through a totality of *things*. And each thing *is* the Absolute in a particular mood or phase, for there is nothing else for it to be, and in that mood or phase it has all that pointing to everything, and that explanatoriness of everything, which the Absolute, wherever it may be, possesses. The close union of the various aspects of the thing, and the relatively loose, contingent union of the things which coexist in space, also has its justification: by realizing close unity in the small, it also realizes diremption in the large, and so enlarges and enriches the *task* of overcoming diremption which is the Absolute itself.

If we turn to the development of things in time, and their interaction with other things, we see the same understandable resolution of problems in the Absolute. The limitations of descriptive discourse, building on what can be imagined or perceived, breaks the continuous *growth* of one state into another, into a set of disjoined, existentially separate phases, having all the gay inconsequence of the notes sent forth from an instrument without any hint of the instrument's necessary persistence. What is most peripheral and parasitic and capable only of existing in the interstices of what endures, becomes the model on which endurances are themselves interpreted, and we wonder why the instrument continues to be dully there and does not change and fade like the notes it gives rise to. Whereas the diremption of the Absolute into seemingly separate things would be nothing if those things had no definite persistence, no firm retention of character. This again is no dilemma of thought but of being. Characters which are infinitely and accidentally variable, and which do not specify some thing's invariant background, nor weave to and from other specifications of the same background, are not characters at all: their invariant background likewise only is or has a character

D

because it can thus specify itself. Without so much, we may say, all character would be dissipated in the inane. The growing of phases of things into other phases assumes more dramatic form when the phases are widely different, or when they are located in separate things. Here we have the classical problems of causality, either in the wonderment as to why disjoined phases engender definite expectations, or the nature of the mysterious 'law' which holds their sequences in check, or in the wonderment as to how cause and effect manage to be separate at all, why causation does not detonate, we may say, in a single flashing transaction in which origins and outcomes are one. Neither of these possibilities would, however, accord with the essential *deviousness* of the Absolute, its need to give seeming separateness to its stages as well as content and living reality to their outcome, an outcome in which all the stages that led up to it are livingly retained. The causes of things lead on to certain effects because they are only in imagination separate from them, and the 'laws' which connect causes with effects are merely the specific inseparabilities in which the Absolute, as the universal connectivity of all with all, manifests itself in particular contexts.

From substance and causality we pass on to natural kinds, the third pillar in the façade of scientific induction and of the ontology which such induction presupposes. The far-flung things of the world, themselves growing into ever other things, and helping other things to grow into yet other things, fall and must fall into a finitely denumerable set of last kinds, each marked or defined by a finitely circumscribable set of properties. Variety and differentiation there must be, and their subspecies and cases may be indefinitely numerous, but the *heads* of such variety and differentiation cannot be infinite in number, nor can the range of variety comprised, covered under each such head, if we are to have variety and differentiation at all. For only what covers a definite range of variety, and has its place in a definite range of such ranges, can have definiteness of character, will not merely be dissipated in the inane. This again is not *our* dilemma, but a dilemma of being; finitude, τὸ πέρας, is essential to what is. Even the transcendent excellences which are the Absolute embody such finitude: infinite in their possible instantiation, they are none the less specifications of finitude. We may expect then to see that things will fall into a limited number of ultimate *genera*, adjusted also to the powers of the minds present in our universe and representing its self-understanding. The possibility of rational induction will be vindicated, and the nightmare multiplication of alternatives checked, and allowed to exist only in the interstices of what is measurable, delimited, definite in scope. And the pattern common to far-flung instances represents a genuine identity, as it cannot be on a view which turns instances into Absolutes: they are, we may say, the generalities of Absolutist resolve under which particular instantiations are, in a real sense, subsumed. It is to the general resolves of the Absolute that science penetrates, even though it must penetrate to them through a welter of instances.

The cunning of the Absolute is no less successful in guiding us through the labyrinth of life and mind. Here, as Hegel maintains in the *Naturphilosophie*, the *Aussereinander* and attendant mechanism of Nature is being steadily overcome: we are approximating steadily to the all-in-allness characteristic of the Absolute. Life is, in fact, an excellent monogram of the Absolute: it is always totally present in its distinct parts and functions, and jiggles them about when they fail to realize its total purpose, and this total purpose is further simply itself, to go on living. It also ramifies into a real genus of individuals, capable of many forms of social recognition and co-operation. Modern science and philosophy recognize all these things, but they too often fear to do so explicitly. Life too, like the Absolute, covers up its tracks by approaches to mere mechanism: it embodies its functions in many special vehicles, and so lures the scientific mechanist on to the perfect piecemeal solution which lies just round the corner, only to dash him on the rocks of life's capacity to do substitution-tricks with its vehicles. There is rich amusement and irony in the course of biological research: everywhere there are approaches to that pure mechanism which can neither be thought of nor be, and everywhere there is a swing-back to the organic totalism which for the mechanistic thinker means frustration. Life is no doubt an inadequate and absurd expression of the Absolute, in which integration is always at odds with disintegration, and this is why it points beyond itself to states less involved with special 'vehicles' that will concern us in the next lecture.

From the problems of life we go on to the problems of mind, by which we unabashedly mean the phenomena of interior experience, intimately related as these necessarily are to near and remote worldly situations as to situations unreal or impossible, and necessarily flowing over into overt action or into readinesses for such action. Interior private experience offers us an amazing two-sidedness, being welded, on the one hand, into an indiscerptible subjective unity, the unique me-relevance of whatever is there-for-me, yet having, on the other hand, a direction to matters immensely diverse, which in acquiring a common me-relevance do not therefore acquire real relevance to one another. On the one side, unity, on the other side, utter diremption, on the one side privacy, on the other side possible publicity, yet the two sides are linked in a single phenomenon, the intentionality or 'of-ness' of our private experience, which not only takes us out of ourselves into a common, natural world, but also leads us back therefrom to our own and other people's privacies, and so ends by putting privacy back into what is public, as it puts publicity back into every privacy. All the infinite swings from a subjectivity parasitic upon an objective order to an objectivity parasitic upon a subjective order, and vice versa, here have their origin, and can be teased out in an infinite progression: there can be no decision as to the priority of the in-itself or the for-me. This paradoxical intentionality, this living transcendence of self in the very process of remaining most intimately at one *with* oneself, and the transcendence of such transcendence when it is seen as at one with this immanence, is plainly the Absolute in its most unveiled perspicuous form, the most unveiled form, certainly, to be met with in this present life. Why conscious intentionality arose in the world is not at all mysterious: it arose because nothing could be or be conceived without it, because it embodies the non-diremption which is the *raison d'être* of all diremption.

The Absolute will stand us in good stead in most of the philosophical problems that surround the interior life of mind. That this life should be led up to by organic, material processes which seem but a shade separated from full-fledged conscious intentionality, and that it should constantly pass away into the same, is not at all extraordinary, even though it readily prompts the view of conscious intentionality as a mere offshoot of organic, material processes. Bodily processes lead up to conscious ones because, we may say, they are at all times labouring to divest themselves of their mere bodiliness, to rise to the undiremptedness which their surface diremption belies. It is because they are never merely mechanical, a product of independent part acting on independent part, that they can be raised to that supreme fusion where there are not, strictly, any separately acting parts at all. We think with our brains, undeniably, but the thinking brain is a brain that has lost its mere corporeality, its structure of part acting on external part, however much its mere appearance may continue to suggest the latter. In the same way concentrated internal resolves and realizations readily pass over into those neutral deposits from which they are always ready to be elicited, and into those long drawn out semi-automatisms of behaviour which they only at long range and on occasion steer and guide. Were we dealing with separate things in such cases, or, worse still, with a wholly uniform thing mysteriously posing as two, we should have no key to all these transformations.

Another range of problems of the mind are those that are concerned with knowledge. There is, we take it, a thoroughgoing conformity of human beliefs, of the ontic pressures we experience in our references, with what we take to be the reality of things. This conformity is not to be discounted on the mere ground that what we take to be the reality of things is bound to accord with our beliefs, since these last are our specific reality-experiences. Such a move fails to explain the immense mutual support given by belief-experiences to one another, especially in the region of compulsive, perceptual experience, and also, more remarkable, the thoroughgoing anticipation of what we shall meet with in such experience, and how we shall interpret it, in the unfulfilled sector of our thoughts. In all fields we successfully divine, in advance of detailed encounter, the sorts of phenomenon we are about to meet with, the relations to other sorts of phenomena that they will show, and most astonishingly, we understand what interpretation to put on such phenomena and how to test it. Thus we unthinkingly know and apply those techniques of looking for the invariant under and in the variable which enable us to say what bodies are like 'in themselves' as opposed to how they seem to observers: we are not hesitant in exploring bodies from many sides, calling on the witness of others, probing them with instruments, sifting the idiosyncratic from the constant, until in the end we arrive at that residuum which we take to be the true gold of natural reality. Our confidence in these explorations is so firm, and the questions we ask so definite, and asked on such a seeming background of knowledge, that it seems meaningless to regard them all as anything but an advance intimation of the reality of things. If things have a reality, we may say, this is how it would intimate itself to us. All this is odd enough, in the great welter of possibilities, to suggest that secret cooking-up of data by the human psyche of which German epistemology has been so fond: the difficulties of this epistemology have, however, been well exposed by Anglo-Saxon criticism, from which only deep ignorance still saves the Germanic mind. But in the light of the Absolute and its alienation in nature and return to self in mind, all this is explicable: the unreflective person's thought-techniques are the techniques through which alienation is overcome, through which the world 'out there' in all its dispersion and disunion, comes to be truly one, grasped and enjoyed in mind. Much the same is true of our confident use of the notion of mental otherness, whenever we encounter a creature that behaves faintly as if endowed with a unitive grasp and with spontaneous purposiveness, a notion without analogy or illustrations in our direct experience, yet strengthened by the use of analogy once it has been used. In this instant understanding of mental otherness, so clear to children but beyond the inferential approaches of philosophers, we may well see the Absolute at work: the unity systematically dispersed among various separate persons intimates itself in each person's advance knowledge of that systematic separateness, and how its content can in detail be determined.

I am led on, finally, to consider the philosophical problems which centre in value and evil, and which only are problems from the standpoint of an absolutism which alone can hope to solve them. If we reject absolutism, and believe only in a radical contingency of whatever exists, including human desires, then we can assign no absoluteness, no deontic character, to the various goals which seem to us absolute and mandatory, though it will remain an interesting problem how they come to seem so. It is clear, however, if we reflect with some care, that our so-called mandatory values all radiate from a single, central aspiration, which is nothing but an aspiration to transcend the specificity of personal interest and the particularity of the person, and to pursue only that which would interest us no matter who we imagined ourselves as being and no matter what we happened to be interested in. Moved by this aspiration, we rise above an interest in horse-racing or in oriental philosophy or in the strategy of seduction, and become interested in such shareable ends, as happiness pursued by all for all, as power, freedom and successful endeavour pursued in a similar manner, as justice or the refusal to be arbitrarily swerving or partial, as moral zeal, or the impartial devotion to all these ends.

It would take us too long to show how all our higher-order ends are merely specifications of this desire to rise above the specificity and the personal particularity of interest, and we can only here argue that it is a plausible view. Our mandatory values are not like the values studied by Stevenson, to which we declare ourselves to be partial, and politely recommend to others. What, however, is extraordinary and worthy of comment, is the whole aspiration upon which such mandatory values seem to rest. This involves what many a philosopher would reject as quite unmeaning: the attempt to determine what one would feel if one were someone quite different, and to do this in a whole round of cases, and to do it in all of them together, and then to take up the attitude of what Adam Smith called an impartial observer, who is all and none of these parties at once. The difficulties of all these proceedings, faced with frankness and not covered up by empty, formal talk of 'universalization', will show how transcendently metaphysical are the foundations of our most ordinary moral valuations. They involve, we may say, an attempted ascent to the Absolute, to a unity which indeed specifies itself in the distinctness of conscious persons, but which also asserts itself against their separateness, which puts itself forth as their one true source and goal, and which is to be found in everything that they are, and in all they can be. At the mere level of personal separateness, there is no morality but one of high-grade prudence, and there are no values but the ends that we personally happen to like. It is even doubtful whether we should not go further and confine ourselves to the values and pressures of the moment. The notes of omnitude and quicunquitude which are part and parcel of our impersonal norms and values can indeed be deduced from a general aspiration towards impersonality, but the existence and strength of this aspiration, and its central position in human practice, can be explained only by the Absolute. It is because we are all variously alienated instantiations of one Absolute, whose essential nature it is to alienate itself only in order to overcome such alienation, that we are unable to live unto ourselves alone, that we are compelled to rise, with what seems even logical absurdity, above the limitations of being the particular person we are, with our particular interests and place in the world.

The problem of evil, like the problem of values, is likewise no problem if we reject Absolutes. That there should be things in the world from which we shrink profoundly, and that some of these shrinkings should be backed by what may be styled 'deontic pressures', are indeed circumstances requiring explanation, but not raising issues of a fundamental, philosophical sort. It is only if we accept the existence of an inescapable, self-determining, all-determining Absolute, and believe values to be part of its self-expression, that we can be puzzled by the many forms of defect and untowardness that confront us in this life. The devious Absolute we have been putting to work is, however, well-accomplished to account for evil, and that without taint to its profound goodness. For it is only a very naïve vision that conceives that one can instantiate good without instantiating deviations and fallings short from goodness, and fails to see that the latter are not a sad accompaniment of the former but of its essence. The very nature of instances is that they should be one-sided even in their goodness, that they should be capable of mutual interference: an instantial world is essentially a rough and tumble world if not grossly and wrongly interfered with by celestial gardening. It is clear, further, and has been clear to many, that the highest excellence is the self-alignment with high values when other choices are possible, and that the highest excellence consists in the overcoming of evil. The Absolute, we have seen, is essentially self-determining, endowed always with a branching power of alternatives, and alienating itself in forms endowed with further powers of alternatives without end. The possibility of divergence from the absolutely good must therefore be granted in the absolutely good: it is part and parcel of its self-alienation. Evil must even inhabit the ideal interstices of the good, organically part of it, and parasitic upon its substance. The Absolute must certainly contain all these malign possibilities, and must by direction or indirection release them in existence, but while they may be practically the whole soul of some of its embodiments, they cannot, if we may speak so, be the soul and heart of the Absolute. And they will suffer attrition in this world and in time, since they are eternally, logically overcome in the Absolute.

I have now completed my sketch of how a suitably constructed Absolute might overcome some of the abiding difficulties of philosophy. I have seemed to be constructing a sort of cosmological or physico-theological proof, arguing from contingent being and its characters to the being of an Absolute. Really, however, I have been proceeding ontologically, for an Absolute that fails to bring light and unity into every contingent field, is an

Absolute infected with contradiction, one that is not and that cannot be. But now that my hasty sketch has been completed, I am sure that you will have been left with misgivings. Have my arguments not been too smooth and too easy? Have they not merely developed a particular view of the Absolute, and shown that much can be explained by it, and does this mean more than that I have tailored my account of the Absolute to fit the difficulties that I wanted to explain? Have I really succeeded in disposing of the alternatives that *might* obtain, whether of alternative Absolutes or of radical contingency or of superficial pragmatic piecemealism? And is there not something arbitrary and complacent in my rationalistic optimism, especially in view of many irrationalistic and existential protests against it? May not the Absolute after all be the difficult and bloody, but to some strangely fascinating Absolute of Kierkegaard, or the blind Germanic Will to Power of Nietzsche or the quite uncharacterizable mixture of Despair, Guilt and Nullity conjured up by Heidegger? I confess myself unsympathetic to these alternatives, which do not even make sense to me, but have I really abolished them? Have I not merely shown my own unrepentant eighteenth-century enlightenment, tempered with some early nineteenth-century, speculative touches, without saying anything about reality? I must admit that these questions strike home. The paper-arguments I have built up are not a sufficient bulwark against our contemporary weight of terrible and tragic experience. We live in a world, it seems, in which nothing is too terrible not to happen, and not even to be deliberately sought and wallowed in by some. And the world of motels and supermarkets and computers has not even the comforting promise of light and reason that existed in the salons of Paris and Versailles. We must, it is clear, retreat to higher ground, find the justification of our assertions in higher strata of being. It is this that will be attempted in my last lecture.

THE ABSOLUTE AND RATIONAL ESCHATOLOGY

In my previous lectures I first developed the idea of an Absolute in what seemed its most profitable, most theoretically useful and illuminating form: though an Absolute, if there is one, will not necessarily represent the peak of explanatoriness, and may even have unexplained contingencies alongside of itself, and side-by-sidenesses of necessary being within itself, still *our* only reason for toying with the notion is that Absolutes reduce side-by-sideness and underived contingency as much as possible, that they render them minimal even if they do not completely explain them. What we are therefore after in constructing the idea of an Absolute is that of something self-explanatory, which it does not make sense to suppose not there, and likewise all-explanatory, in regard to which it does not make sense to suppose the being or being the case of anything for which it is not, with supreme lucidity, responsible. Both the Absolute that will do this theoretical work and the lucidity which will guarantee it, are, however, desiderata rather than actual possessions, but Absolute-theory presumes that we may at least have glimmerings of such lucidity, which will show us at least what the one Absolute, if there is one, is not and cannot be, even if it does not fully show us what it is. At all points in our researches we may encounter ruin: we may come to see incoherences in, or what is a case of the same, to see alternatives to, some Absolute we are constructing, which will at once abolish all claims it may have to absoluteness. But even if this does not occur, incoherences may so burgeon, and alternatives suggest themselves so abundantly, that it may not seem worth while to go on with the whole venture. A glimmering insight did not, however, deny itself, and we were led to reject Absolutes in which all-explanation amounted to all-necessitation, or Absolutes that were value-indifferent, or Absolutes that were merely a re-assertion of our rough-and-tumble world, or Absolutes that were merely ideal systems of Platonic entities, or Absolutes that were merely concrete and individual in however exalted a manner, or

58

THE ABSOLUTE AND RATIONAL ESCHATOLOGY 59

Absolutes that were merely 'spiritual', in whatever individual or social, exalted or common form. What we were led to was an Absolute conceived as an eternal task or work or achievement, an achievement that was its own end, rather than as a worker or wonder-worker or field or material or august ideal blue-print connected with the work in question. The Absolute was something done or a-doing, and the categories mentioned were parasitic on it, rather than it on them. And if we were asked what sort of work the Absolute is or might be, then the answer was simple: that it was precisely the task of asserting Absoluteness, profound, necessary, self-contained unity and internal interconnection, over what appears to be the opposite of these, but which really, as the foil of absoluteness, can be regarded as part and parcel of absoluteness itself, i.e. dispersed plurality, loose aggregation, sheer contingency, all in short that the logic of description finds most basic in the world. Since talk of the Absolute must make use of an anthropomorphism which can only with difficulty be avoided, we may say of the Absolute that it is devious, cunning, even ungrateful and cruel—most of these are epithets used by Hegel—it advances towards certain limits only to retreat from them, gives colour and substance to certain independences only to nullify them, gives rein to plurality and contingency only to bring them to heel. All this, has, however, the misleading implication that the Absolute stands outside of the process in which it develops and reveals itself, that it devises this from on high, and that we are the poor pawns and victims in its game, whereas it *is* the game, and in its utmost alienation, *we*. The dispersion and disunity which we and other creatures represent is as much a part of the Absolute as is its unitive, blessed heart.

In our second lecture we tried to show how our Absolute was not merely fainéant and abstract, but could be put to work in resolving philosophical tensions, or in justifying the values and norms which guide our activities. We associated ourselves with the seventeenth- and eighteenth-century tradition, of making an Absolute, a God, do something for its living, if only to remove worries and to guarantee and justify what we should in any case do. An Absolute conceived as we conceived it, required Time as we know it, rather than showed up antinomies in it: it required the gay show of self-contained constancy and the evanescence that erodes it, and that makes it pass over into and become a mere past in something else. It required both the standard map of Time, frozen into coexistence like space, which physicists and philosophers have found so endearing, and also the realization that each point on the map is the not-yetness and the no-longerness of other points and had its whole content in being this and this alone. Time both separates and analyses and also annuls separation and analysis, and is always inseparable from whatever it arrives at or departs from, and is therefore a fit monogram of the Absolute. Much the same applies, *mutatis mutandis*, to Space, where every distance that separates is also a route that connects, and where there is really nothing that does not on examination show itself to be a transition, and an articulation of transitions, between something and something else. Existence in Space is also the kind of existence which, while retaining an aspect of holding together, goes as far in the direction of the fragmented and discrete as to suggest a sort of being that one cannot, in fact, ever have, which is suggested only to be negatived in the Absolute, but which for that very reason retains such a deep attraction and permanent fascination for our thought.

It is, further, what we have called the devious, indirect strategy of the Absolute which explains the gradual overcoming of dispersion and disunity at many successive levels, and at the level of the substantial thing, whose properties and parts have a deep mutual belongingness belied only by their surface appearance and the tricks of the Humean imagination, but which yet stand opposed to other similar things, with which, in a large number of connections, they have nothing to do. And it also explains the various points at which this mutual irrelevance suffers limitation and erosion, the causal transactions among separate things, which again show how little distance the Humean imagination can penetrate, and the natural kinds which likewise forge bridges of identity among dispersed specimens, bridges not merely there for us and for our abstractive comparison, but without which inductive arguments would have neither purchase nor sense. And the various forms of organic and conscious unity arise as living refutations, true existential protests, against the dead environment that seems to extend peaceably and logically around them, but which in fact illustrates the true logical absurdity and the total incredibility which organic and conscious being only seem to embody. It is only the long drawn out approach to disunion that we have in time which explains how the world could have gone on so long without that crowning presence.

Life and mind, however, introduce as much surface dispersion as they introduce unity, and here the presence of the Absolute shows itself in the cognitive registerings of remote facts and the readiness for such registerings, which we everywhere manifest, through which, in fact the dispersed world is gathered together in a unified perspective, and through which the unified perspectives in which it is gathered together also announce themselves to each other. If asked what the unity of the Absolute means in practice we may point precisely to these cognitive transcendences: they *show* absoluteness asserting itself over surface dispersion and multiplicity. The unity of the Absolute also expresses itself in those various higher-order goals of happiness, knowledge, love, sensitivity to beauty, etc. which are, as we held, merely special forms of self-transcendence in the field of interest. They are all an endeavour on the part of the finite person to be rid of his finite personality and the limitation of his interests, and to achieve some sort of a halting identification with the Absolute. And, as we argued towards the end of our second lecture, even the misfits, mishaps and deliberate misdeeds that we meet with in our world have their explanation and justification in the Absolute, which must extend itself, in an alienation which comes close to the limit of an impossible otherness, in order to reassert the unity, the redemptive self-identity which such alienation presupposes, and which is real only when alienation has both been enacted and overcome.

At the end of our second lecture we came, however, to see something all too facile in these marvellous doings of the Absolute. Like a wonderful elixir guaranteed to cure all disorders, it inspires doubt as to whether it can cure any. Will the face of the world not permit itself to be seen in other sinister, more senseless lights? Do we find, once we have seen it in the light of our teleological Absolute, that all other ways of looking at it lose their haunting grip? It is plain, on the contrary, that these other ways of looking at the world are not exorcized by our absolutist constructions, and that the existence of such unexorcized alternatives renders the explanatory claims of an Absolute empty and nugatory. We remain haunted by the presumption that diremption and looseness and mechanical encounter may still be the basic truth of things, and that the unitive inspiration of life, mind and our higher values may be due to some improbable chemical accident, occurring only once in world-history and in a single part of space, and doomed to die out quite tracelessly and irrevocably. The empirical data assort well with such a way of regarding things. We have an ever diminished reason to believe that life, mind and the higher values occur in a planet other than our own, or at another time than the present, and on this planet at this time they manifest infinite fragility and corruptibility. Changes of climate disrupt them, technologies destroy them, the mental vagaries of a Hitler soon corrupt them utterly. It is true that the view of life, mind and value as an improbable scum on a surface of chemistry is itself inherently improbable: it is an absolutism, and an absolutism that fails to recommend itself by its indifference to the values which must always confront it as a rival, and whose strange deontic pressure it leaves wholly unexplained. There remains however, a deep difference between what is inherently likely, fully understandable, and what is possible, free from internal incoherence, and it is not clear that the epiphenomenalism now revived as an identity-theory is inherently unthinkable. While utterly rejecting any Humean theory of the possible, we must still respect the solid witness of the empirical data confronting us. They bear witness, if not conclusively, to a life and a mind and a set of guiding values which have a merely superimposed, irrelevant character, which are parasitic upon states and events which have, for the most part, no similarity of basic nature. How can these ancient but quite genuine difficulties be dealt with? Is our only recourse a piecemealism which directs itself to immediate issues and refuses to ask absolutist questions? And how shall we exorcize the intellectual and moral despair to which such a piecemealism leads?

I am not, however, an existentialist wallowing in gratuitous despair, nor a gamester concerned to go on playing language games that mean nothing, but a rationalist, a child of the enlightenment, one who believes in justifying the ways of the Absolute to man. In my personal experience I have known things of such transcendent illumination and goodness as to make any radical scepticism, any radical moral despair, even any mere piecemealism quite unacceptable. What way shall I take out of these ancient difficulties? I expect some derision when I say that I propose to take an ancient way out of these ancient difficulties, a way that looks for their solution to another world, another state of being, another life. It is well known that this particular solution has been used to solve the problems of morality: a 'future state', it was believed in the eighteenth century, will redress the unfairnesses of this present life, will see the wicked punished and the good rewarded, and Kant thought it would enable us to make that unending progress towards ideal morality which the categorical imperative demanded. 'On earth the broken arcs, in heaven the perfect round' was a typical utterance, also, of Victorian moral optimism. The moral vision of Plato, basing himself on Orphics and Pythagoreans, likewise saw a future state as one in which Minos and Rhadamanthus would judge our naked souls, in which tyrants would suffer endless anguish in Cocytus, while true-bred philosophers and men of virtue breathed the upper air of the true earth, and could survey the many-coloured dodecahedron which was the shape of the universe. Plato, however, made use of another life as a solvent of epistemological as well as moral problems: in that life we should contemplate the eternal, blessed Forms and their lucid relations as we cannot hope to do in this life. And it was given a position *before* as well as after our present life, and it was our memory of the blessed forms and their lucid relationships which enabled us to frame dialectical definitions or to solve mathematical problems without teaching and without research. It has been too readily presumed that all this is mere myth, and was taken by Plato to be such, that Plato in fact had the cave-complacency that is now almost universal. Other philosophers have likewise used a future state as a solvent of metaphysical problems, notably McTaggart who believed in a final state which was not really a final state, since in it we would realize that we always really were in it, and so be free from those contradictions of temporality which McTaggart dwelt on so zestfully. Plato too thought that the contradictions of instantial half-being would be dissolved in his upper world of the Forms, and that such contradictions were valuable as serving to drag our minds towards true being. Other thinkers have given the upper world or life no necessary pastness or futurity: it was something that could be entered now and explored now. The Hindus and Buddhists of India, and the Buddhists of China and Japan, had their techniques of Yoga or Dhyāna, running up through stages of successive abstraction to the culminating, contentless enlightenment of Samādhi, or Satori, or Kaivalyam. St Paul ventured into the Seventh Heaven and encountered things not lawful to relate, yet infinitely more awesome in their obscurity than the splendid detail of St John's Apocalypse. St Teresa had her own complex *scala mystica*, all vouched for by her own experience, in which she ascended from her conventual worries in Avila till she lost herself in her Creator's larger life and light. All these schemes of transcendental life and experience, whether located in the past, the future or the present, have a strong air of the informative about them, which is yet belied by their almost total lack of content. When the soul with its chariot drawn by two horses saw the Forms shining in pure light, what did it really witness? When St Teresa's small bucket lost itself in her Creator's large ocean, what really happened to her? At the lower levels detail is sometimes impressive, as when we read Swedenborg on Heaven and its Wonders and Hell. But always we end up with an attenuation of description, and an approach to the empty or the self-contradictory: the situation is very puzzling indeed.

Our point of view is, however, different from anything extra-sensory or quasi-empirical: it is a severely logical, dialectical approach like our approach to the Absolute. The Absolute is a notion constructed by us to render this world, and our approaches to it, intelligible, to deprive it of some of its gross absurdity. The notion of another world is introduced to make such a construction viable, to remove or lessen the philosophical surds of this existence, and in so doing make Absolute-theory possible. We are not speculating about strange contingencies and seeking empirical confirmation of them, but we are trying to tailor the notion of another life to the surds of our present existence: it must remove these surds and nothing else. To those whose conception of the logical does not go beyond descriptive diction, and which makes no built-in use of the notions of determination, necessitation and explanation, it will of course appear that we are not doing logic, only a confused sort of speculation. To us, however, explanatory and self-explanatory discourse is as fundamental as merely informative, descriptive discourse, and involves its own irreducible modalities and connectives, and to work out how we may best talk self-explanatorily about the world is a logical and not a speculative venture.

We do not, however, wish to deny that our logical construction may involve certain empirical promises: it may prefigure the sort of experience that will fit in with the sort of construction that it is. That logical systems have empirical implications will of course be contested by many. But just as the low-grade logic of mere description has been used to justify a metaphysic of colourless objects and atomic facts, so the high-grade unitive logic of interpenetration will justify a metaphysic of high-level interpenetration and unity. Heaven, the other world, will be the place where this high-grade logic has its *most* appropriate application, though it will of course also have an application down here. Geometries, too, fit some states of the world better than others.

This brings me to my next point: that any other world or life that we construct is not, strictly speaking, another world or another life, but the continuation, the reverse side, if you like, of the world, the life that we are involved in here. There is no explanatory service done to thought if we resolve our philosophical difficulties *somewhere else*, while they remain rampant here. Their removal must be their removal *everywhere*, and our whole present world and life must assume lucidity and well-formed meaningfulness, when we supplement it with another world and life. I shall go further and say that the same absurdity and incompleteness which infects our present world and life, if not seen in the context of another world and life, must infect that other world and life if not seen in the context of this one. Our two worlds, or two hemispheres of one world, must be *mutually* parasitic, must take in each other's washing, as it were, if a viable Absolute is to emerge from their commerce. Everyone knows how silly, how utterly lacking in credibility, are popular religious or spiritistic accounts of the life to come, and everyone knows how empty of content, and hence of interest, are some accounts of the mystical consummation. This is because both afterlife and mystical consummation have suffered a severance of the umbilical cord binding them to *this* world and to this experience, which are as necessary to *their* meaning and being as they, in their turn, are necessary to the things of this world. I for one shall never sever that umbilical cord, and shall never overlook the crucial, the central significance of this dirempted, tortured life. I may here refer you in parenthesis to Hegel's venture into two-world philosophy which occurs in the *Phenomenology* and also in the *Logic*, which stresses the complementary character of the two realms and their mutual inversion, building on illustrations which derive impartially from the New Testament and from contemporary science. It is the same sort of *mélange* of different sorts of problems and discourse that I shall be carrying on this evening, no doubt to the pain of many.

I must, however, go to work if I am to sketch other-world geography before this lecture closes. I shall therefore lay down that the other world is a spectrum of states, terminating at one end in the dirempted, externalized condition that we call our

E

world, and at the other end in the absolute unity which more poignantly and pregnantly expresses the Absolute. The Absolute is everywhere throughout the system, nor is there anything in it that is not the Absolute in some guise, but it is more poignantly and pregnantly itself, more free from self-alienation, in the unitive pole of the system. Between our dirempted state and that unitive pole stretch, as I have said, a whole spectrum of states, achieving more and more unity and interpenetration as one progresses towards the pole, and more and more divergence and externality and concretion as one progresses towards our region of existence. This transitional spectrum is as essential to the limits of the system as they are to it: each dirempted item on the cosmic periphery has its life-line to the centre by way of this spectrum, along which, as we shall hold, there can be a going back and forth, and the absolute unity is only a unity in relation to the many life-lines that radiate from it, and that end in the most forlorn reaches of creaturely being. The Absolute, we may say, is redemptive, reclaiming activity, and such activity presupposes the creaturely periphery that it constantly transforms and reclaims, and in so doing can enjoy its unitive, central life. These diagrammatic sketches will, however, require a richer elaboration.

I shall now suggest the following characterization of the other-world spectrum we are considering. In harmony with Brahmanic, Buddhistic, Platonic, Neoplatonic and Thomistic accounts, I shall hold it to be a spectrum running from the extreme of sensuousness, at the one end, to the extreme of non-sensuousness, of purely noetic givenness, at the other. In our own private interiority there is a whole spectrum from sense-perception, through imagination, through symbolic reference, to purely notional apprehension: we can see a man stealing someone's purse, we can picture it, we can speak of it understandingly and we can realize it in an inward flash of grasp without even a trace of imagery or of spoken or imagined words. The whole essence of our inner conscious life is its capacity to *concentrate* multiplicity into unity, to be of a multitude without at all being many, and it is in this respect a good analogue of the Absolute. In our interior spectrum, all the members are parasitic upon one another: there would be no content to our concentrated understanding of some fact, could it not be deployed and fulfilled in imagination and sense-perception or carried out in perceived, felt action, but equally there is no content to perception, imagination and external behaviour which cannot be distilled into interior experience and set apart in the isolation of thought.

The same sort of spectrum obtains in what we may call the other world. While its lower ranges will be practically indistinguishable from the world of sense-perception, as had often been found ridiculous in the reports of spiritists, it will soon rise to something of the free variability of imagination, and that will manifest a curious and continuous irruption of the private into the public, that will be very disquieting to a positivist. So they will in fact no longer be able to say when they are perceiving and when imagining, and when others are sharing their vision and when not. As we move further up the spectrum, sensuousness will fade and the pure notion will predominate: we shall live more and more in a region where nothing is strung out in tedious illustration, but all is pure gist, concentrated meaning. We shall experience the world as we experience an opera when we have heard it out, with the utmost concentration, to the end, and it lives on, to quote Lotze, as 'an abiding mood in the soul'. And the concentrated presence of a whole system in one thought will not be the mere metaphor that it was to Wittgenstein. All this is not gratuitous speculation, but designed to clear up our philosophical problems, how our pure notions always have application to sensuous things, and how it is possible to think non-sensuously of the sensuous. Sense and thought are not two disparate modes of experience, nor is the second a mere substitute for the first: they are phases of a single spectrum and shade necessarily into one another, and their spectrum has a real and cosmic, as well as a personal and subjective, meaning.

With the spectral variation from sense to thought, will go a variation in what may be called materiality or corporeality. There is not, and cannot be, that sudden passage from the embodied to the disembodied, from the fleshly to the immaterial, that some have posited. There will have to be a gradual passage in which bodiliness, materiality, will be more and more attenuated till it vanishes altogether, remaining, however, as a notional gesture even in the most advanced states of immateriality. The snubness of Socrates' nose, which involves materiality as well as mathematical concavity, has been acknowledged to be a part of his Form or notion, of his immaterial soul. In the lower reaches of the upper world there will be things having many of the characteristics of bodies: they will be in large measure inert, subject to definite law and the same for all. But even at that level, as I am sure sometimes at ours, there will be breaks in that uniform rigour, and as we go up the spectrum materiality will become more and more of a gesture, a matter of useful illustration. There will cease to be public, unchanging bodies as we know them, until there cease to be bodies altogether. And this will of course apply to those special bodies, those vehicles or ὀχήματα, in which conscious beings display themselves, and exert influence on other bodies and on one another. At the lower levels such bodies will certainly exist, even if they lack the heaviness and unmalleability of this too-too-solid flesh, but as we go up the spectrum we may expect them to be attenuated to convenient shades, until they end up in those mere suggestions of characteristic atmosphere or presence which play a large, but unrecognized role in the phenomenology of persons. The solidity of bodies down here is, however, necessary to give a reminiscent content to the bodiless being up there, and the atmospheres left by a voice, face, gait and so on, will continue to individuate the being yonder.

Together with an overcoming of bodiliness will go an increasing overcoming of the externality and long drawn out successiveness of the spatial and the temporal. Near and far in space will increasingly lose meaning, as Dante and others have testified, and will more and more depend on inner affinity: journeys may well involve the strange property mentioned by Plotinus of carrying their starting-point with them. As regards time, we must avoid any facile leap from the long drawn out successiveness of being and experience down here to the *punctum stans* of eternity, but we must also avoid any brushing aside of the categorial character of temporal distinctions, of the inexorable difference between past, present and future, and of the constant passage of live content from one to the other. Scientific and metaphysical theories which try to play fast and loose with the categorial distinctions of tense, play fast and loose with the most intelligible, characteristic and precious feature of the universe, with what is most absolutely absolute in it. But though this is so, there may well be, at higher levels of being, what may indifferently be called an acceleration of passage or a widening of the scope of the present, so that a thousand years, or the *mahakalpas* of Indian imagination, become concentrated into one day. We shall more and more approximate to a limit of sheer momentariness in which none the less, as in a point from which lines radiate, there will be a sublated vestige of succession. It is not necessary to believe that, in the Absolute, such a limit exists, any more than the sheer diremption that opposes it ever exists: both, however, have a meaning as part of the continuous spectrum which is the Absolute itself. It is not necessary for me to spell out in detail how the curious properties of our space and our time, where continuity and unity come close to overstepping the externality which likewise comes close to destroying them, and where we are influenced by what is most remote in space and time, and even at times feel the self-shaping of the future, will pass over into the far more intimately collapsed versions of space and time that will exist yonder, till they draw close to an ultimate simplicity. The upper world spells out in detail what we always feel with our bones: that everything, however pinned down in location, is to be reckoned with everywhere and at all times.

The upper world will also show forth, we may be sure, an attenuation of that most vexatious, unintelligible feature of our present experience, numerical difference and particularity. Constantly down here we meet with differences which are not differences since they have nothing to pin down their empty repetitiousness but the vanishing distinctions of the here and the there, the this and the that, the then and the now. A repeating wall-paper seen from a bed of sickness, and nightmarishly extending itself towards infinity, is a good example of this surd repetitiousness of which no rational account can be given. Plato and Aristotle knew the elusiveness of the merely particular, and Hegel exposed it in the *Phenomenology*: it has been left to modern analysis to find its Absolute in this insubstantial region. Even in this world, sheer particulars elude our grasp, but in the upper regions of being they will not even *appear* to exist: profoundly like things will more and more coalesce in identity. We shall experience in an unconfused form that strange identification of what down here are distinct beings, such as occurs in dreams and in the thought of the unconscious generally. Even down here we have friends who mysteriously seem mutually replaceable, dittographs of one another, and in dreams it regularly happens that persons, things and places shade into one another, wherever there is an identity of role to connect them. Dreams, we may say, are at once the most rational and the least rational of experiences. While they confuse the common-place order of mutually external things with their mutually exclusive properties, which some think the paradigm of the logical, they also suggest an order, with higher claims to be considered logical, in which what we may call a unity of meaning operates through a large number of vanishing vehicles, and passes without let or hindrance from one to the other. Though dreams are not the product, as primitive thought supposed, of the soul functioning free of its body, but are perhaps rather the product of the body functioning free of its soul, still they illustrate something arguably beyond both soul and body. The ultimate vision of the real must have many of the characteristics of a lucid dream, and a River of Light may understandably transform itself into a still, white Rose, as in Dante's *Paradiso*. I shall not here stress how a seriously entertained upper-world realism of universals will explain inductive policies, as they are not explained by a serious acceptance of the dispersed particularity of things down here, which will neither allow us to expect continuity of behaviour in the individual, nor affinity of behaviour among dispersed things classified by us as belonging to a single, common sort. There will of course be levels of upper-world being where specific distinctness is as developed as individual distinctness is down here: the ultimate drawing together of such specificity will lie yet higher.

There are other forms of distance and separateness which obtain down here, and which will, we may be sure, be steadily attenuated as we progress upwards. There will be a reduction in the distance between cognitive approaches and their objects, between objects as they are onesidedly given or presumed to be, and objects as they in their true fulness are. The coincidence of intentional with real objects, only partial in this life, and troubled with many errors and confusions, will become more and more perfect, and with this will vanish the whole mysteriousness of intentional reference as we know it, the inexistence in consciousness of what transcends consciousness. We shall rise to something like the intuitive intelligence of Kant, or the active intelligence of Aristotle, or the Νοῦς of Plotinus which is only the unitive aspect of the νοητά that it contemplates. In the light of such an upper-world coincidence we shall no longer be perplexed by our strange power to refer to what is quite unlike ourselves, or to what exists nowhere, or not yet, or no longer, nor by our strange power of advance outline vision of what experience will subsequently fill in. All this will represent only a seeping down to lower levels of what is fully carried out yonder, and it is because our cognitive endeavours are even now *continuous* with those higher-level transparencies that our various knowledge-claims have substance and justification. Otherwise nothing but the sheerest scepticism would have more than a self-destroying vestige of justification.

Another form of distance and separateness that will be attenuated as we progress upwards will doubtless be the distance and separation of persons. The 'sharing' which is a mere metaphor down here will become more and more of a normal, understandable reality, and there will be no problem in communication or community. As in dreams, which again offer us an anticipation of upper-world experience, it will often be perspicuous what other people are intending, and the whole distinction between *their* conscious references and *our* awareness of these will become redundant and inappropriate. In many cases it will become a silly, empty question in just *whose* experience something is occurring. The state that Dewey pretended to have achieved in *Experience and Nature* will be actually realized, and the perplexities of Wittgenstein's *Blue Book* and *Philosophical Investigations* will happily lapse into total meaninglessness. All this does not of course mean any sheer elimination of personal distinctness in upper-world unity, any more than it means the sheer elimination of spatio-temporal distinctness there. When *A* comes into coincidence with *B*, it will bring into the coincidence a vestige of its former apartness, which it can again resume, and it will conceivably be in this perpetual flux and reflux of alienation and identification that upper-life social intercourse will consist. This is a better account of the social life of angels than is to be found in St Thomas. When we consider the unity of persons which obtains at higher levels, we can understand the anticipations of it that exist down here: the transcendent leaps of love, the extension of justice to beings wholly alien to ourselves, etc. etc. None of these phenomena have the slightest intelligibility on the separatist logic and philosophy which many apply to all the phenomena of our present life.

The third gulf that we must expect to see attenuated yonder is the gulf between existence and value. There is a strain of the absurd in the contrast between the absolute claims which certain values make upon us, their unconditional ought-to-be-ness, and the indifference men frequently feel towards them, and that the world, in its mechanical, and even in many of its organic and social aspects, shows towards them. From a point of view which rejects the authoritative, deontic character of such values, and which regards them as goals arbitrarily set for us by peculiarities of our psychological and social make-up, there is of course no problem in all this, but for anyone who fully experiences the phenomenon of value, its repudiation by men and nature can only be seen as inexplicable and absurd. This absurdity is lessened when we see the world's approach to value-indifference as a reflection of its approach to diremption, its approach to the mere side-by-sideness and brute indifference which in fact it never does and can achieve. From this point of view it will not be remarkable if, in the drawing together of the dirempted threads of being in which upper-world being consists, values, which consist precisely in the demand for such a drawing together, become ever more richly in evidence. The beauty which consists in the precise accommodation of outer form to sense or meaning will become ever more prominent where there is nothing inert, resistant, merely mechanistic about that outer form. The justice which consists in equal respect for the interests of all others will become a stronger force where others are all perspicuous versions of the self, and the same will apply to the love whose supreme achievement is the emotional and practical overleaping of immense personal separateness. The knowledge and insight which consist in notional penetration of what is objective, and the subjugation of oneself to it, or of it to oneself— it matters not how one phrases it—will likewise be raised to a maximum. And, lest the whole picture be too monotonously brilliant, let us consider that the greatest evils will also have a place there, even if coerced and encircled by the good things just mentioned: the incredible remorse for wrongs done to others whose enormity is now felt in that they seem done to oneself, the compassionate reliving of pains suffered by all beings in all parts of the world and at all times, the moral evil of the higher perversities carried up even to this level and sustained in the face of the absolutely good. For if there are infernos in the upper world, as there doubtless are and must be, it is not an alien anger that makes them infernal, but the resisted love of the absolutely Good: to be excluded from what one most necessarily and burningly must desire, must be the extreme of anguish for a rational being, its true self-damnation. All these evils will, however, exist in an interstitial and parasitic manner in that upper world and much more plainly so than they do down here. For their roots in the good from which they deviate will be clear, and they will be set apart and ringed off by their own interior conflicts. Evils will not be the utter mysteries and inexplicabilities that they are in this life.

The upper world is accordingly to be conceived as an extension of this world which transforms its problematic absurdities into reconciliations and coincidences, and enables us to make sense of it. And though it may end by being deeply antithetical to this world, it must be continuous with it and must diverge gradually from it, so that there will be nothing unintelligible in its connection with the things of this life. It will merely accentuate and bring out the living unity which is always at work among the dispersed things of this world, and which only extreme conceptual atomists fail to notice. And it will be parasitic upon this life and existence, as this life and existence will be parasitic upon it. Without the dispersed diversities and chance collocations and extreme deviations of this life to rearrange and restate, it would have no true content whatever. The bliss of Nirvana, of the ultimate dissolution, depends on the content of the whirling cosmos that is dissolved in it: they are in fact, utterly the same thing, as the later Buddhists of the Great Vehicle came to perceive. It may also be held at this point that just as complete independence and dispersion represents a limit which can be approached, but never achieved, so the utter unity which counts as the opposite pole of the system is likewise an unattainable limit, a transcendental Idea, in Kant's phrase, rather than anything actual.

If we now therefore are asked where God will be located in a system like ours, the answer will be everywhere and nowhere. If we locate Him at the central pole of the system He will answer to the Nothingness and the Emptiness of the later Mahayana, and to the corresponding notions of Neoplatonism and their pupil Dionysius the Areopagite: He will also have the properties of a transcendental, regulative Idea, rather than that of an actual cosmic phase. Having nothing of instantiation in Him, He will move the system as its transcendent goal which can as readily be expressed in terms of emptiness as of fulness, of ideality as of reality. If, however, the term 'God' is reserved for spiritual, conscious life as it exists near the unitive pole, then a language of theism may very well be appropriate, though a language of polytheism, as used by the Mahayanists or the Gnostics, might well be less restrictive. But perhaps it is best to reserve the term 'God' for the Absolute itself, the endless living overcoming of diremption and its subordination to unity, which however eternally presupposes and requires the diremption that it overcomes and subordinates. Of the three supremely paradigmatic men that our race has produced, Socrates, Buddha and Jesus, one was a polytheist, one an atheist, and one a monotheist, a fit reminder that those best qualified to perceive and enjoy the Absolute also perceive it quite differently.

If we now inquire as to the position to be allotted to Man in this complex world-circulation, it would appear that he is best regarded as a stage on the great return movement from maximum diremption and inert mechanism which confronts us in the more drearily material sectors of our world, to the unitive, interpenetrating life which must lie at the opposed pole of the cosmos. Of any movement *from* the unitive pole to the diremented periphery, and any phases to be met with on this course, we disclaim all knowledge, which could only spring from a profounder logical meditation than we have been able to perform. As far as we are concerned, there may be no actual process of *Entaüsserung*, of self-externalization, corresponding to the *Erinnerung*, or self-internalization, which we see everywhere in process. *Entaüsserung* may be merely *Erinnerung* seen in reverse, and from the end of the process. Remarks of Hegel on the identity of the concepts of Emanation and Evolution would seem to show that he would agree with this view. In the higher phases of unitive being and experience we see the earlier stages *as if* dependent upon these higher phases, as having their sense in it, though in the process they were the *prius* and it only an ideal goal. There are, in the eschatology we are elaborating, last things but no first things, or rather the first things are the last things seen from their own final standpoint.

The place of Man is obviously at a fairly advanced stage in the progression towards absolute unity, in which corporeality has not only acquired unitive, organic functioning, but also the deeper concentration of interior experience and thinking. And in the activities of social life, and in the rise to suprapersonal values and goals, there has obviously been a yet further movement away from diremption: interpersonal interests are directing and governing the life of man, rather than first-order, personal ones. If we now see Man in the light of phases of existence less diremented than our own, it is probably simplest to see him, in terms of the Orphic-Pythagorean-Platonic picture, as alternating between the gross immersion in corporeality and sensuous concretion that we call our present life, and the passing over into states where such corporeality and sensuous concretion, with all their attendant diremption, are more and more attenuated. Such an alternation, of course, works in both directions. It will place the great spiritual trials and temptations, as well as the great encounters and advances, in the maximally corporeal sector, where there will also be the Lethe, the water of forgetfulness, which will limit and concentrate vision, while the wider vision, the reminiscent Aletheia, will be the prerogative of existence yonder. We shall develop in this dark cave the insights and decisions which will be the ultimate glory of the upper world. In all this our total spiritual history will resemble our ordinary conscious life, which also alternates regularly from interior to overt phases. And I should hold it not unreasonable to believe in something like the ultimate liberation from corporeality and diremption, which one authoritative tradition postulates. The eschatology I have mentioned is of course that of Brahmanism and Buddhism, and is therefore readily thought of as foreign and Asiatic. It is, however, also the eschatology of our own greatest, classical philosophers, and it should be taken seriously and not dismissed as a tedious, Middle-Period Platonic myth. The merits of this eschatological tradition must not, however, close our eyes to the possible merits of the complex Christian tradition, where a single movement from this life to the next perhaps accords better with what we have said above about *Entaüsserung* and *Erinnerung*.

It is not, however, my purpose in these lectures to enter deeply into the merits or demerits of various eschatological hypotheses. What we are arguing is that some such eschatology must be accepted if we are to make full sense of our existence, of our various rational enterprises, and not merely of such as are lofty and transcendental, but also of very ordinary, basic ones. It is only in the light of an upper world drawing the threads of creatureliness together that we can understand the unity-in-dispersion of space and time, the existence of causally interacting things and of natural kinds scattered in space, the existence of organisms with their interior life, of human knowledge with its extraordinary gnostic capabilities, the existence of our understanding and love for others, and of our feelings for the deontic values which are in the main specific forms of that love. It is only because there are upper reaches of unitive experience, which always impinge upon us marginally, and which we have enjoyed and shall enjoy more fully when we are not so grossly immersed in corporeality, that the degree of unity we detect in the things around us, and the confidence which we feel in our various rational enterprises, are so strong and certain. The eschatology we have elaborated is a rational, and an *a priori*, not an empirical eschatology: it bases itself on the philosophical surds of our present existence, and suggests the supplementation necessary to resolve them. But, though rational and *a priori*, it is not absurd to hold that complete insight into the detailed form it must take must wait upon our experience of sectors of being that are now hidden from us. The whole structure of the colour-pyramid is in a sense implicit in every one of its members, it is utterly and purely *a priori*, yet it is only fully evident to those who enjoy a complete colour-experience. We who are acquainted with the complete round of hues, can see how they are all the colours there could be, and that all their relationships are necessary: but a colour-blind or partially colour-blind person would lack insight of this kind. It will be in less corporeal attenuations of our present life and being, that we shall understand the full structure of the sensible and noetic cosmos, and our own place in it and our circulation through it.

We may end on a note of some importance: of the permanent scepticism that must always be present as a foil to the rational, mystical faith emphasized in the present lecture. *Sentimus et intelligimus nos aeternos esse*, but our life is likewise lived in the shadow of a death that will, it seems, put an end to all feeling and understanding. Nothing is fully understandable except in the light of a rational eschatology, but our understanding, and the eschatological vision it projects, may be no more than marsh-lights dancing upon some inexplicable, accidental, chemical process. Piecemeal rationality, or a rational opting out of everything, may be the genuine alternatives before us. It is important to stress also the necessary obscurity of last things from the point of view of an absolutism that believes in them. The Lethe that surrounds our cave, and in fact constitutes it a cave, is no accident, but a necessary feature of cave-life, and hence also of the life that extends beyond the cave. It is only because everything is so rent apart that even logical atomism seems entertainable, that there can be the sense-making restoration that occurs at higher levels of being. Death, the final epitome of senselessness, is the most distressing of all the appearances of the cave, and its impossibility can only be understood and enjoyed in a setting in which its possibility and even its certainty have at first been brought vividly before us. The sublime uncertainty of the draught of hemlock, the dark doubts of the stormy night under the Bodhi-tree, the anguish of Gethsemane and Calvary, are not dispensable preliminaries to the serene safety they lead to: they are part of, preserved in, the latter. It is only on a background of despairing scepticism that supreme dedication is possible, a dedication which can live in and for the mere possibilities which a deepening insight will then show to be the only possibilities, and hence the necessities of all being.

IV

THE TEACHING OF MEANING[1]

Modern philosophy is distinguished by the emergence of a new question: how we give meaning to the expressions used in ordinary and philosophical discourse. Earlier philosophers simply inquired into the truth of this or that assertion, without troubling to raise the prior question as to what precisely such an assertion meant, or whether it really meant anything at all. When the question of sense had been raised, it led to yet another inquiry: in what way or ways a sense had been *given* to some assertion, or in what way or ways a sense *could* be given to it. This question led to yet another question, which is our main concern on this occasion: in what way or ways the sense of an expression could be *taught* or imparted, so that many men could use the expression in an identical way, and give it the same sense. This obviously is a truly fundamental question. For it is plain that most expressions acquire sense for us through a process of teaching. And even in the rarer cases where we ourselves act creatively, and arbitrarily give senses to expressions, there is still some teaching in the process, though it is we who are the teachers (or teachers *in posse*). For to legislate semantically is to desire others to use expressions as we do, even if only for the space of some discussion, and if we do and can attach sense to expressions for our own quite private purposes, this is at least a singular and not very valuable performance, of which it is not easy to give a plain instance. In each field of discourse, therefore, teaching plays a necessary role: it must be possible for us to be taught the use or sense of an expression by others, and it must be possible for us to teach the use or sense of the expressions *we* use *to* others. And if it can be shown that no such teaching has occurred, or that for some reason it cannot occur, then we may be spared troublesome inquiries into the sense or the truth of some assertion in question.

[1] Presented at the Oxford 1962 meeting of the International Institute of Philosophy on 'Thinking and Meaning'. Published in *Logique et Analyse*, Nouvelle Série, No. 20, Nauwelaerts.

The purpose of this paper is not, however, to pursue the method indicated, but to inquire into its foundations. It is to ask whether we can hope to understand the possibilities of giving sense to expressions, by considering the ways in which such sense can be taught or imparted, and whether we should not rather strive to understand what teaching is and achieves, by considering the senses we *do* manage to attach to expressions.

This is after all the method we adopt in other fields. We do not determine whether a man has been taught French properly by considering the way in which he was taught it: we see whether the man really knows French at the end of his course, and by his proficiency we assess the method of his teachers.

It will perhaps bring out the light thrown by the study of teaching on the communication of meaning if we consider the familiar case of the ostensive teaching of descriptive adjectives: words like 'blue', 'hot', 'loud', 'round', etc. which we are taught to use by having our attention directed to objects to which these descriptive words are applied. It has long been clear that the success of such ostensive procedures is mysterious, and that nothing in the mere rite of uttering words in the presence of objects makes clear how the understanding of their meanings 'gets across', nor even what precise meaning does get across. I may murmur the word 'red' in the presence of a geranium, and you may show by your subsequent use that you take the word to be a proper name for this geranium, or a name for flowers in general, or a name applicable to all objects warm or deep in hue or which attract attention or which please the eye, etc. etc. Only close examination of your subsequent utterances, in situations themselves requiring interpretation, will show whether the meaning I wished to teach has in fact been communicated, and it is notorious that even extended examination of your usage need not *conclusively* show what sense you attach to the word in question. If I can never be sure a man understands a word from his actual use of it, how much *less* can I be sure of it by examining the way in which he was taught it?

The points I have brought forward are commonplace, but they invalidate two arguments that modern philosophers constantly employ. The first argues from the fact that some circumstance mediates our learning the sense of an expression, that this circumstance enters crucially into that sense, that it represents a 'criterion' essential to the use of the expression. The second argues from the fact that some circumstance is *not* actually present on an occasion of teaching, that it is *not* an essential part of the use or sense taught. By the 'presence' here talked of is meant the sort of presence that a scientific 'observer' might recognize, not the sort of presence that requires divination, intuitive understanding, imaginative supplementation and so forth. Now it appears that both of these types of argument are misguided: they suppose that the world of the learner and student of meaning is the artificially stripped, standard world of the scientific 'observer', whereas it essentially must be his *own* world, with the distinctions he recognizes in it and the peculiar stresses he puts upon it and the unseen co-ordinates and standards that run through it, a world which we enter when we become deeply familiar with a man's use of expressions and see things as he sees them. I should therefore like to frame the two following counter-assertions: (a) that it is never right to argue that because some observable circumstance mediates the communication of a meaning, it necessarily plays an important role in the communication, or that it does more than touch it off; (b) that it is even more wrong to argue that because some circumstance cannot be observed when an expression is taught it is not playing a vital role in the teaching. Whether a meaning *has* been put across satisfactorily is shown solely by the interpretability of a man's subsequent use. A man might learn what it is for something to be so and so, or for such and such to be the case, by being shown something that illustrated the exact *opposite* of the sense we desired to impart, or by being shown something that *vaguely approximated* to it or pictured it, or by being shown something of which it was in some sense a *natural complement*, or even by wild words and ritual gestures that somehow 'got it across'.

If we are to evaluate the teaching of meaning by considering what it successfully imparts (as measured by our own successful interpretation), I think the following propositions may be laid down:

1. The sense communicated by a process of teaching always has a much wider generality than the materials used in teaching, how much wider, and wider in what directions, being something that only long study and careful interpretation can throw light on.

2. The senses collected from presented instances are almost always more extreme, simple and pointed than any sense which the instance on careful examination really illustrates. The paradigm

meaning of many words, e.g. 'round', 'empty', 'linear', 'equal', 'free', etc., is paradigmatic in the Platonic rather than in the recently current sense.

3. The sense communicated by a process of teaching often involves elements going quite beyond the things used in communicating that sense, and not, if we speak with a care for scientific observability, strictly illustrated by those things at all. Our understanding of ordinary terms descriptive of people's states of mind arguably involves much of this sort.

4. A process of teaching may successfully communicate senses which it is plain never *could* be illustrated at all. We all understand, after a few pregnant indications, what it is to 'go on for ever', or what sort of difference there is between *your* feelings and *mine*. Whether one cares to talk of the innate or the *a priori* in such contexts is a matter of taste.

5. It is never legitimate to deny that there may be obscure, dubious, queer, even contradictory elements in the senses of ordinary expressions merely because the cases in which we were first taught to apply them had no such *observable* oddities.

The outcome of this paper is negative: it is to suggest that an examination of the circumstances in which we learn the use of words throws comparatively little light on our learning or on what we may learn. It is also to suggest that if we are to find a model for the process of teaching meaning, the Platonic model of reminiscence is perhaps more suitable than any. The teaching of meaning may, with some pardonable exaggeration, be said to be the use of inadequate indications to achieve the more or less doubtful communication of a sense whose subsequent application is itself always doubtfully correct. The wholly correct use of an expression, and the wholly successful communication of its meaning, are in short Platonic paradigms like the meanings they presuppose.

DISCUSSION

Prof. Joseph MOREAU

Quand j'ai accepté d'engager la discussion sur la rapport de M. Findlay, je n'en connaissais que le titre, qui éveillait en moi une vive curiosité; car il soulève un problème d'un intérêt capital.

F

Mais les procédés d'analyse de M. Findlay, le caractère technique de ses considérations, ne me sont pas très familiers; aussi devrai-je me borner à présenter deux remarques, et à déplorer l'absence de M. Nikam, autre orateur désigné, qui aurait pu sans doute apporter des observations plus précises et plus complètes.

Ma première remarque est une réserve concernant l'assertion initiale du rapport de M. Findlay. Avant de s'interroger sur la vérité d'une assertion, il convient observe-t-il, de s'assurer de sa signification. Cela est incontestable; mais est-il certain que cette question préalable n'intéressait pas, comme l'assure M. Findlay les philosophes du passé? Il est permis d'en douter, si l'on s'en réfère à deux grands exemples.

Le premier est celui d'Aristote. Il est, suivant la doctrine des *Analytiques*, des choses qu'il n'est point nécessaire d'enseigner, qui ne font l'objet d'aucune science particulière, d'aucun enseignement particulier; par exemple, que toute proposition est vraie ou fausse. Si l'on vient recevoir l'enseignement d'un géomètre ou d'un physicien, il ne nous enseignera pas ces vérités générales communes, que nous sommes tous censés connaître; mais il nous enseignera, par exemple, ce que c'est qu'un triangle, quelles sont les propriétés essentielles de cette figure. Mais pour cela, précise Aristote, il devra nous expliquer d'abord ce qu'on entend par triangle, ce que signifie ce nom. C'est seulement après nous avoir expliqué ce que signifie (τί σημαίνει) le mot triangle, quelle est la *signification* de ce nom, qu'il nous montrera que la figure ainsi désignée *existe* (ὅτι ἔστι), c'est-à-dire qu'il est possible de la tracer. Car il peut y avoir des significations qui ne soient pas effectuables. De même, il nous faut entendre ce que signifie une proposition comme celle-ci: la somme des angles d'un triangle est égale à deux droits, il faut qu'on nous ait enseigné la signification de cette proposition, avant qu'on la puisse démontrer, c'est-à-dire prouver qu'elle est vrai (ὅτι ἔστι). La distinction que propose M. Findlay entre *enseigner une signification* et *établir une vérité* est donc une distinction qui n'est point nouvelle, mais classique.

Ce n'est pas tout: non seulement la nécessité d'enseigner une signification (*to teach a meaning*) avant d'en prouver la vérité a été reconnue par Aristote; mais on peut citer l'exemple d'un auteur ancien pour qui seule la signification peut faire l'objet d'un enseignement, non la vérité (*only meaning can be taught, truth cannot*). Cet auteur est Saint Augustin. Son traité *de Magistro* est consacré à établir qu'un maître peut bien nous présenter certaines propositions, nous en faire connaître la signification; mais pour ce qui est de la vérité de ces propositions, c'est à l'élève seul d'en juger. Une signification peut être enseignée, montrée, car elle s'explicite en un énoncé, qui est un contenu objectif de pensée; mais la vérité est une valeur que nous reconnaissons à tel énoncé, à tel contenu de pensée. Reconnaître cette valeur est un acte qui relève du sujet seul, qui ne peut lui être imposé; c'est affaire de réflexion, de jugement personnel, prononcé dans le for intérieur, en consultant la souveraine vérité, qui nous éclaire intérieurement. Dieu seul, ou le Maître intérieur, présent à notre conscience, peut nous instruire de la vérité; lui seul est notre Docteur.

Ma seconde remarque se réduit à une demande d'explications; ou plutôt, je dirai d'abord comment j'entends les explications de M. Findlay dans son rapport, et je lui demanderai de me dire si je l'ai bien compris.

Comment peut être enseigné le sens d'un mot? Il ne suffit pas pour cela de montrer l'objet qu'il désigne; cela n'est pas suffisant (exemple des géraniums) et cela n'est pas non plus nécessaire; il faut que celui qui m'écoute comprenne mon *intention*.

Mais comment puis-je faire comprendre mon intention et m'assurer qu'elle est exactement comprise? Comment vérifier si celui qui m'écoute s'accorde avec moi sur la signification d'un mot? Cela n'est possible, semble-t-il, que si la signification se ramène à une opération.

Si notre esprit se bornait à recevoir des impressions, à accueillir des représentations, aucune communication ne serait possible; ma représentation ne saurait en aucun cas être comparée avec la représentation d'un autre sujet. Mais nous sommes capables d'opérations; or, l'opération que j'accomplis peut être accomplie aussi par un autre, et chacun peut voir si elle est accomplie pareillement par lui et par moi. Là réside le principe de la communication entre les esprits, la condition pour qu'une signification soit enseignée et comprise. Faute de telles opérations, susceptibles d'être accomplies identiquement par divers sujets, il n'y aurait pas de communication intellectuelle, ni d'objectivité. On saisit par là pourquoi il ne suffit pas de montrer l'objet pour que la signification du mot soit comprise; c'est qu'il n'y a pas, à proprement parler, d'objet, tant qu'il n'est pas désigné par un nom, tant qu'il n'est pas constitué par une signification.

Or, une signification ne se définit et ne peut être enseignée qu'au moyen d'opérations. Cela me paraît attesté par deux exemples:

1° l'exemple des définitions d'objets usuels: un objet usuel se définit par son usage, par la façon de s'en servir, par une opération. Un couteau, c'est pour couper; c'est un objet qui sert à couper. Un objet de cette sorte est défini par référence à une opération;

2° l'exemple des définitions mathématiques: les objets mathématiques se définissent par leur mode de construction. Le cercle, c'est la figure engendrée par telle opération.

Cette théorie opératoire de la signification, il me semble l'apercevoir à travers les explications de M. Findlay. Ai-je raison de l'entendre ainsi? Du moins, peut-on la reconnaître chez Berkeley.

Toute représentation, observe Berkeley est singulière; c'est la représentation d'un objet singulier chez un sujet singulier. La connaissance objective n'est possible que par le moyen des mots qui ont une signification générale.

Or, comment un mot peut-il recevoir une signification générale? Comment le mot « triangle » peut-il désigner n'importe quel triangle? — A condition, dirons-nous, de ne considérer dans chaque triangle que les propriétés qui résultent de sa définition, autrement dit qui correspondent aux opérations par lesquelles une telle figure est construite. Le mot « triangle » s'applique à toutes les figures sur lesquelles telles opérations déterminées sont possibles. Les choses sont toujours singulières; si les mots peuvent avoir une signification générale, c'est parce qu'ils ne désignent pas immédiatement des choses, mais des opérations délimitant une catégorie d'objets, à savoir l'ensemble des objets qui se prêtent à telle ou telle opération. Les mots ne s'appliquent aux choses que par l'intermédiaire des opérations, qui seules peuvent être immédiatement désignées, dénotées par des signes.

Berkeley illustre ces vues par l'exemple de la numération, parlée ou écrite, utilisant des *noms ou des caractères*; les uns et les autres sont des signes qui ne peuvent s'appliquer aux choses, aux objets nombrés, qu'en vertu des opérations par lesquelles se définissent les nombres, et d'où les nombres écrits (les caractères), ainsi que les noms de nombre, tirent leur signification. « *The names are referred to things, and the characters to names, and both to operations.* »

J. HYPPOLITE

M. Moreau ne peut pas faire l'économie d'une synthèse d'identification en rejetant l'identité sur l'opération seule. D'autre part, le progrès dans la signification s'effectue par la distinction des significations à partir de situations confuses.

M. MERCIER

Après la première remarque de M. Moreau, il me paraît impossible que M. Findlay pense que le problème d'enseigner, de communiquer des significations ne se soit jamais posé autrefois. Si donc il dit que le problème de cet enseignement se pose aujourd'hui différemment, c'est d'une façon qui fait de lui un problème nouveau. Quelle est la différence, qu'y a-t-il dans l'enseignement des significations que les anciens auteurs ne pouvaient voir?

M. ZARAGUETA

Il y a lieu de distinguer entre la transmission du sens et celle d'une conviction. Elles sont parfaitement séparables. Il y a des convictions sur des propositions qui n'ont pas de sens, qui sont même un contresens ou tombant sur un sens étranger à celui qu'on veut et croit transmettre. Cela vient de ce que la conviction s'attache souvent à une simple formule verbale, ou à une formule prise dans un sens figuré ou topologique. De là le cas fréquent où deux personnes croient être d'accord alors qu'elles ne le sont qu'en apparence, ou par contre se croient en désaccord total ou partiellement apparent.

Prof. A. J. AYER

I agree in the main with what Professor Findlay has had to say against the Wittgensteinians. There are, however, one or two points which I should like to see further elucidated and one or two on which I should like to enter a mild protest.

It seems to me that the reason why the Wittgensteinian school lays so much emphasis on the ways in which words are learned may be that it assumes that if a child can acquire a concept by being shown a certain state of affairs, then the extension of the concept must be identifiable with states of affairs of the type in question. I should like to know whether Professor Findlay rejects this assumption or whether he holds only that his opponents take too narrow a view of what can be shown. For example, I agree with him entirely that Professor Malcolm's account of dreams is very perverse. But may not the trouble be that Malcolm oversimplifies the context in which a child learns the use of expressions like 'I dream' ignoring the fact that the child not only reports the dream but also remembers it?

I am a little puzzled by Professor Findlay's use of the phrase 'detached observer' which he seems to equate with 'scientific observer'. He seems to be suggesting that such an observer can only deal with what is public. But since Professor Findlay holds, I think rightly, that it is possible to communicate information about one's inner states, why should they not be amenable to scientific treatment? I don't think Professor Findlay wishes to hold that a scientific psychology must be behaviouristic.

Neither can I follow Professor Findlay in his denunciation of Ockham's razor. He seems to overlook the fact that the principle states that entities are not to be *unnecessarily* multiplied. The question at issue is what one takes to be necessary. To some extent this is a matter of temperament. I tend, as it were, to go in for landscape gardening. Findlay's outlook is more romantic; he likes the scenery to be lush. Still, there is more to it than this. If it turns out that certain types of entities are eliminable, we have discovered something of interest about the world. Even the attempts at reduction which don't succeed may be illuminating. An example would be the phenomenalist programme which I am now disposed to think cannot be carried through. But surely the attempt to carry it through has thrown light on the nature of physical objects and on the problem of perception. If we gave up philosophizing in this fashion, I think we should feel the loss.

Finally, I think it may be a little dangerous to reify meanings to the extent that Professor Findlay and others have been doing. We must not lose sight of the fact that meanings are properties of signs. What we still lack, it seems to me, is a satisfactory theory of what it is to use or interpret a sign. What exactly happened to Helen Keller when she realized that the tapping on her wrist *meant* water?

Prof. H. ROTENSTREICH

Prof. Findlay rightly opposed the genealogical view which attempts to derive knowledge from simple data, pre-knowledge ones. Yet he himself suggested in a way a genealogy in his allusion to Plato's theory of reminiscence. Anamnesis is a state of pre-knowledge and it suggests a primordial art of knowing. As against this I would like to suggest that there is no primordial art at all. Every art of knowledge presupposes in terms of arts and in terms of meanings a former art and a former meaning. This regression implied in every knowledge is due to the fundamental structure of meanings. Meanings are interrelated—e.g. if one knows the meaning of 'uncle' he knows by the same token the meaning of 'father' and 'brother' and if one knows the meaning of 1 he knows the meaning of 2. One can be taught the meaning of 'B' because one knows already the meaning of 'A'. This structure of a regressive and progressive continuum of meanings is reflected in human reality in two parts: (a) human reality is a reality permeated with language—and meanings in language refer to other meanings; (b) human reality is a reality of roles—composed of roles of being a father, a teacher, a friend. To grasp a role is to grasp a meaning.

One can teach a meaning because one knows a meaning beforehand.

Prof. M. BARZIN

Nos entretiens portent sur la notion de signification. Mais nos premières discussions font ressortir la confusion de cette notion et l'urgence d'établir à ce propos de nécessaires distinctions.

1° S'agit-il de la signification de notions ou de l'interprétation du sens d'une proposition affirmée vraie?

Le premier problème est d'importance mineure. Les définitions de mots sont conventionnelles. Il n'y a pas de vraies ou de fausses définitions. Les définitions de mots peuvent seulement être plus ou moins pratiques.

Le deuxième problème est au contraire, cardinal, car il touche aux notions de vérité ou de fausseté. Il a une portée ontologique.

2° La deuxième distinction, plus nécessaire encore, s'il est possible, serait de mettre entre les significations ne comportant pas d'élément de valeur, et les significations qui comportent de pareils éléments. L'enseignement peut servir ici de pierre de touche.

Je puis parfaitement enseigner à quelqu'un qui n'en connaît pas le premier mot, une théorie objective. S'il a ce minimum d'activité qui s'appelle l'attention, la théorie passera de mon esprit au sien, sans perte ou tout au moins sans grande perte. Tandis qu'il est impossible d'enseigner une signification comportant un élément de valeur, à quelqu'un qui n'éprouve pas, au moins inconsciemment, cette valeur. Les conditions de réceptivité sont très différents dans les deux cas. Il faut donc les traiter à part.

M. DEL CAMPO

Deux questions:

1° Quand vous parlez de *teaching of meaning* doit-on comprendre une autre chose que communication? La notion de communication n'enveloppe pas celle de *teaching*.

2° Vous croyez que le phénomène de la signification naît seulement avec l'enseignement ou bien plutôt la communication est-elle un phénomène inextricablement lié et inséparable de la pensée? Peut-on enseigner sans avoir déjà la signification?

Réponse du Professeur FINDLAY

In reply to M. Moreau, I must admit that my statement that philosophers in the past discussed the truth of statements without first asking what they meant, is very exaggerated. Certainly Aristotle realized that one must be clear about meanings before inquiring into truths, and I am not surprised that St Augustine showed a similar clarity of perception. But *in his practice* even Aristotle very often affirmed statements, particularly those about the mind, of whose precise meaning he did not give a clear prior account: what, e.g. does it mean to say that the mind is the place of forms, or that it contains the forms of things without their matter, that it is potentially all terms, that it is raised to actuality by an intelligence that is actually all forms, etc. etc. These are not propositions one can readily assent to or reject, for it is not clear what they assert. The same holds of St Thomas's assertion that in God essence and existence are the same, that the minds of angels contain 'similitudes' of things, etc. etc. Of post-Renaissance philosophers it is likewise throughout true that they discuss many issues to which no clear sense has been given. That it is all important to clarify sense *before* discussing truth *does* seem to me have been *more* emphasized by recent thinkers than by any previous philosophers.

To what M. Moreau says about 'operations' I am less sympathetic. In the case of *some* meanings operations are central, in the case of others only the operation of emphasizing some aspect or pointing to some limit is relevant, and here the 'operational' aspect is not the important one. As far as I can see, M. Hyppolite agrees with me that M. Moreau wishes 'operations' to doo mre work than they properly can.

In reply to M. Mercier I think that modern thinkers have been incomparably more *rigorous* than ancient ones in their demand that a precise meaning should be *given* to every expression used in philosophy, and that it should be shown *that it is possible* and also *how it is possible* to give certain expressions to certain sorts of meanings, e.g. meanings involving reference to private experience. Many such questions were certainly never raised in the past.

I agree with Monsignor Zaragüeta that the communication of meaning is quite a different thing from the communication of conviction, and that a person often *accepts* what I am trying to communicate in a form which only indirectly or inadequately represents its true meaning, or which positively misrepresents it. One of the uses of the word 'true' is to *assent* to formulae one perhaps cannot repeat and certainly cannot understand.

I do not disagree with Professor Ayer that Wittgensteinians can be said to have too narrow a view of what can be shown. But I still think that we probably should not use the word 'show' so widely that it covers any case in which we make plain to a person the sort of thing a word stands for. I doubt, e.g. whether A can show B, what it is for B to have a dream. As regards my use of the term 'scientific observer' I of course did not wish to suggest that information about inner states is unamenable to scientific treatment. I think, however, that protocols have an importance in theories about inner states, that they do not have in the case of theories about physical things, if for no other reason than that the interpretation of these protocols is infinitely more obscure in the former case than in the latter. I am not ashamed of my romanticism: I like the universe to be rich and full, though I also believe that it is so. And I agree that to talk about 'meanings' too hypostatically is extremely dangerous.

I think I agree with Professor Rotenstreich that the teaching of meaning is only possible on a background of pre-existent meanings.

In reply to M. Barzin I do not agree that the communication of meaning is of secondary importance. The notion that it is easy to communicate meaning, and that it requires little proof of success, seems to me to be one of the prime errors of past philosophy. I agree that the communication of meanings involving values is much harder than the communication of merely descriptive meanings.

In reply to M. del Campo I hold the now unfashionable view that meanings often exist in thought before being attached to words, but that few abstruse meanings are communicated except by teaching people how one proposes to use words.

V

SOME REFLECTIONS ON NECESSARY EXISTENCE[1]

The present note assembles some brief reflections inspired by an all too rapid, but deeply interested, reading of Professor Hartshorne's forthcoming book, *The Logic of Perfection*.[2] I have read it in proof, a mode of confrontation which always makes me aware how difficult it must have been to read Aristotle in the scroll: the rewards for my effort were in this case fortunately commensurate. I am contributing my note to the *Festschrift* for Professor Hartshorne, partly because I want to keep my foot in the door of the argument and partly because I wish to pay a tribute to Professor Hartshorne for his originality and courage in bringing the whole topic of necessary existence back into circulation and philosophical respectability, and for having done this in so systematic and persuasive a manner. Part of the thoroughgoing rehabilitation of the great philosopher who sleeps in Canterbury Cathedral had of course been begun by Professor Malcolm in a recent article, but this may have seemed to many—though not to myself—as a strange intellectual excursion of Professor Malcolm's, an intrusion of a personal Kierkegaardianism into a field where such quirks are merely curious. The 'infinite guilt' felt by Professor Malcolm for delinquencies unapparent to the secular eye, seems a poor reason for making major innovations in the sphere of modality. Professor Hartshorne, however, by being Anselmian in so well-worked out and contemporary a fashion has at least shown that the theses and arguments called 'ontological', are no trivial sophisms, but have the same sort of place in philosophy as the arguments of Zeno, of which refutations are numberless, but which, by their uniform survival, have revealed more of the essence of space and time than any merely positive analyses. Anselm's notion of the one unique case where existence cannot be accidental seems to point to some pole or horizon of discourse, a perfectly well-defined

[1] Published in *Process and Divinity*, Open Court Company, 1964.
[2] The Logic of Perfection and other Essays in Neoclassical Metaphysics (La Salle, Illinois: The Open Court Publishing Co., 1962).

limiting ideal position or region, which can be too easily judged void of actual occupancy, if we expect its geography and geometry to conform to those of nearer regions.

It is not possible for me, within the limits of my time and this paper, to consider all Professor Hartshorne's detailed theses and arguments, nor do I indeed know how I stand towards many of them. My thought on the topics with which Professor Hartshorne deals is itself in motion, and in directions not unlike his own: I have moved far from my simple *Mind* 'disproof' of God's existence, and I cannot say how far from each other we shall ultimately find ourselves. I have been powerfully moved by Professor Hartshorne's suggestion, so strange to theological tradition, that it may be feasible to recognize both a necessary and a contingent 'side' in God, that they in fact require each other and fill in each other's defects, and so enable us 'to eat our cake and have it' in the way religion needs, and that my *Mind* 'disproof' judged impossible. My aversion from theism, even when qualified as 'panentheism' is, however, constitutional: like Professor Hartshorne I have been much influenced by Gotama Buddha, the best man in my acquaintance, and I always recur to his battle under the Bo-tree against the spells and threats of positive religion. I certainly dislike the thought of 'one up there', whether developing or undeveloping, who seems to retain something of distinct existential status, and to act otherwise than through rational personal insights and decisions. There is an externality, a suggestion of being one among others, even in Professor Hartshorne's fine portrait: it makes deity 'finite' in the Hegelian sense, and so a defective object of religious deference. The best way to rationalize these protests is, however, to develop them fully, and I shall therefore try to reconsider in my own idiom, the feasibility and propriety of affirming categorically necessary existence, as well as the sort of object to which one might apply it.

I shall say, at the outset, that I do not think the sort of question under consideration can be dealt with in a formal way, whether this formalism achieves the final formalization of symbols, or the mere fixity of clear, closed, rigorously functioning ideas. No formal treatment can tell us whether or not we should include among possible axioms the assumption that there is, or necessarily is, any sort of object, nor whether we should so choose our axioms, definitions or patterns of inference that this follows from them. As little could it tell us whether we should or should not postulate a necessary God or a necessary giraffe. It cannot tell us these things, since they are not the sort of things a formal system can tell us: they involve asking what we should say in a situation where there are as yet no rules and principles to go by, a type of question precisely excluded by the notion of formality. If a formal system can without absurdity be made to refer to a part of itself, and to comment on its own structure and workings, and if it can be so extended as to include evaluations of its own assertions, asserting some to be valid, some contravalid, and some neither, and perhaps also to include prescriptions to the effect that this or that should be asserted, or this or that inferred from that, its assertions about itself will still never be more than idle endorsements of its actual procedures, and condemnations of those it does not follow. It can never rise to a consideration of what should be asserted or inferred in a situation where there are no rules to go by, or rules to which we are not committed, or a plurality of conflicting rules among which we must choose. It is plain that the issue under debate is one that requires the free, unformalized thought that lives in the interstices of formal systems, and that may be called 'dialectical' in a valuable and appropriate sense, a form of reasoning that tries out reasonings and assertions and sees how it likes their outcome, and which is not even clear as to the borderlines of its concepts till it has found out whether the picture they yield has the satisfactory contrasts and unity which make for 'intelligibility'.

All this would be trivial, were it not so readily forgotten. And it is forgotten whenever the exigencies of logic, in an august and truly important sense, are confused with those of some formal system. I am not clear whether Professor Hartshorne makes such a confusion or not. He wishes to make the existence of God a logical necessity, not anything relative or natural or psychological, but he defers greatly to existent formalisms, and he wishes to bring in his theology as an 'interpretation' of these logics (see p. 99) rather than as a new version of logic altogether. This deference to existent formalisms is, in my view, misguided. Formalization has no other philosophical merit but to show up the resources and limitations of certain basic conceptions and assumptions, so that we may freely decide whether to adopt them, add to them, alter them or reject them totally. By itself it can be construed to recognize anything or suppress anything, to bring out any distinction anyone finds important, or to relegate it, by a suitable *lettre de cachet*, out of all sight and mention. A formal system can be constructed so as to imply the determinism of the future or to leave it open and un-determined, to imply an ontology of at least one, or of a definite or indefinite finite number of individuals, or of an infinite number of individuals, or of no individuals at all, or of individuals variable in number through time, and capable of dividing or coalescing. It can likewise be so constructed as to admit of any number of irreducible categories, for which anyone might find a use. But, however constructed, it is, like all formalisms, potentially sinister: we can be tempted to read a philosophy out of it, instead of putting one into it. This is not a senseless warning. One has but to think how Russell became the prisoner of his own formalisms, still pliant and malleable when the *Principles of Mathematics* were being written, but set beyond remoulding once *Principia Mathematica* had been published. One has but to think how he imprisoned whole generations after him, so that even today a great logician dares to connect ontologies with odd issues of quantification and the use of variables. I do not accuse Professor Hartshorne of these errors. But he has not demoted symbolism and formalism to the quite ancillary part it should play in discussions of the sort he is conducting, the place of a secretariat invaluable in preparing or executing philosophical decisions, but quite unfitted to take part in them.

Decisions regarding the notion of necessary existence as applied to deity will, however, require general decisions regarding *existence* and *necessity*: one must determine their content and mode of functioning. Here I can do no more than indicate, without making out a full case, how I stand on these points. I reject all Russellian approaches to existence: that something exists does not mean that something or other has certain properties, or that a certain description has application. Existence is not primarily connected with descriptions or with general notions: it is primarily applicable to individuals, or to abstracta thought of quasi-individuals. It is I, you, the butcher, Professor Hartshorne, Julius Caesar, the number 10, the quality of mercy, etc. that exists or has existed, not primarily men in general, or number or qualities in general. And it does not matter whether the entities said to exist are named or merely described: St Teresa existed not otherwise than the saint of Avila. If men in the plural or numbers in the plural, can be said to exist, it is because individual men or specific numbers exist—John, Paul, Harry, 124, 209, etc.—and the existence of men or numbers does not mean that the properties of being a man, or of

being a number, apply to something. The reasons for my somewhat startling denial are many, and can only be given summarily.
One reason lies in the almost universal rejection of Russell's
equation by those not specially drilled to accept it: all those who
have taught the 'theory of descriptions' to pupils know how
relentlessly they say 'There is something that is King of France
etc.' before acquiring the aseptic 'Something is King of France,
etc.' thereby showing their unextinguished sense of the difference
between the *existence* of the something that is King of France, and
the mere fact that he *is* King of France. Another reason lies in the
way in which it prejudges the whole issue of the possibility of
there being nothing at all, and so furnishes a gratuitous ontological
proof of the existence of something or other, a prejudgement
which even Russell saw to be a defect. Another reason lies in our
plain need for what may be called judgements of acknowledgement, or judgements of 'hailing', judgements expressed in such
words as 'There's that!', 'There's something!' or simply 'John!',
'Something!', 'That!' Whitehead admirably suggested the
symbolic forms 'Lo *a*!' and 'Lo *x*!' as the general expressions
of such judgements. The judgemental character of our attitude
appears in the possibility of a negation: we can always say 'No
John!' or 'Nothing!' or 'That's gone!' Another reason lies in the
fact, manfully acknowledged by Moore, that while it may be
strange and redundant to say of an entity before us 'This exists',
it still is significant since it excludes the plain possibility that *this
particular entity*, not another, *should not have existed*, should not
have been part of the universe at all. To think of the possible
non-existence of an entity is implicitly to recognize its existence.
And a last reason lies in the grammar of desire and of other
intentional experiences. For plainly to desire that there *should* be
something having certain properties, e.g. a beautiful bride or child
for oneself or for someone else, is *not* to desire that one or other
among actually existent things should have been, or should become, such a bride or such a child. It is to desire nothing concerned with the mere character of anything, but with the prior
existence of what shall sustain such a character: to make it impossible for us to utter this intelligible thing is to create a dangerous
form of aphasia. We are driven unavoidably towards drawing a
distinction between what Meinong called facts of *Sein* (being
simpliciter) and facts of *Sosein* (being such and such), even if
we refuse to take his further audacious step of making *Sosein*

independent of *Sein*. To assert character, we may hold, implies, though it does not actually assert, existence, just as to assert existence demands, though it neither implies nor makes, some further assertion of character. All this must not be forgotten because it is often obscure whether we mean to assert existence, or character, or both.

As regards necessity, we need not be so contentious. We must say, however, that the necessity to be considered must not be the merely arbitrary necessity of some formal system, nor yet a necessity dependent on the existence of actual states and relations of things which exist in the world, whether this necessity circumscribes the 'nature' of open classes of existent things (the so-called 'laws of nature'), or of particular things in particular predicaments. It must be a necessity which emerges as we deepen our hold on our notions, and avoid all facile applications, identifications and subsumptions, and it will show itself, not so much in a passive, descriptive *Wesensschau*, but in what may be called the profound protest of our ideas, their screaming fight for significant survival, when subjected to various dialectical manhandlings. It is the sort of thing we encounter when we see that something which, at a facile, formal level, is free from contradiction, and would have taken in a Hume, does not, at a deeper level, admit of being thought out clearly, or when we see that some innocent simplification or substitution really mauls, maims, deforms or rends asunder the whole tissue of organized discourse. And in the battle for significant survival no holds are barred: ideas change their form and their characteristic strategy, positions are abandoned and lines reformed, examples and counterexamples serve to reinforce or to wear down. The battle for ideal survival is normally conducted in words: it is in fact necessary that it should be so. It has been as honourably and as well fought by many who have professed merely to investigate the use of words as by some who have professed to deal in naked essences. It has, however, always involved going beyond mere words or their actual use, to the live protest of our notions, to what we feel we must or cannot on reflection say. And the necessity it brings to light is always the upper limit of a long series of notional probabilifications, of cases where notional protest is muted rather than wholly absent. There are things that we can conceive, but only with strain: they are rebarbative, grotesque, intellectually repellent. There are things whose contradictories can only be entertained with strain, which make doubtful sense:

it is these whose upper limit is true notional necessity. There are also things that we can conceive as well as, or nearly as well as, their alternatives: here is the field for all that 'saying what one likes' of which recent philosophy has been so profligate. The final outcome of the steady rise in the acceptability of a notion is its formal canonization: its content and working are set forth in a system which it would seem self-destroying to question. It is not my task to inquire how far we have reached, or may hope to reach, this peak of philosophical uninterest.

I shall now proceed to apply these broad reflections to the question of necessary existence in general, and of God's necessary existence in particular. Here what I have said of the distinction between assertions of existence and assertions of character is extremely relevant. Anselm thought, or can be interpreted as thinking, that one can reason from a mere determination of the divine character, of the sort of thing a God would be, if He were at all, to the fact of God's actual existence, and he rightly included in that character the higher-order property of existing necessarily. A being who might or might not be, would, however excellent, not lie at the point of intersection of all those exacting demands which make up religion, and could not therefore be a perfect being or a God. And there is nothing obviously wrong in a notion of necessary existence in which it functions as a higher-order part of a thing's character. Things, if any, of which it was true that there had to be such things, would certainly deserve to be distinguished from things of which this was not true, and the attribution to *them*, as a character, of such a feature of the fact that they are, would be no more oblique and far-fetched than any other higher-order attribution, e.g. having all the properties of a great general. What remains clear, however, and what the whole traditional criticism has emphasized, is that the existence of anything cannot be inferred from anything in its character or concept, even if this includes a reference to existence, since its character or concept only tells us what sort of thing it would be *if* it existed, from which no conclusion involving existence can be inferred. I do not think Professor Hartshorne has shaken this traditional line of criticism nor am I sure that he wished to do so. The only hint that he may have wished to do so stems from the fact that in his formal proof (pp. 51–2) he argues to God's existence from the logical possibility of perfection. The suggestion is that this possibility is a small thing to concede, and that, once conceded, its immense conclusion follows. But the possibility of a necessary existent is no ordinary possibility, precisely because it is not a possibility if it is not also more than one, i.e. an actual fact, so that, in consideration of this immense consequence, one might well find the option of impossibility more attractive. There is, therefore, no route to existence from anything notional or characterizing, even if the latter in some way relates to existence.

If there is to be a valid ontological argument it must proceed, not from concept or character to existence, but in the reverse direction, from existence to concept or character. One must be clear, in the first place, that there must be something, and it must then follow that only what is of a certain character can necessarily be. Or perhaps the two could be established in unison, as it were: one could be clear that there must be something of a certain sort. The principle thus arrived at is not really derived from higher premisses: it can at best be buttressed indirectly by showing that all other affirmations or denials of existence of anything else alike presuppose it, which is rather a means of exhibiting its axiomatic character, than of deriving it from anything. The Cosmological Proof, enlarged to argue equally *a contingentia mundi* and *a contingentia absentiae mundi* would be a better expression of this line of argument than the Ontological Argument: Kant was wrong in giving the latter the prerogative. But it would not be a strict proof, but rather the sort of 'elevation of thought' that Hegel held the theistic proofs essentially to be: the sudden decision, informed by insight, to shape one's thought and one's language so that, whatever may be or not be, divinity certainly is. We must now ask whether we are prepared to 'take off' in such an 'elevation of thought'. Do we feel, in reflecting deeply on all we can conceive or assert or deny, that we are always residually committed to affirming the existence of something, and of something presumably exalted and unique?

There are much stronger grounds for holding that we are, and should be thus committed than are commonly allowed. Even Russell showed such commitment when he shaped his logic so that, on his own admission, it 'contains the admission that there is something'. And Wittgenstein made it in the *Tractatus* in failing to provide explicitly for the possibility that there might be no linkages among 'objects', and so no 'world'. Many people feel, and Professor Hartshorne among them, that something at least must exist to make affirmations and denials significant, though

G

there need be nothing necessary in the number of kinds of what thus exists. I myself am not hospitable to this conviction, since it seems to me to belong to a confused family in which what is incapable of illustration and fulfilment *for us*—placed as we are placed, and for reasons that we quite well understand and that are involved in what we mean—is confused with what is intrinsically and absolutely incapable of illustration and fulfilment. There is a predicamental difficulty in picturing one's own funeral which is quite different from the logical difficulty of imagining the end of infinity, and the difficulty of conceiving that there should be nothing whatever seems to me to belong to the former class. If the possibility of there being nothing whatever is to be ruled out, it must be on stronger ground than that we should not then be there to talk or think, or that someone is unable to imagine what such a situation 'would be like'.

It appears to me that the one hope for a successful ontological argument lies in the region of value: we must be able to show the existence of something to be necessary because it would be good. That it lies here is perhaps felt by Anselm and Professor Hartshorne when they connect necessity with perfection: the trend of their argument is, however, logical and ontological, and the 'must' of greatness rather than the 'should' of value predominates. That it should be possible to argue from what is to what should be, is of course a suggestion now universally suspect and evocative of horror, but suspicion and horror pale before an argument from what should be to what is, especially when the 'should be' hangs in the void, and depends on nothing beyond itself. None the less such an argument seems to me to have force, and force of that ultimate, notional kind that deserves the name of 'logical'. Despite all that I have read about the emotive or prescriptive or non-natural character of ethical utterances or their content, I cannot call anything 'good' or 'fitting' in full seriousness, without thinking it likely, and intrinsically likely, that it will recommend itself to others, and I cannot do so without thinking it to some degree likely, and intrinsically likely, that even *things* will show some tendency to conform to what I feel to be good and fitting rather than the opposite. I call the likelihood in question 'intrinsic' because it is neither based on experience nor capable of being removed by experience, though experience may possibly increase it. And that it is intrinsically likely is shown by the fact that I do not think reasons need be given, in certain profound and ultimate cases, when things are as they should be, but only when they *deviate* from this state. It is not, e.g. at all remarkable, nor requiring explanation, and yet not a matter of definition, that things should reveal themselves more and more completely when studied by science, and that our observations should more and more chime in with scientific expectations, whereas it would be remarkable if they did not do so. Many will of course see in my remarks no more than a relic of teleological superstition. Everyone knows, it will be said, that the 'survival of the fittest' explains the adaptiveness of things, that the order of nature is what our minds and our language put there, that all science is fortunate guesswork, etc. I am unrepentant. I find in my deepest thought a persistent linkage between the 'should' of likelihood and the 'should' of value, so that I cannot conceive, except facilely and superficially, what either would mean without the other. And I detect a similar linkage in the thought even of those who would reject it most explicitly. There may be divergence in detail, but there cannot be systematic contrariety or mutual irrelevance between the two 'shoulds'. It is not, however, necessary to argue this point strongly, nor to resuscitate any grand-scale traditional teleology. It is only needful to ask whether, if such a linkage obtains at all, it will entail the existence of anything, and in particular of anything of a superlative and unique kind.

It might appear plain that, *if* there is an argument from value to existence, then it would surely prove the existence of what is perfect, the synthesis of all values in their highest form. This argument would previously not have held water, since the notion of perfection seemed plainly self-contradictory. Not only did it involve a purely conceptual necessity of existence, which seemed absurd, but it involved also a synthesis of countless incompatible ways of being good or an impossible choice among them, as also the notion of an apex where no apex is conceivable. Professor Hartshorne has suggested a way out of *one* of these difficulties: a synthesis of the necessary and the contingent in the being and nature of God. That there should be a God is necessary, and that, being a God, He should have certain deific properties, e.g. capacity for realizing all excellence, uniqueness, etc. is likewise necessary, but that God should reveal Himself in this way rather than that—in *some* way He must—is not necessary but contingent, and necessarily contingent. This contingency in God would affect, presumably, not only His relation to His creatures, but also His intrinsic being: capable of all things, He might elect to be one sort of God, e.g. a somewhat austere mixture of justice and mercy, rather than another. Professor Hartshorne has given this divine marriage of necessity with contingency a temporal form. God, rather like the immortal soul in Kant, seems bent on removing the element of contingency in His being by realizing an ever wider round of possibilities: if He cannot achieve all goodness at once, He will at least achieve it by endless approximation—an aspiration in my belief vain, since the *order* in which goodness was realized would remain contingent. Possibly I am reading more into Professor Hartshorne's picture than he really would allow: I am interested but not deeply moved by his notion of a developing deity. His conceptual marriage of the necessary and necessarily contingent seems, however, to be an important idea, and one in which I can see no obvious flaw; that it should be necessary for something to be, and that what thus necessarily is, should necessarily have these or those properties, not only does not *exclude* its having farther contingent properties, but even *entails* that it *should* have some, since no complete being can avoid 'coming down' among various incompatible possibilities. Nor is such 'coming down' necessarily an imperfection, since it merely reflects an incapacity for the impossible, and since it does not affect the divine power to achieve each incompatible possibility separately. God, in short, cannot be *actus purus*, since the idea is, in this connection, self-contradictory, and He has never, outside of the pronouncements of official theology, been thought to be so. His necessary nature necessarily completes itself in a freely chosen contingent nature—He is by preference the God of Jacob and not of the Edomites, by preference forgiving rather than absolutely exacting, etc.—and possibly the thought of the creative Logos, or Second Person of the Trinity, was framed to express this fact. The possibility opened by Professor Hartshorne smites me with awe, but I cannot say that I wholly like it. Perhaps I feel obscurely that I might not personally care for the sort of God God has contingently chosen to be.

In another direction, however, I do not think Professor Hartshorne has worked at all hard enough to remove contradictions in the notion of perfection. His God presumably enjoys a personal consciousness distinct from that of contingent beings, though He sums up and sympathetically relives all that they do and suffer. I am not able to see how this squares with Hartshorne's 'panentheism', or even with the perfection of God. For a God that has even the exclusiveness involved in being one conscious person among others, even though reliving all that the others live through and more besides, has not in my view the absoluteness necessary for a perfect, truly religious object.

I feel, therefore, that the antinomies in the idea of deity have not been eliminated, and, moreover, that one does not perhaps wish them to be so. I am not sure that religion really desires a possible, and therefore an actual God. If the divine lineaments emerge from conceptual mists there is always something dreadful about them (religiously dreadful), and they make those whose thought about them is not nebulous into somewhat dreadful people. Or if one approaches the matter from the standpoint of an argument from value to fact, I am not sure, paradoxically, that it would be good for there to be something perfect, or not in any straightforward first-order sense of perfection. The argument from value to fact is in any case never felt to be a rigorous one, as, e.g. Plato felt when he held that divinity only made things as good as possible. We do not feel, further, that it could conceivably be made rigorous: the being of the good cannot rise above probability. If it is absurd to conceive of a complete divergence between what is and what should be, a complete coincidence seems as inconceivable, and as destructive of either notion. These are old antinomies, part of the deep 'duplicity' of our value-consciousness, that nothing has overcome. It seems to be the case that the perfect or best, in an ultimate sense, is also always a higher-order perfect or best, and that it demands, as part of its meaning, the *non-existence* of what is straightforwardly perfect or best. The really best, in short, is a state where rational purposive activity always has some work to do, and this, it would seem, is a state from which the redundant, ready-made perfection of a God is necessarily absent (though it has, of course, unlimited room for saints and gods, of which I hope there are many). All this is what I believe Hegel understood by 'the Idea' and its 'reconciliation with error and finitude', which practically amounts to making our own world, and our own rational struggle in it, when looked at in a special transfiguring light, as both being what necessarily is, and what is as it should be. So that if I were to believe in any sort of necessary existence—a plunge I have not yet taken—I should make my necessary existent something much more like the Hegelian Idea than Professor Hartshorne's developing and suffering deity. I am not concerned to argue for such a conception. What I am concerned to argue is that Professor Hartshorne's defence of Anselm has left the whole question open: one is still in doubt whether to say anything necessarily exists, or to say that it is of this or that sort. This, however, is precisely Professor Hartshorne's merit: he has reopened a question that for so long had seemed closed.

VI

FREEDOM AND VALUE[1]

The aim of this contribution is to stress a number of logical relations among certain of our fundamental ethical concepts: the concepts I am about to consider are those of freedom, of value and of moral goodness and badness. It is my belief that there are few fields in which there is such an abundance of close inter-connections among our various notions, some of these inter-connections being wholly necessary and admitting of no excep-tions, while others are merely relations of mutual adjustedness and belongingness, so that we find it more or less 'odd' if the notions are not exemplified together, whereas it appears quite 'natural' and unsurprising if they are jointly exemplified. The application of these fundamental notions to actual cases is profoundly obscure and controversial: we may very well question whether some of them apply to anything at all, and certainly whether they apply in this or that particular case. All such obscurity should not be allowed to affect the clarity of the relations among the concepts themselves, and the nice way in which they play in with each other's variations, and build upon or supplement one another.

The first concept that I wish to consider in this connection is that of Freedom. I shall say that anything is free in a given situa-tion if it may be credited with a readiness to act or react in a manner A, but may equally well be credited with readinesses to act or react in certain alternative manners B, C, D, etc., these various readinesses together entailing a disjunctive readiness to do either A or B or C or D, etc. none of whose members represents a vacuous addition which is not an independent readiness. (Though the thing conjoins the readinesses for A, B, C, D, etc. it does not, of course, have a readiness for their conjunction, since A, B, C, D, etc. are incompatible.) And I shall say, further, that anything is free if the precise member of the disjunction that is afterwards realized can be held to be realized merely because the

[1] Presented at the XIIIth International Congress for Philosophy, Mexico City, September 1963.

thing in question is the sort of thing it is, in the situation in which it finds itself, and not because we know or suppose the presence of some further factor or feature from which, in company with suitable laws or rules, the precise alternative realized deductively follows. Freedom, in short, is a negative notion connected with potentiality, actuality and time, and concerns the logical relations between what is potentially true of a thing at one time and what is actually true of it at another, or between what can be validly anticipated of something at one time and simply predicated of it at another. Very loosely and inaccurately it may be said to involve something like a self-narrowing disjunction, a readiness for either A or B being succeeded by a realization of A (say), no further explanation of this circumstance being looked for beyond the mere fact that there *was* this readiness for either A or B. (The term 'self-narrowing disjunction' is inappropriate since the additional positive notion of a 'readiness' qualifies the whole bracketed disjunction and is not represented in the outcome.) The logic presupposed by our concept is no doubt peculiar, and probably involves some such consequence as that, when all is yet in readiness, it is false of any definite alternative A, B, C, D, etc. that it *will* be realized, though at a later date it is true that one of them *is* so. The thought of poised states afterwards coming down on one side need not, however, have the logically untoward consequences it is often thought to have, since the futurity of not-A need not be taken to be the true logical contradictory of the futurity of A. We need not confound 'It is not the case that A will be the case', which covers the poised and unpoised state alike, with 'It will be the case that not-A will be the case', which applies only when the poise has been resolved. Some patience and a little logical skill will give our forms and rules the means to cope with the concept we are here considering; it should not be ruled out merely on account of simplifying prejudice.

The objections to the notion of freedom just outlined are not, however, logical: they are much more weighty and concrete. Some would doubt whether our notion is capable of empirical illustration, and so possessed of a definite, discussable content: others would doubt whether it corresponds in the least to what we ordinarily mean by 'freedom'. Yet others would doubt whether, though capable of imaginative illustration, it can have any use in weaving the fabric of knowledge and science. As regards the first point, I think we should distinguish between illustration and completely verified presence: a roulette wheel that comes to rest in a certain position, though its whole behaviour illustrates an equal readiness to come to rest in other positions, completely illustrates freedom, even though in reality, to an eye that takes in innumerable unknown circumstances, it may not exemplify freedom at all. For what a case illustrates is what the mind collects from it, what it sets before us or introduces us to; and this is almost always more pointed, more abstract, more neatly representative and more shorn of context than what is really there. One cannot determine, as many students of the 'paradigm case' have too readily thought one could, the significant content of one's references by considering the *actual* circumstances in which one hazards them: one must consider those circumstances as the speaker sees them, or as they are taken by him to be. And if the roulette wheel is a low-grade instance, then one has but to pass to the utterances and actions of a truly intelligent and sensitive person: at every point they exhibit the faintly fresh, yet not crassly surprising character in which freedom is best illustrated. While falling within assignable limits, they are never completely foreseen. That they might have been foreseen by an angel or cosmic demon does not alter their power to illustrate.

As regards the second point, it is undeniably the case that there is a more elementary, less interesting concept of freedom, having intimate logical connections with the one we are studying, which can with some justice be regarded as covering 'what we ordinarily mean by "freedom"'. This is specifically the freedom *from* compulsions and hindrances, from factors shaping something's line of activity or inactivity in directions in which its own contribution is negligible or non-existent. This freedom is, in the plain case, one from external intrusion or obstruction, in more subtle cases one from internal pressures and blockages which, in the case of reflecting, deliberating persons, seem to fall outside of the various fully formed or half-formed decisions which they none the less help to inspire. It may even seem that the freedom involving a radical openness to alternatives is merely a distortion of this ordinary freedom, a lack of alternatives, though coinciding with an individual's unforced line of development, being misconceived as a sort of internal compulsion. One might, however, say that the distortion worked in the reverse direction, an absence of hindrances being misconceived as freedom since it is necessary to and completes every exercise of freedom, since it is *hypothetically* open to such alternatives as freedom may take, and since it is often the only factor in an exercise of freedom which is of interest, since open to some doubt. It is, however, perhaps best to admit that we have here two quite different, interrelated concepts, both involving an initial disjunctively qualified readiness afterwards narrowed down to a single, non-disjunctive outcome. Only, whereas in the case of the one concept this involves an extraneous factor, the other involves only the force and sense of the disjunction as such. The vicissitudes of life certainly lead ordinary speakers and thinkers to form such a concept, and if 'spontaneity' be thought to be a better name for it than 'freedom', there need be no quarrel on this point.

It may, however, be held that the notion just dealt with, though readily formed, free from contradiction, and capable of superficial illustration, is none the less not one with which responsible, deep-level thought can operate, certainly not the thought of natural science nor the thought which seeks to probe the choices and conduct of men. Such responsible thought, it may be argued, must necessarily seek to make the passage from a disjunction to the assertion of one of its alternatives deductively compelling: there must be some new factor recognized, whether as operative cause or internally moving reason, as well as a rule stating how this cause will act or this reason move, until all but one member of the disjunction have been eliminated, which residual member will be thereby completely 'explained'. It may, however, be held that spontaneous freedom, wherever its presence is conceded, is as unmysterious and as fully explanatory as are other sides of the developing behaviour of things, and that the role of science is not to exclude it as inadmissible, but to find out precisely where and when it exists, within what limits it manifests itself, as well as the degree to which it is manifested or could be manifested in given circumstances. For the presence of spontaneity in natural and human affairs does not mean that anything and everything can happen—such an assumption would certainly disrupt organized thought and discourse—its presence is necessarily confined to certain sorts of agents, in definite sorts of circumstance, it must operate over definite ranges of alternatives, and it must achieve some outcomes with more difficulty and consequent infrequency than others. It would be the task of science to map and measure all these factors: to determine what sorts of performance are, for a given agent or type of agent, well within, or well beyond, or on the limits of its range, the sort of assessment we roughly perform on the characters of our associates, and which it is not absurd to suppose that science might learn to perform on its electrons and other objects. For spontaneity has only not become fully acclimatized in science because its presence there has been judged obnoxious and provisional.

We may note, further, that the notion of spontaneous freedom, if given a place within the developing fabric of knowledge, need not be equated with that of chance. Chance reflects the element of random collocation among the disparate things lying side by side in the world, an element which, while with suitable laws it may indefinitely explain later collocations, and be itself deduced from prior ones, still never loses its hybrid inconsequence: if necessarily sequent upon prior unions, it none the less always continues their irregularity. Spontaneity, on the other hand, covers the variability of response regularly found in a certain agent or type of agent, precise as to the circumstances of its exercise, and measurable in its range and degree, perhaps itself also subject to a higher order of variability according as it has been thus or thus used or abused. While a 'randomizer' may conceivably counterfeit spontaneity, the imposture will surely break down. Statistical uniformities based on stray distributions of independent factors have not the enduring, characteristic variability of single things.

Spontaneous freedom is of course most interestingly displayed at the level of cool, conscious choice, rather than at the level of primary impulse, and much rather than at the level of unconscious or inorganic behaviour (though we need not exclude its presence there). At the level of cool, conscious choice we have at least the *appearance* of the arbitrary, the wanton, the gratuitous, the reckless, the capricious and the perverse, and, though one may seek to base such phenomena on a wholly different substructure, it is not 'in their idea' to be so based. In the idea of an arbitrary choice there is no idea of a hidden cause which leads one alternative to be embraced, much less that of a secret reason. In the idea of a perverse choice there is even the idea of action in deliberate opposition to reasons or to personal drifts and tendencies. It is not our task to argue for the granting of hospitality and employment to these notions rather than rejecting them as delusive. What we may, however, attempt to point out is *why* they seem to be illustrated at this level rather than at lower ones.

Arbitrariness and wantonness, or their appearances, are found at the cool, conscious level, since this is the region where there is a detachment from or a distancing of primary impulses and interests, where they come to be replaced by mere symbols of value, to which our attitude is calculative rather than overtly desirous. Cool, conscious choice tends to occur at a level where we are secondarily interested in the *interest* we know objects have for us, rather than in those objects themselves, which may be quite unwanted at the time. Being thus remote and secondary, the region in question is also a region of liquidity, where sums can be totalled and exchanges effected, where one personal value or interest can be added to or balanced against another so as to yield a single overall outcome. But being a region thus secondary and representative, it is also a region where the frail reasons that stand for warm personal needs and commitments, can be readily discounted or resisted, where the fine poise of our detachment can readily be brought down in a perverse, capricious or arbitrary manner. If these notions have application anywhere, it is here that they find their best field.

But, as we have said, the region of cool choice is also the region where higher, ever more abstract and generalized notions of value arise, and have a shaping influence on our conduct. The zone of the arbitrary, of *Willkür*, would seem strangely enough to be the region from which the norms, the rational, interpersonal standards of conduct and valuation descend, and Kant would seem to have been right in accommodating in the same practical will both the prescription of impersonal imperatives and the personal decision to adopt them or not adopt them as one's maxims. For the detachment from primary impulse which makes caprice genuinely possible, is also the detachment which enables us to range our diverse interests together and devise plans which harmonize them all. And it is also the detachment which quite readily, having made the great initial leap from primary interest, overleaps the relatively trivial distinction of different persons, sets their interests side by side, and discovers outcomes satisfactory to them all. And the same detachment readily leads on to a love of the justice, the impartiality implicit in its own procedure, and to a hatred of all that transgresses it. It is not our task on this occasion to show that the whole firmament of our impersonally approved values including knowledge, love of beauty, mutual understanding, etc. may be deduced, not perhaps rigorously but none the less persuasively, from the impersonality which characterizes even our first steps into the cool, detached survey of our own interests.

We have said enough to show, however, that the sources of caprice and disinterested rationality lie extraordinarily close to one another, and to this we may add the further observation that the sources of moral excellence and obliquity seem to lie in the same region. For, whatever we may concede to deterministic theory, we measure a man's virtue or wickedness by the seeming gratuitousness or seeming inevitability of his voluntary espousal of purposes good or bad, the voluntary espousal of a good or bad purpose being more excellent or depraved the more energetically spontaneous it appears to be, whereas it becomes less and less a matter of moral praise or condemnation the more the irresistible appears to replace the spontaneous. These propositions are not novelties: what would be a welcome novelty is that they should be taken seriously in philosophy.

CHAPTER VII

METAPHYSICS AND AFFINITY[1]

The aim of this paper is to analyse and recommend a policy of inquiry and reasoning that may very well be called 'metaphysical', though whether it accords with any policy of reasoning that may have been called 'metaphysical' in the past, whether with praising of dispraising intent, may very well be doubted. It is, however, a policy to which I, and a certain number of other nurselings of what has been called 'analytic' or 'linguistic' philosophy, have felt ourselves increasingly drawn or driven, and which has brought us to feel increasing sympathy with the phenomenologies and speculative deductive systems of the past, as well as—despite many reservations—with the wilder 'ontologies' and 'existentialisms' of the present. Briefly, it is a way of thinking that holds that there is a truth *to* appearances, *to* experience, *to* real things and characters, *to* the categories and structures that are there, that is quite different from the truth of what is matter of fact, of what must indisputably be acknowledged, of what can be pronounced before everyone without fear of contradiction. If the latter sort of 'truth' comes readily and unhesitantly as we apply the concepts and procedures we have to what lies before us for pronouncement or report, the former sort of truth comes hard, and not without a profound sinking of our mind in the sense of words, an examination of this sense from wonted and unwonted angles, an attrition of case upon case, a giving heed to questions, protests and promptings not normally felt, a descent into minutiae that ordinarily escape notice and an ascent to generalities not ordinarily hazarded, and all in all a continuous screwing up and adjustment of our notional and verbal sights so as to achieve a closeness of fit and a faithfulness of representation that is quite alien to the ordinary workaday ideal of correct or true pronouncement. Truth in the ordinary acceptation is an all-or-none affair: it either hits its relatively broad target, or it falls short of it. But truth *to* the appearances, to the matter before us, to what we

[1] Published in *The Monist*, Vol. 47, No. 2, Winter 1963.

encounter in experience or thought, is an infinitely graded matter: it may vary from the most inadequate sketchiness and the most distorted misrepresentation to a representation ever more subtly accurate, without however being capable of complete adequacy. Truth in the straightforward sense is the fit of *assertions*, whose component terms and forms have well-established senses and uses, to what stands before us for utterance, whereas truth in the sense here under consideration is rather the fit of *notions* and ways of speaking to these same matters, which by its nature cannot be straightforward. What will be the result of the continued effort after 'truth to things' in the sense just sketched is of course not one that we can predict in advance: it may very well be quite remote from the ordinary account of things, as queer in its whole mode of representation as were the 'analyses' aimed at by Moore in relation to the unquestioned deliverances of common sense. Such an adjustment of concepts to things will, if feasible, have all the suggestions of 'lifting the veil', probing 'beneath the surface' into a deeper dimension, which will entitle us to call it 'metaphysical'.

The kind of conceptual transformation called 'metaphysical' might very well occur in a number of quite different ways, which would however always exhibit one salient polarity: some transformations would enrich diversity, whereas others would increase unity. Sometimes our quest for a profounder faithfulness would result in the uncovering of differences that had previously passed unnoticed, sometimes it would result in the elimination of differences that had previously seemed important, sometimes, that is, it would dig down to a deep unity of character under differences admittedly great. These cases would not be hard to illustrate. A philosophical analyst of mind might, e.g. like to bring out the difference between a palpably-intuitive and an impalpably-non-intuitive element in our ordinary acquaintance with sensible things, and he might like, in this respect to assimilate perception to imagination or he might like to see them both as divergent species under a single genus. In like manner the quest for a deeper truth to things might result in the unveiling of articulate structure where no such structure was previously recognized, or the blurring of structures previously admitted, or their replacement by structures not previously suspected. For this kind of philosophical complication or simplification I need provide no illustrations: thousands will suggest themselves. But the quest for deep faithfulness may

go beyond bringing out relatively shallow differences or identities of character: it may uncover profound differences of
category, of basic type or manner of being, where no such
differences seemed evident, or it may build bridges of affinity
which blot out such differences, or it may resume them all under
some deeper identity. One has but to think, e.g. of how the notion
of a relation first distinguished itself in thought from that of a
quality, and was then again assimilated to it in the notion of
'monadic' and 'polyadic universals', or of how Brentano's 'intentionality' first showed itself as utterly distinguishing inner mental
activity from anything physical, and then became a feature as
much present in outward behaviour as in inner mental acts, etc.

Such deep changes in conception will go together with a demand
for changes in propositional form to express them, and may
necessitate logical revolutions: a new calculus of relations may
emerge, or a new calculus of indirect mental and verbal reference,
etc. But, more important than all, it may happen that our existent
modes of conception are felt to be *modally* inadequate: their
classifications as necessary, contingent, impossible, etc. may be
felt to be open to question, and their relations of entailment,
exclusion, independence, favourable or unfavourable relevance
may be felt not to be 'true to' the real natures or characters or
categories that they cover, and to require substantial revision
and remoulding, which in its turn will require to be registered in
the formation and transformation rules of our logic. The necessary, the consequent, the compatible, the impossible are of all
things the least evident in a purely formal perspective, and the
most demanding of a 'deeper' assessment. Bertrand Russell, in
his memorable Lowell Lectures of 1914, first made us familiar
with the view that a philosophy armed with the various liberating
tools forged for *Principia Mathematica*, e.g. the logic of triadic
relations, could find many things 'possible', e.g. the dark mystery
of false belief, that less privileged philosophies could not help
finding 'unintelligible' or impossible: he saw the new notions
made to satisfy the deeper needs of mathematicians as also 'giving
the philosopher wings', as enabling him to evade the all-devouring
elenchus of Bradley, where no possibility could survive but the
existence of an Absolute and its dark prerogatives. But he failed
to reflect that a reform of logic inspired by another subject-matter
than mathematics, by the requirements, e.g. of mental or value-
discourse, might yield contractions rather than expansions of

possibility, that the pursuit of deep faithfulness to the matters under consideration might result rather in our increasing feeling that certain things really 'wouldn't make sense' in the absence of others, that the former only superficially seemed imaginable or conceivable without the latter, that 'at a deeper level' the possibility of their divorce did not really represent a possibility at all. Thus Bertrand Russell's successors have denied the real possibility of the world having been created five minutes ago together with its fossils and memories, of the people around me being mere 'phantasms' in my private world, and of many of the other 'possibilities' of which Russell's brain was so fertile. If one's sympathies are often with Russell in these dogmatic encounters, the point of principle remains that what counts as a logical possibility depends on one's logic, and that one's logic depends on the relations of dependence and independence that one may ultimately decide do obtain among one's notions, and that are not necessarily reflected in the relations obtaining among them at a routine level, when we are not concerned to achieve deep 'truth to things'.

The notion of deep 'truth to things' will, however, seem open to many objections. Some of these are general objections against trying to step out of speech in speech, and against comparing one's utterances with the real structure of things. We have long been schooled to think that no mode of speech can be truer to things or truer to thought than another, that the Frenchman is laughably mistaken who thinks that the French language renders things more perspicuously and articulately than any other language, that it is absurd to translate one form of speech into another, and think that one is then setting forth its 'real content' or 'true meaning' any better, that it is basically erroneous to think that the bald utterance 'Brick!' in a language of pure imperatives is more explicitly put in *our* normal form of utterance 'Bring me a brick!'. These doctrines are, however, all part of a systematic confinement of thought and understanding to the manipulation of signs according to linguistic rules, of which most serious question may be made, and they are also the embittered reaction to a frustrated intent to conceive the 'real structure of things' in an atomistic manner based on abstract metaphysical argument, having no illustration among the things encountered in human experience. Obviously a form of speech which recognizes the complexity of a broom's structure, together with the relative

H

simplicity of its function, is 'truer to' the broom's nature and make-up, than one which treats it as a mere complex of ultimate entities or as *penitus simplex* like a Thomist God. And from the simple metaphysics of the household we may advance to a higher metaphysics whose speech and thought is more true to knowledge, to valuation, to thinking, to perception, to material existence than ordinary modes of speech and thought. Certainly the exhaustive minutiae of, say, Austin's treatment of the language of sense-perception do nothing if not screw up our sights to a more detailed, accurate, unhazy and astonishing account of our language than our ordinary concepts of that language ever rise to: though only professing to analyse what we say, they abundantly illustrate the proposition that to be 'really true to' what we say is to go beyond what we should ordinarily, or in superficial philosophizing, say that we say. The researches of Wittgenstein likewise amply show that to be 'true to' the uniform characters we *say* are there is often to recognize unsuspected, complex networks of 'family relationships', and that what we say or think we can conceive, and what is accordingly 'possible' at a certain level of examination—the 'feelings' we project into chairs, or the 'room' of our neighbour's imagination into which it seems that sorcery or telepathy might give us an entry—are not really thinkable or possible when the matter is thrashed out more deeply, that they are surface-modalities of unconsidered speech which do not accord with the depth-modalities of further reflection. Certainly the performance of the linguistic analysts gives the lie to the view that no mode of speech can be 'truer to' fact or dig deeper into being than another, if ever they have been so foolish as to maintain this. (Austin, I am clear, never made these relativistic pronouncements.)

In the same way, we may reject the objection that there can be no modal qualification, no necessity, impossibility, possibility and contingency, no entailment, contradiction and independence, that is not a mere reflection of our chosen way of speaking, of the rules of our language, and which has some sort of root in the natures of things. Obviously we learn by deep reflection and meditation, by *approfondissement* in meanings and in cases, what things can and what things cannot be otherwise, what things cohere together ineluctably, or what exclude each other totally. We may then choose to reform our rules of language so that what was discovered by deep meditation now goes without saying: anything we like can become part of the meaning of our terms, can be built into our linguistic procedures. An attribution of all things to a Spinozistic God or Substance can as easily be so built in as the secretly materialistic metaphysic of individuals, qualities and relations which is basic to most modern calculi. But it is profound, non-formalized reflection that alone can decide what shall be held to be truly possible, impossible, contradictory, independent, etc. and no formal procedure can help us here.

It is in fact a profound objection to some current forms of linguistic philosophy that they have obstructed deep meditation on modality: in tacit conservatism they have endorsed certain forms and procedures that we have, denied that alternative patterns could be 'truer to things', and then proceeded to look on all things as 'possible' which these patterns did not rule out, while tacitly treating as impossible all that they could not readily formulate. And they did so always with a bland air of neutrality, of making no factual assertions, of leaving the matter of experience untouched, while they in fact *showed* (though they might not assert), by the sheer limitation of their forms, the outlines of a highly determinate metaphysic. Through the defects of their symbolism they insinuated, e.g. the impossibility of there being nothing at all, through their self-restriction to predicative and relational functions and their refusal to countenance anything intensional, they legislated conscious and semantic phenomena out of existence, through their poor symbolism for identity and their refusal to countenance tenses, they excluded the possibility of two distinct individuals achieving fusion, or of what is the case ceasing at a later time to be the case. What they did was sometimes admirable, though always done under the wrong rubric or pretext, and if they sometimes did screw their sights into closer alignment with the real, they did not admit that they were doing anything of the sort. What must accordingly be written over the gateways of an analysis of language is that there is no acceptance of language which is not also tacitly assertive: to elect to talk of the world in certain ways is to say subvocally that the world is of a certain general sort.

It is of course a great merit of speech that it can be conducted at varying levels, and it is not one that we should ever wish to eliminate. There must, e.g. be a fairly superficial level of speaking in which vastly many things are possible, and ever more deeply reflective, concrete ways of speaking in which more and more of these superficial 'possibilities' are ruled out. There must be a basic, pluralistic, extensional form of diction suitable for mathematics and the like, and more tightly knit, subtly formed kinds of diction, suited to physical, mental, axiological, metaphysical and other higher forms of discourse, and what is absurd or inescapable at the apex will not necessarily be so at the base. That there are some ways of thought and talk that are 'truer to things' than others does not, however, mean that we must always speak in the truest manner and spurn the less true. A probing microscope or an electronic telescope are not always the best visual instruments. The less true may be the right way for innumerable limited purposes, and may also be a necessary foundation and background for the more true.

The notion of an adjustment of our concepts to the 'truth of things' has, however a genuine intrinsic difficulty in addition to the mock difficulties we have just been considering: it implies an extraordinary internal dualism in our own notions themselves. That we revise our conceptions is certain, and that we do so by considering instances, reflecting on obscurities, voicing misgivings, etc. is also undoubted, but what does it mean to say we make them truer *to* the real characters, categories, structures, modalities, etc. that they cover? Can it mean anything but that we amend concepts by comparing them to other concepts, and those as much our own as those to be amended, since it is not clear what could be meant by 'real characters', 'real structures', 'real categories', etc. if these are not mediated by our own modes of speech and conception? Plainly, it is not 'experience', in the sense of a dumb encounter with single things and occasions, that can be held to amend our first imperfect notions, and if it is 'experience' in the sophisticated sense of Husserl, the developed internal grasp of what it is to be this or that, how can this be other than the formation of a new set of conceptions by means of which our first rude notions are corrected? How can 'looking at the phenomena' or the essences mean more than conceiving them, and how can one mode of conception coexist with and illuminate the other? Only a belief in an Aristotelian active intelligence, possessed of forms in a manner which our passive intelligence only emulates, and capable of communicating their pattern to the latter, would seem able to perform what is here presupposed and demanded.

If the matter is looked at carefully it would seem that, here as elsewhere, Aristotle has, in an account which at first seems strange and arbitrary, really gone some way in pinning down the actual 'phenomenon' that is involved in the philosophical 'deepening' of our concepts. For we do feel, when we try to be closely 'true' to the content covered in some concept, that there *are* two ways in which we are conscious of an identical coverage. We have, on the one hand, a relatively condensed, inexplicit concept of what it is to be this or that, and we have, on the other hand, a relatively expanded, developed concept having the same coverage, or at least professing to have it: the inexplicit concept, however, contrary to the Aristotelian image, is the one by means of which we test the correctness of the explicit one, and it has an abiding prerogative in virtue of doing so. It is only when the explicit concept appeases all the obscure demands of the implicit one that we feel that we have done justice to what it is to be such and such, or for such and such to be the case, and *then*, in the final result, we have something like the Aristotelian *intellectus in actu*. It makes no difference whether this final result is a clear-cut Socratic or Platonic circumscription of essence, or a loose Wittgensteinian pattern of 'family relations': both represent the 'truth' of a mode of conceiving of which superficial conceptions are very far from the truth.

What we have said will of course seem the rankest mysticism to all who believe that correctness of utterance always has a conventional public basis, and who would assimilate attempted self-correction *in foro interno* to such things as the vain testing of a piece of news by a desperate buying up of identical newspapers, etc. Plainly, however, what we say describes what we actually do, and what we need not do *in foro interno*, but in the public forum of discussing philosophers. Always in such discussions, if they are not grossly at cross purposes, there is a well-known, commonly accessible corpus of sense on the table for dissection or reassembly, and there are deviant proposals as to how such dissection or reassembly should be carried out. That senses, meanings, coverages, scopes of terms *are* such lucid, publicly accessible matters, is of course obscure to many philosophers, who think tables, chairs, mountains, etc. the only things capable of public exhibition, forgetting the immense obscurity, the infinite many-sidedness of the physical individual, and the impossibility of seeing or showing it except in some limited, one-sided conceptual 'light', in short, as an illustration of a more or less clear-cut concept or meaning, to which alone such clarity as there is in the situation truly belongs.

This meaning may, in fact, not be *really* illustrated by the individual before us, which exposes the rank absurdity of supposing that it is this individual as such that is really pointed at or shown. What it is easy to show to people, what they readily collect from a process of showing, is not what it is to be a *minimum sensibile*, or a perspectivably distorted penny, or a subtly motivated man, but what it is to be round, fast, endless, instantaneous, free, etc., in short, all the highly simplified Platonic paradigms which physical or sensory realities never adequately exhibit. The world of *abstracted* Platonic paradigms may not be the world in which we most readily move and discourse, but neither is the world of inexhaustibly rich, erratic individuals: the world we move in most readily is a world of *seemingly* illustrated Platonic paradigms, and this means that nothing can be clearer, more accessible to many, than the simplified senses thus seemingly exemplified. Meanings, conceptual scopes are just the sort of things of which clarity and communicability can most significantly be predicated, and if philosophers find them obscure they can hardly be clear about anything else. All this is of course not to deny the 'open texture', shifting focus, systematic ambiguity or 'family analogy' of our meanings which modern researches emphasize; the most openly textured, shifting, ambiguous or family-structured meaning is, however, clearness itself beside the obscure physical individuals that may be said to hide behind it.

We may say, further, that the kind of adjustment of explicit to implicit conceptions involved in a philosophical 'deepening', is not well represented by a model in which we correct our sketch of something by repeated looking at its actual original. The 'reading off' inspired by simple looking is not closely like the conceptual adjustment in question: the former is relatively passive and somnambulistic, whereas the latter is intensely active and argumentative, concerned to run through cases, explore alternatives, elucidate ideas, look for objections, etc. It is the masterly procedure of Husserl when he wrote the *Logische Untersuchungen*, not the increasingly unclarified, dogmatically assertive procedure of his later writings, whose faults the existentialists further magnified and multiplied. It is not remarkable that once expressions like 'intuition', 'survey of essence', pure 'description', etc. had gained ground, the fine edge of Husserl's insight became blunted: what he said had less weight because no longer carried out in detailed argument and illustration as against every conceivable alternative or objection.

If there is, then, a desire to be 'true to' the profound content of our notions which may fitly be called 'metaphysical', there is a further desire which presupposes this one, and which is perhaps even more deserving of the title. This is the desire to understand the world better by *reducing its contingency*, its independent variability and variety, by finding more necessary or near-necessary connections among the concepts in terms of which we approach it than at first appeared feasible. This second metaphysical impulse is closely akin to an impulse which inspires all empirical science. If empirical science first assembles before it a well attested array of observed facts, and then tries to go behind these facts to laws and hypotheses which connect them in many remarkable and unforeseen ways, so that there is much less disjoined accident, much less merely factual connection in the empirical world than at first seemed to be present, so the metaphysician, having achieved some measure of 'truth' to his various concepts, may be on the look-out for signs of internal mutual requirement among them, for an inability to make separate sense, so as to reduce thereby the looseness and independent variety of his whole conceptual system. He must have a positive interest in showing that in cases where A appears to be totally irrelevant to B, there is not in fact the total irrelevance that at first appears, that while A might, e.g. do without particular B's, it could not do without any B's whatsoever, that to suppose A's without B's would disrupt the whole sphere of discourse and being in which A's and B's alike have their place, etc. His interest in showing this need not be one that stoops to pious fraud—that refuses to bow, after careful consideration, to the plain conceivability of an A without a B. But he must definitely try, and try with seriousness, to overcome the bleak deadness of irrelevance, or the superficial imaginabilities which, like opium dreams, confused the philosophical perceptions of Hume, and he must not abandon the fight till a strategic retreat and a counting of losses is inevitable, much as the empirical scientist must at times give up looking for laws in certain directions, or must abandon kinds of hypotheses to which the facts have proved peculiarly inhospitable.

The procedure of the metaphysician will of course be quite different from that of the empirical scientist, since the connections which he seeks to establish are such as will be intrinsically understandable, deeply rooted in, part of the profound sense of the notions he employs, whereas there need be no such 'rooting' in the case of the concepts linked together in empirical laws. But this would not, of course, mean that what started as a mere constatation or empirical generalization might not, on more profound reflection, reveal itself as having some notional justification—those philosophers are to be praised, not abused, who try to show that space *can* only have three dimensions, that life is intrinsically evolutionary, etc. even if we are not always clear as to the value of their 'proofs'—while a notional insight might be tried out, and to some extent confirmed or disconfirmed, by empirical instances. The things we are suggesting are of course totally monstrous in terms of the orthodoxy to which we were long enthralled. On this orthodoxy what is necessarily true reflects the actual use of our terms and the content of our concepts—we do not *have* a concept if we are not clear what it necessarily covers or does not cover— nor is there any sense in which deep reflection—as opposed to formal manipulation—can bring out anything more about it, or can deepen or revise our view of it, particularly in issues involving modality. We have, however, thrown this sort of view overboard —our concepts are not, we hold, adequately represented by our first definitions or our unconsidered or ordinary uses—and we may very well come to see or decide that concepts are *not* independent, though our first instinct was to treat them as if they were. Philosophy may well, therefore, have the task, of putting the philospher back into the chains of necessity—chains willingly and happily accepted—after he has enjoyed the intoxication of a liberating logic—such as that of Russell in *Principia Mathematica*— which has given him too many wings.

We must, however, make plain at the outset that it is not part of our philosophical programme to achieve that complete abrogation of contingent particularity in necessary universality which for some seems the ideal of speculative philosophy. Spinoza is often credited with an ideal of this kind, though it may be doubted whether his plain recognition of a 'natured' as well as a 'naturing' nature, and of finite as well as infinite modes, lays him open to a charge of this kind: in a necessity of the natured or finite he certainly believes, but it is a necessity, not intrinsic, but only *relative* to the existence of other natured or finite modes. And if we turn to Hegel, it was Krug, not Hegel himself, who demanded the 'deduction' of such a thing as a quill-pen, a demand quite at odds with Hegel's belief in an irremovable contingency at the lower levels of existence, and in his farther belief that the most profound demands of the 'notion' in various spheres might be violated by many factual exceptions, which thereby stamped themselves, in his diction, as 'low and untrue existences'. It is not, in fact, till we reach the relatively enfeebled thinkers of the late nineteenth century, men awed by the claims and prestige, rather than by the actual achievements of materialistic, deterministic science, that an equation arises between the contingent or merely possible, on the one hand, and the imperfectly understood, on the other, and that the 'really possible' is made to coincide with the actual, which, as being without an alternative, coincides with the necessary. Everything should and can, on this view, be made 'intelligible', and to be 'intelligible' is to be the only coherent and therefore only genuine possibility, which, as unique, is also necessary. Every connection posited in this unique possibility must likewise be a necessary connection, an entailment and no mere factual coincidence. This opinion does not, perhaps, deprive the modal categories of all sense, since they are allowed to retain their distinctness 'for us' and 'for our knowledge'. But it certainly places our search for necessary connections, and our removal of particular contingencies, in a depressing light, since our results will not differ 'in the end' from the most casual coincidence of fact, there being as intimate a connection between, say, being the sum of the first n odd numbers and being a perfect square, as between being John Smith and living next door to Ada Jones. Or if this is not conceded it is not clear why it should not be. Whereas the whole point and force of the necessary, as well as its peculiar dignity, lies in its *contrast* with the contingencies which take place within its framework, and of which it represents the matrix. Aristotle may have been too hasty in his 'essentialism', in his setting apart of a range of traits which, on deeper examination, are felt to 'belong together' and to make up a well-defined form or species, while other traits merely nest in their interstices or give final determination to such an essence, but these are, for better or worse, the conditions for intelligibility, which are not less characteristically sought by those who propound general theories of our concepts as involving 'family relations'. Even philosophers like Hegel who have set 'individuality' alongside of 'universality' and 'specificity' as 'moments' of our notions, have seen in such individuality the necessary foil and complement to the other notional features, intelligible in their required, imperfect intelligibility, rather than as something reducible to these other features.

Our procedure, in a metaphysical system, would then be to lay bonds of necessity, in an increasingly straitening series, on our previously clarified notions: to do so would represent an attempt to be more closely 'true to' their content. Indirectly we should be steadily reducing the contingency of the facts in the world: more and more 'mere' possibilities would be extruded into the impossible, while the contingents which were their realized counterparts passed into the circle of the necessary. At the bottom of the hierarchy would be found the most liberal range of 'possibilities' compatible with the most abstract choice of fundamental categories: the necessities of this level would do no more than state what was implicit in this choice of categories. Some sort of conflation of mathematics and formal logic, some sort of *mathesis universalis* in the sense of Husserl, would obviously be in place at this stage, and no one would wish its simplicity spoiled by the injection of relations of a deeper-going sort. What would be wrong would be to regard it as absolutely basic, since it might on reflection show itself to be basic only by abstraction. Its categories, e.g. might make no sense except as employed in a context involving certain more advanced categories, which lay quite outside of its explicit scope and purview. Thus the 'possibilities' contemplated in mathematics and mathematical logic may imply, though they do not refer to, background facts guaranteeing permanent distinguishability and identifiability of units, recurrence of character, etc. Upon this basis would be then imposed increasing restrictions of the possible, each definitory of a certain stratum of being or abstraction, in which certain categories would be dominant, e.g. the category of physical thinghood, of mental life, etc. The advance to these higher strata would sometimes, as just mentioned, represent the mere undoing of an initial abstraction: sometimes, however, it would represent a narrowing of possibility that obtained only on a background of contingently presupposed existence. Granted that there are coloured objects, or organisms, or minds, such and such possibilities are excluded, and such and such counter-possibilities are raised to necessities. We should arrive at what Husserl called a 'regional eidetic', a system of notional connections governing a certain 'region' of possible existence. At the top of the structure we might admit the 'necessities' and 'possibilities' which have little or no intrinsic intelligibility, but which arise inductively out of our acquaintance with the ways of particular individuals or classes of individuals. It would not, however, be right, as observed previously, for us to draw too tight a line between the understandable connections which define the fields of *a priori* investigation and the merely factual, though general, connections that we learn *a posteriori*. Things that stand on one side of the barrier might end up on the other, or receive reinforcement and correction there, and men of science would not advance far if a certain knowledge of the sort of thing likely to obtain in Nature *überhaupt* did not guide their study of nature as she actually is.

All that I have said is of course preposterous and absurd to all who believe that necessary connection never involves anything genuinely ampliative, or who seek to reduce cases where there seems to be such ampliativeness to cases where there is obviously none. They are not to blame since Kant, the author of the synthetic *a priori*, could believe in its 'possibility' only by running through an extraordinary subjective circuit: it was as deeply unintelligible to him, as to the empiricists he criticized, that we should have substantial knowledge regarding particular things that we had never encountered in experience, and he could only explain the possibility by the most revolutionary of hypotheses. Whereas, for the true *a priorist*, *a posteriori* knowledge or learning by experience is only possible on a background of *a priori* understanding which would delimit the kind of thing before one for empirical examination, and it would be the mere empirical confrontation with something regarding whose character or even category we knew nothing whatever that would represent a true problem for philosophy. To the question 'How is pure *a posteriori* knowledge possible?' the answer should be that it is not possible at all: on reflection we see that something so transcendent of the individual and the moment as knowledge is, must necessarily embrace matters going beyond the detail of our empirical encounters and constituting its necessary framework. It is not, however, our task to argue all these vexed questions here, but merely to suggest that it is not unreasonable to assume that we can only empirically discover facts about particulars of this or that sort by an advance knowledge of the connections which make them into particulars of the sort in question, a knowledge that can if we like be made trivial and verbal, but which can just as well, and with greater 'truth to its notion' be made genuine and substantial.

So far what I have said does not go far beyond the programme that Husserl sketched for himself in the first part of his *Ideen*, and might be fairly called 'phenomenological'. Now, however, I wish to pass on to an idea which has for me an Hegelian inspiration, though I also find it widely applied in contemporary philosophy. This is the idea that the most important of the *a priori* connections among our notions are probabilifying connections, *connections of mere probability*, rather than connections of strict necessity. What we know in advance of encounters with individual realities, and what we know with double clearness when we seek to deeply 'true to' to the content of our notions, is not that a case of *A must* invariably be a case of *B*, but rather that it is likely to be a case of *B*, that it will be a case of *B* in all but a strictly limited number of exceptional cases, or perhaps that there is some deep *tendency* for an *A* to be a *B* which will be increasingly displayed the more cases we consider, or the more certain hindrances are removed. It is true, in other words, that *A* and *B* are found to have a certain 'mutual belongingness' or 'affinity' which we discover merely by reflecting deeply on *A* and *B*, and not merely by considering their joint occurrence in cases of a certain sort. Corresponding things can of course be said regarding non-belongingness or notional disparity. It is this 'affinity' which I think so important which has given its title to my paper. It is important for metaphysics because its assertion more plainly represents something substantial, informative, not so readily reducible to tautology— though this will no doubt be attempted—than an assertion of some absolutely necessary connection. If notions have affinity they *may* none the less be instantiated separately, and this makes their joint occurrence true by experience, as well as notionally likely. And we may have our sense for notional affinity whetted by facts of empirical coexistence, just as such facts may likewise suggest a notional disparity where an affinity has been too readily presumed. Such cross-fertilization occurs of course in the realm of the strictly necessary as well, even in the realm of mathematics, but its fruitfulness in the case of the notionally probable is much more obvious. Metaphysics in this field therefore plainly makes statements having empirical content, even if their modal features, in this as in similar cases, are not displayed at the lowest phenomenal level. What it establishes also has empirical value as plainly setting the stage within which learning by experience and theory-making may proceed, by expounding the background presuppositions without which they would not be possible. That those who find the notion of *a priori* synthetic necessity unpalatable will be any better disposed to the notion of *a priori* synthetic probability may be doubted. We may note, however, that the recognition of an *a priori* element in probabilities was a part of the earliest theories, and that, despite attempts at radical empiricism, it is doubtful whether it has ever really been got rid of.

We have not done much to illustrate previous claims regarding metaphysical aims and procedures: we must at least try to illustrate what we mean by 'affinity' and by *a priori* probability. We shall choose our examples from every quarter of the philosophical firmament, not fearing the ridicule that a frank statement of what everyone secretly believes is likely to occasion. There is, we may first hold, a basic *a priori* likelihood, underlying all forms of extrapolation or argument by analogy, that whatever exists should exhibit little diversity rather than much, and that the unlimited combinations of characters which make some treatments of probability so wearisome and so silly are in fact wholly impossible. What we are enunciating is, moreover, not a heuristic principle nor a regulative maxim which holds only for us: we leave such devices to the radical empiricists. Our principle is, if one likes, a principle for 'nature' or 'being', as well as for that small segment of it which falls within our minds, and our assurance of it, stated with probabilistic limitations, so much exceeds that of all wilful assertions of contrary 'possibilities' as to amount to knowledge. It is moreover a principle overriding the artifices of a formalism for which adjectives which stand only for trivial far-fetched resemblances count on a level with adjectives which stand for resemblances that we all recognize as weighty. We are are well aware that the resemblance covered by an artificial concept like the 'bleen' of Goodman—coinciding with 'blue' up to a certain point in time and thereafter with 'green'—is more attenuated and therefore exerts less analogical force, than the resemblance covered by a natural concept like 'green' or 'blue', and we also know this to be no mere fact of language or of human psychology, but of the larger sphere of being as well. If our symbolism fails to register the difference between close and far-fetched, or between weighty and trivial likenesses, then it is a poor symbolism or one irresponsibly operated.

In the same way there are *a priori* likelihoods, or rather unlikelihoods, more or less covering the ground traditionally covered by such principles as the permanence of substance or that of universal causation: the comparative unlikelihood and essentially exceptional character of *detached events*, not growing continuously out of other events to form the history of a thing or a number of interacting things, the impossibility that such events should exist otherwise, if they exist at all, than as a sort of detritus in the interstices of well-rounded, enduring substantial realities with their own inner coherence and momentum. The 'looseness' of happenings which for Hume's imagination (in one sense of his 'imagination') was the norm, must in short be seen as the marginal exception or the near-impossibility. The principle we have tried to state, as certainly one without which talk about 'happenings' makes no sense at all, is much vaguer and looser and probabilistic than the principles it replaces, but in one respect it is stronger: the continuous growing of events out of events that it postulates is most probably a growing of the neighbouring out of the neighbouring, and of the like, in no artificial formal sense, out of the like. That every event has *some* cause—in Sirius perhaps, and having nothing obvious to do with it, and connected with it by some law of unfathomable complexity—such a principle is rightly censured as empty and laughable. Far-fetched complex connections there may be, but their intrinsic likelihood diminishes with their far-fetchedness and their complexity, and these are part of a 'probability' more basic and better known than the probability of a misapplied 'theory of chances', which sees all laws as infinitely improbable, both before and after instantiation, and for which the divinations of the scientist are only audacious guesses.

From these cosmological affinities we may proceed to some governing the relation of mental life to physical existence and to other forms of mental life. Here I shall not be afraid to shock those who hate to apply causal notions to sense-perception, or who have been seduced by Gilbert Ryle's questionable doctrine of 'verbs of success', by saying that I think it intrinsically more likely that the objects around us will impress our senses in a manner representing their true character and structure than in a manner which grossly misrepresents it, and that they are likely to reveal this 'true character' increasingly, both by improvement in the senses and by pooling of their data, the more closely they are examined. And I think further that, apart from all causal influences, the preparatory ideas that we form of what we shall encounter in sense-perception, and the frameworks in which we try to locate them, are intrinsically more likely to fit what we shall encounter and the true nature of the things thus encountered, than that the contrary should be true. I believe, in short, in an affinity between thought and being. To me it seems that the notion of a pre-established harmony between the realities of the environment and our perceptual and notional approaches, which Kant, with his repressed, background empiricism thought less acceptable than long fables regarding the productive imagination—is thoroughly acceptable *a priori*: it is a harmony that permits of countless distortions and exceptions, but which it is quite absurd to imagine universally absent. What we are here stating is no mere postulate embodying the faith of the scientist, nor some arbitrarily conceived definition of 'reality' and 'truth': we are stating a substantial principle governing the relations of things in the world to such minds as are also present in it, and which is known to us as certainly as anything is known. The same difficulty which characterizes lying misrepresentations, and makes them evident to close students of human behaviour, may be held to characterize nature: she too finds it hard to hide from us what she is, especially if we probe her carefully.

From this we may proceed to the various likelihoods governing psycho-physical relations, the *a priori* likelihood, in particular, of the profound, if queer, analogy, that obtains between the occurrences of our segregated 'inner lives' and the 'outer' bodily existence and action with which they seem continuous. The notion of inner experiences, actual or possible, which have a merely factual, contingent connection with 'outer behaviour', so that *any* inner experience might conceivably go with *any* kind of outer behaviour—the kind of assumption guided by abstract 'logical possibilities' which has bedevilled and rendered nugatory the whole contemporary treatment of the problem of 'other minds'— is not only a notion untrue to what we know of the detailed character of our 'inner' and 'outer' lives, it is also a notion that cannot but be untrue. A recurrent misfit between 'inner' and 'outer' is of course conceivable and frequently exemplified—the felt grasp of a principle which does not issue in the ability to apply it rightly, the ability to discriminate which does not go with a perceived 'aspect', the dry preparedness for something unaccompanied by a felt tension, etc.—but they can only occur because they do not always do so, because there are some cases in which what is 'inward' completes itself in a suitable, i.e. intrinsically likely 'outward' manifestation and vice versa. The characteristic momentum with which a sense-encounter passes over into a more or less corresponding 'private imagination', and thence into a mere thought, and with which the last moves over again and illustrates itself in the second, and the second in the first—a momentum in which there is throughout a deep 'fit', and an intrinsic likelihood of sequence—the imagination being in a queer sense a continuation of the sense-encounter, and the thought of the imagination—all these are matters governed throughout by affinity and intrinsic probability, and at no point manifesting the hiatuses, the profound gulfs, whether between 'public' and 'private' or between contrasted privacies, which a too absorbed preoccupation with 'scientific observability' leads us to suppose. The ghostly passes, and must pass, continuously over into the bodily, and ghost may be said to commune with ghost through the continuous corporeality in which both terminate, and only the strict intersubjectivity required by certain forms of science introduces a cut into this continuity, and suggests a hiatus of being where there is only one of approach and method.

I now wish to suggest as a final field of the probabilistic *a priori* that there is some sort of affinity between the *existence* of a dispersed physical world-order in space and time, and the *existence* of minds which in some sense concentrate that order in conscious enjoyment. I am not maintaining the idealistic thesis that the dispersed physical order *cannot* be thought of as existing without the concentrated mental order, nor any converse thesis, but I am maintaining that the one is in a sense the natural complement of the other, and requires the other to be fully what it is—the physical order requires to be gathered together in unity, as the mental order requires something that it can thus gather together—and that it is not therefore an empirical accident that the world should at appropriate times concentrate itself into sensitive, cogitative points in which its whole order and history becomes perspicuous and surveyable to itself. I have no doubt that what I have said will be felt by many to be irresponsible and wild, but I can only ask whether we ever really believe that the presence of rational spectators in the cosmic scene is really a mystery and a superfluity, and whether it is rational to believe this? Do we not in fact think that the pre-established harmony of which I spoke earlier points to a more fundamental existential conspiracy, a need of the two sides for one another, a tendency of each to lead up to and evoke the other? This may be pursued further, and I do not doubt more shockingly to many, by holding to some sort of affinity between the course of the world and the rational ideals of the conscious beings which emerge in it, some sort of profound relevance of fact and reality to value and vice versa, which need not entail a denial of the profound gulf between these. It seems to me plain that I cannot attribute goodness to anything in a certain profoundly disinterested reflective manner, without thinking it in some degree likely that the facts of existence will tend to conform to what I thus appraise as good, that it will not be remarkable if they ultimately do, whereas it will be strange and requiring explanation if they persistently do not. The very words of my language recognize this connection, since the verbs 'should' and 'ought' almost always have *both* a probabilistic and an evaluative meaning and the same tie-up is recognized even in the thought of professedly naturalistic thinkers when they make use of such terms as 'normal'.

I have not said enough so far regarding the problem of the 'control' of our assertions of *a priori* probability and affinity. Plainly we do not want anyone simply to *say* that it 'does not make sense' to suppose the existence of a feature A without some frequency of accompaniment by a feature B. Profligacy in the postulation of necessities and near-necessities of connection is plainly as bad a disease as the unlimited postulation of possibilities. Here I can only suggest that while we must be ready to listen to the faintest whisper of intuitive plausibility in considering necessities and near-necessities, such whispers should not be given authority till we have carefully considered how wide a rot will set in if they are not heeded. We must, e.g. consider what it would be like, and whether it would really be thinkable, if *no one ever* modified his chosen line of action to fit in with what he found to be the case, if *everyone* deceived *everyone* on *every* occasion, if we could live a life of pure thoughts that were *never* carried out in sensible confrontations, etc. It is not, further, the single conceptual connection that must be affirmed or denied in isolation, but it must be seen in relation to a whole field of other relevant concepts that provide its setting or its alternatives, so that our decision is always a decision for a whole field. Such a systematic justification of basic concepts is not unlike that attempted by Kant in his various transcendental proofs: in modern times it has been brilliantly applied, in, e.g. Strawson's attempt to conceive of

I

discourse in a world of objects without position in space. Metaphysical method therefore remains basically intuitive, but there is a vast difference between intuitions of an isolated sort, and intuitions systematically worked out in relation to other intuitions: the latter alone constitutes a worthwhile metaphysical exercise. Since, further, the notion of 'truth to things' does not work exactly like the concept of 'truth', there is a possibility of systems of concepts 'true to things' in varying respects and degrees, as we commonly recognize to be the case, so that divergences among metaphysicians may have a complementary role, rather than the refuting role of disagreements among scientists.

VIII

HEGEL'S USE OF TELEOLOGY[1]

I wish to devote this paper to considering an aspect of Hegel's thought which, I think, enables us to understand him better than any other, i.e. the thoroughgoing teleology of his manner of thinking. No other philosopher has approached him in this regard, with the sole exception of Aristotle, who is perhaps also the greatest single influence in Hegel's inspirational background. If one regards Hegel as an Aristotle in whom teleology has been carried to the limit, so that it becomes transformed into something else, one will perhaps have achieved a good way of regarding him. The teleology of Hegel's thought differentiates him from all the philosophers, however idealistic, whose procedure is what I may call axiomatic, all philosophers who start with a clear body of formulated principles and who deduce elaborate and detailed consequences from it. It sets him infinitely far apart from Spinoza, and it sets him infinitely far apart from the dogmatic rationalism of the Bradley who wrote the second part of *Appearance and Reality*. For Hegel the true, the philosophically adequate account of things is an account that emerges out of a great deal of transformed inadequacy and error, which has no content whatever without such inadequate, erroneous preliminaries, which in a sense preserves them all in the ultimate result, and is in fact nothing beyond the fact of their ultimate transformed preservation. (I should argue further, with some evidence to back me, that Hegel means by the ultimate result the provisionally ultimate result.) Hegel's teleology sets him infinitely far apart from all those idealistic or spiritualistic philosophers who put mind, spirit, rational subjectivity at the *origin* of things, who make it the ontological background for whatever exists or appears to exist, whether they do so in the manner of scholastic theism or in the manner of Berkeleyan idealism or in the complex qualified manner of Kantian phenomenalism. For Hegel the spiritual, the ideal, the self-conscious which is the ultimate meaning of everything, does not lie at the beginnings of thought and being,

[1] Published in *The Monist*, January 1964.

but rather at their end: we may decide that it is the logical and ontological Alpha of the cosmos, but only after it has first emerged as its logical and ontological Omega. All this means that at the *origins* of philosophical truth lie much necessary thought that is abstract and formal and mechanically analytic—the thought of the British analytic school will do admirably as an illustration— whereas at the origins of being lie many states of things that are inert, external, purposeless, mechanical, contingent, irregular, em- pirical and brutally real. The spirituality that arises out of them all is a painfully educed, glorious result. I should like to say that, if Hegel's system is rightly described as one of absolute idealism or spiritualism, it is also rightly described as one of dialectical materialism: it is in fact the true dialectical materialism of which the dialectical materialism of Marx and Engels may be said to be an incompetent, amateur travesty. These sweeping assertions require, however, a good deal of backing, which I shall now endeavour to give.

I shall first seek to apply these teleological perspectives to the dialectic, the peculiar self-critical, self-transcendent method of thought which hardly anyone has learnt from Hegel, and which distinguishes his philosophy from any other. The dialectic is in my view primarily a method of persistently reapplied higher-level, or metalogical, or second-order comment, in which we pass from a situation where we merely employ a concept to a situation where we consider the content and operation of a concept from *outside* as it were, and assess its success in doing whatever it sets out to do. It is also, secondarily, a method where we use such metalogical thought-transitions to understand a series of strata or layers of being in the world, or a succession of phases in personal biography or in world-history.

That Hegel's method is reiteratively metalogical no one who studies him closely can for a moment doubt. We consider, e.g. the thought-stance involved in a mere assertion of *being*, and see that, while purporting to be rich in content, it is utterly empty and abstract, and indistinguishable in what it really covers from the thought-stance which asserts the total *absence* of anything. We then see that in our whole previous procedure we have been experiencing the inherent instability of abstract concepts, in other words their *becoming*. Modern semantics suffices to show us that novelties of principle persistently emerge as we proceed to comment on what went before. What was unformulable or unprovable in an object-language may be formulable and provable in a metalanguage and so on. And quite apart from modern semantics, common sense shows us that what is true *of* an idea differs from, and is often opposed to, the content of the idea itself. The idea of the concrete is very abstract, the idea of beauty is not beautiful at all, the notion of moral worth is itself devoid of moral worth, the absence of any of our family and friends at Christmas is not itself absent but woefully near and present, the Wittgensteinian arguments that one cannot talk about one's own or other people's private experiences show a perfect understanding of what it is to be, or to have, just such a private experience, a behaviouristic analysis of mental life perhaps points by its sheer brilliance and synthetic comprehensiveness to the existence of what is not behavioural, etc. Most of the current objections to Hegelian dialectic rest on the persistent assumption that it is thought that operates on one level, rather than persistently revisionary thought that is always commenting on and criticizing itself.

I now wish to connect the various steps in Hegel's dialectic with the notion of teleology, and to suggest that they always involve comment on a notion and its content and operation from the standpoint of an *aim*, a *Meinung* or intention which the notion secretly involves, and that this comment assumes at least three standard forms.

(a) The notion does not at all achieve what it sets out to perform. While it sets out to be the thought of X, it is such as not to strike its target at all, but as much, or even rather, a target opposed to X. The notion in short breaks down under metalogical scrutiny. This breakdown is itself dysteleological—we do not frame concepts in order that they should *not* do their work—but it clears the deck for a mere positive teleology.

(b) The notion, in not achieving what it sets out to perform, intrinsically points to another notion which effects what the first only tries to effect. It can be regarded as a confused, implicit form of the latter notion, and the latter is the notion we are trying to frame when we frame the former. This type of step is plainly teleological; an inadequate notion is seen not merely as inadequate, but as being inadequate in a respect which implies consciousness of a corresponding adequate notion.

(c) The notion, while not seeming adequate, none the less can be seen by the removal of a few confusing demands and suggestions to be in all essentials adequate. This, the most characteristic teleology of all in Hegel, and the one least understood by his students, is the sudden finding of oneself at one's goal for the very reason that at first seemed to place one far from it. It is the solution of one's problem by turning the problem into its own answer, and resembles falling in love with a woman for the very qualities that at first made her unattractive. I shall now give cases of each of these three dialectical transformations.

Of the first, the breakdown of a notion as achieving the opposite of what it claims to achieve, the above-mentioned passage from Being to Nothing is a good example. Pure Being is a would-be concrete notion, but it does nothing to substantiate its claim. What it sets before us, an object that is and no more, and which is without definite character, is also indistinguishable from the absence of an object which it claims to exclude. Another example is the transition in the *Phenomenology* from absolute revolutionary freedom, which by forcefully abolishing every difference of status which enables men to tyrannize over one another, itself becomes an absolute tyranny, in which the guillotine is the ultimate leveller and equalizer. These then are moves involving a dialectical breakdown: a notion collapses and nothing positive as yet takes its place.

Of the second type of move in which a notion reveals itself as an implicit form of a more adequate notion, there are countless examples. The empty senseless Being which simply is, reveals itself as an inadequate attempt to think the Definite Being which involves contrast in itself, which is Being-there-and-thus, and involves content and opposition. The notion of a genus as a type out there in the natural world, which passes from individual to individual, points ineluctably to the notion of a genus as a type capable of being abstractedly present in the mind of a scientist who surveys and studies that world. The abstract difference of objects which, as it seems, have nothing to do with one another, is likewise seen to be an inadequate expression of the kind of polar difference in which each thing presupposes its opposite, and has it in a sense built into itself.

And of the third type in which we suddenly find ourselves at our goal by a sort of reversal of aim and perspective, I can find no better example than that of the transition, continually repeated in various forms, from the so-called Bad Infinite to the True Infinite. The Bad Infinite is a notion exemplified in any logical progression or series where each term introduces a next term which continues the progression, and where the frustrated yearning emerges to complete a series which can never be completed, to achieve the infinite by merely passing on to a wider finite. This Bad Infinite swings over into the True Infinite, not by any mystical flight beyond finitude, but when the essential futility of trying to outsoar finitude emerges, when one realizes that in each term and step of the series one in principle has all, when one replaces the shackling finite that merely exchanges one set of bonds for another by the freely variable finite which in all its variations is self-same and free. Finite existence in the here and the now, with every limitation of quality and circumstance, is, Hegel teaches, when rightly regarded and accepted, identical with the infinite existence which is everywhere and always. To live in Main Street is, if one lives in the right spirit, to inhabit the Holy City, a view that will be deeply surprising and shocking to many of Hegel's transcendental interpreters. Another example of the arrival at a goal by the simple removal of a false perspective and the substitution of a better one, is the famous transition at the end of the *Logic* where the content of the Absolute Idea, the goal of the dialectic, is simply said to be 'the system of which we have been hitherto studying the development', i.e. dialectic itself, where the end of the journey is simply seen to be the journey itself, and the method that has been followed on the journey. It is by the capacity to understand and accept this last type of dialectical transformation that the true Hegelian is marked off from his often diligent and scholarly, but still profoundly misguided misinterpreter, who still yearns after the showy spectacular climax, the Absolute coming down in a machine accompanied by a flock of doves, when a simple arrest and return to utter ordinariness is in place.

To have indicated the threefold use of teleology in the dialectic, in respectively breaking down, in positively transforming, and in quietly stabilizing our notions, is quite insufficient unless one shows the steady operation of a teleological *nisus* in the system considered as a whole. I want therefore to say something about the implicit role of teleology in the three parts of Hegel's official system: the *Logic*, the *Philosophy of Nature*, and the *Philosophy of Spirit*. I shall say nothing about its role in the *Phenomenology of Spirit* though all that I say would find abundant illustration there as well. In the *Logic* teleology is throughout implicit in that the Notion, with its basic principle of Totality—the principle that *every* aspect of a thing is built into *any* aspect of it, so that complete separateness of aspects is everywhere unthinkable—the Notion with this principle of Totality can, I say, be seen retrospectively to have been obscurely at work in the two 'spheres' of Being and Essence which lead up to the sphere of the Notion. In the sphere of Being, Totality is anything but explicit: the categories of Being give themselves out as surface-categories, categories of quality and quantity, none of whose applications implies any other. To say that A is like this does not seem to involve that it is also like that, or that anything else is like this or that, and it does not seem to allow that A can pass gradually from being like this to being like that without sacrificing its identity altogether: its quantity or amount is likewise wholly irrelevant to its quality, and can be increased or diminished without let or stint. The effect of Hegel's dialectical comment in the Doctrine of Being is to show that this sort of surface independence of aspects is really unthinkable; qualities only qualify in relation to other qualities which are in a sense part of themselves, and which show their internal dependence by perpetual change into one another, qualities likewise are nothing except as involving quantitatively variable determinables, which link them intelligibly with other qualities, while the quantity which these determinables exemplify is nothing except as marked off by, and recognizable in, qualitative change, and so on. In the end the whole brave atomistic Humean structure with which we started lies in ruins and its residuum of truth is sought and found in a sphere of absolute relativism and interdependence, where A points to B as its necessary correlative, while B correspondingly points to A. What is found in this sphere, the so-called sphere of the categories of Essence, is however a wrangling relationship, in which everything seems to be limited by something *else*, precisely because the built-in unity of the correlatives is not manifest. The manifest quality refers back to the permanent essential disposition as the latter reveals itself in the former, the phenomenon points to the law or the force behind it, and the law or force points to the phenomenon. The cause looks to the effect and the effect to the prior cause, and so on. What is implicit in all this is precisely the Notion in which this insensate taking in of one another's washing ceases, in which the various conditioning and conditioned aspects of things come to be regarded as 'the same thing seen from different angles', which is therefore unconditioned and free. It is the free notion of each and everything which determines what it causes and what causes it, what it outwardly manifests and what it secretly is, what impinges on it from without and what springs to meet this from within.

It is worth while stressing at this point the thoroughly teleological character of this central Hegelian concept, that of the *Begriff* or Notion. It is simply the Form of Aristotle conceived as a final cause which is also the full actuality and the achieved goodness of a thing. It only differs from the Aristotelian Form in that the individual, as well as the genus and the species, is part of it: it is of the essence of each general form or type to have individual expressions, and Hegel further suggests, in the section entitled 'The Judgement of the Notion', that the perfection which each type involves is such as to have its individual, as well as its specific differentiations. We all recognize that Buddha and Socrates (say) achieved a perfection of manhood peculiar to *themselves*, and the same applies in the aesthetic field to the perfection of representation or expression achieved by works like Shakespeare's *Romeo and Juliet*, Giorgione's *Concert* and so on. The teleological character of the Notion is likewise shown in the fact that it is not necessarily exemplified in what a thing *actually* does or expresses (in the ordinary sense of 'actually'): a thing can always deviate from, or fall short of, its notion, can be a poor and bad, and therefore, in the Hegelian sense, 'untrue' version of its kind, or even of itself. What Hegel counsels us to do in the sphere of concepts is not simply to study things as they are, and to collect concepts which more or less cover their peculiarities, but rather to see in them approximations to rather full, rich types which they do not adequately represent at all. I may say that I for my part believe that this stress on imperfectly exemplified, normative universals, rather than on painfully discerned, necessary and sufficient conditions for calling something this or that, is of infinite fruitfulness in every philosophical inquiry and that the sustained triviality of certain modern linguistic investigations indirectly testifies to this fact. We may note further that the Hegelian Notion, like the Aristotelian Form, has an objective as well as a subjective status: it may exist immaterially in the mind, but it is also genuinely immanent in outer things, and constitutes the essential inner nature which comes out in all they do and undergo.

Teleology, however, becomes explicit in the last part of the Hegelian Logic, and yields the step which enables us to pass to the last stage of that Logic, the Absolute Idea: we shall not have a glimmer of what that Absolute Idea is, unless we understand the thoroughgoing teleology which it involves. It is the form of the Notion which explains all that went before precisely because it expresses the absolutely comprehensive purposiveness in which all other explanatory and interpretative positions find their place and their sense: it expresses the absolute finality which alone leaves no residuum of unexplained otherness outside of itself. The teleology from which we make our ascent to the Absolute Idea, which *is* in fact the Absolute Idea itself, is not, however, the ordinary finite teleology which we experience in our conscious practical pursuit of personal ends, nor is it even the finite teleology we see evinced in various unconscious performances of organisms, e.g. eating and digesting this or that type of food. It is, Hegel says, an *infinite* rather than a finite teleology, and we shall have the key to the whole thought of Hegel if we know what infinite, as opposed to finite, teleology really is. What is this infinite teleology which is so essential to Hegelianism, and how does it differ from the ordinary finite teleology which we all recognize? Finite teleology obtains where there is a definite result to be achieved, a definite situation in which this result is to emerge, definite means through which the result is to arise, and a definite process of actualizing the result in question, and where result, situation, means and process all differ profoundly in content. Thus, if a University invites me as a Visiting Professor at a certain point in its history and does so by making me an offer by cable, we have a case of finite teleology, and the same would obtain if an amoeba were to devour some food by flowing around it and enclosing it. Such finite teleology is by its nature always variable: as soon as a particular end is achieved by particular procedures or acts, it immediately becomes part of the situation, and is replaced by other ends. Explanation in terms of such finite ends is likewise never finally satisfactory, but points backwards and forwards without end. This bad infinity can only be overcome by postulating the true infinity of a *causa finalis sui*, a *Selbstzweckmässigkeit* which pervades the whole endless process, and which is totally present in its successive phases. This infinite teleology has no specific content, or rather its content is freely variable: one can say that its end is simply purposive organizing activity as such. In this infinite teleology there are various specific ends, but these specific ends are mere orientation-points of self-organization, necessary because one cannot be self-organizing without being so in a specific direction. In the same way, in infinite teleology there is an objective situation which fails to satisfy in some aspect, and so calls forth purposive scheming and trying, but this objective situation can be looked on as subserving, and as therefore a part of, infinite purposiveness, since infinite purposiveness would have nothing to concern itself with if everything were well adjusted. In infinite teleology there are likewise many definite means and many definite practical proceedings which must also be treated as 'moments' of the infinite teleology since it would be impossible without them. The concept of infinite teleology is therefore, in the first place, one of purposive activity undertaken for its own sake and, in the second place, one in which all internal and external conditions of such purposive activity are, by the removal of special finite content from the end, made part of purposive activity itself. Such infinite purposiveness is seen at its most immediate in life. In a living organism all circumstances and available instruments are as much part of its life as are the activities it turns upon them; in all forms and guises of its activity its aim is only itself. Whatever it does or has or works on is part of its living and it lives only in order to live. And the imperfect expression of infinite teleology carried out in the successive generations of perishable organisms has a more perfect expression in the rational thinking life of the conscious person. Here too all activity, and all objective material of activity, can be said to be thinking, and nothing but thinking, and we think in order to think. The Aristotelian inspiration of these crucial Hegelian ideas will be evident.

This doctrine of infinite teleology is even more definitely expounded in those penultimate paragraphs of the Logic where Hegel deals with the Idea of the True and the Idea of the Good, the two opposed and complementary embodiments of the Absolute Idea. The Idea of Truth is the Idea of an Objective order which completely meets the demands of the probing intelligence by being at all points dominated by universals, at all points explained in terms of generic patterns and laws which simply *are* intelligence itself, so that intelligence will simply see in the world a mirror-image of its inherent rationality. This Idea of Truth involves, however, an inherent inadequacy: it *demands* the realization of something which it also implies *cannot* be fully carried out. It demands the final explanatory liquidation of the individual, and this it also demands and implies cannot be completed, since it is of the essence of knowledge to want something hard and individual to confront it which it cannot wholly make or unmake, which is simply *there* for its scrutiny and its explanation. However far the net of explanation may reach there will always be individual details that slip through its meshes, and this is not merely a lamentable accident, but something demanded by the very nature of knowledge itself. The inadequacies of knowledge and truth now point to a more radical overcoming of the gulf between subject and object, the ideal of a practice which achieves what is good. This ideal, it seems, does stretch down to explain the individual, for what is practice but the transformation not of mere notions, but of individual existence? Here, again, however, a seeming flaw vitiates the perfect understanding we seem to be gaining: for rational practice, though it may stretch down to the individual, still demands a gulf between the existent state of the individual and the ideal it seeks to impose on it. If rational practice is to be possible, the individual must not be *wholly* as it should be, and yet rational practice consists simply in making the individual as it should be.

We seem therefore to be frustrated in our attempt to conceive the world in terms of infinite teleology, as being in all its details nothing but an aspect of mind's rational activity: rational activity seems to be impossible without an element of inexplicable individual contingency which it seeks to explain, and must also involve an element of irredeemable irrational badness which it seeks to transform. Here, however, where we seem infinitely removed from our goal, a sudden swing of the dialectic brings us to it. We simply see that, since the gulf between contingent individuality and explanatory universality, and the gulf between such individuality and organized rational practicality, not only cannot, but *should* not, be eliminated in the interests of rational explanation and organizing practice themselves, both gulfs are from a higher point of view already bridged. Since there *ought* to be such gulfs between what is and what ought to be, there are, from a higher point of view, no such gulfs at all: everything from a higher point of view (we may parody Wittgenstein) is in order as it is.

The ultimate step in Hegel's Logic is therefore a step of the kind classified above as (c): a consolidating, quietistic step, one which achieves its goal by suddenly coming to see its goal in what previously seemed only an infinite, hopeless struggle towards it. It is the step we all take in those major moments where we realize that in exerting ourselves to the last for ideals not perfectly attainable against odds that tax our strength to the utmost, and which will never be overcome, we have in a sense reached our goal; we have become one with an infinite actuosity, with the life of God, if you like, which accepts the difficulties which crucify it as teleologically necessary to itself. This is why Hegel in this sort of context employs a language of illusion: the infinite End is achieved when the illusion vanishes which make it still seem unachieved, when it no longer stands in its own light by its own wrong view of itself (*Sc. of Logic*, III, iii. ch. 2B), when we no longer see the absolute Good as something to be achieved but as something actually achieving itself and already achieved, when we realize that the non-achievement of the Absolute Good is, as it were, a shadow cast by its own light, a shadow cast in order only that it may be removed, and that we may see rational intelligent life as the all-in-all of everything. What Hegel teaches in these crucial passages is that an element of ineliminable irrationality, of recalcitrant externality, is teleologically necessary for the life of reason, and that this irrationality, this externality becomes rational, explained, eliminated precisely because it is thus teleologically necessary. It is the old Christian message that the evils of life are there to try us, and that a cross gladly borne will sustain its bearer. How disappointing this simple declaration must be to all who expect absorption in a timeless Absolute or into a timeless society of spirits, to whom Hegel only gives a new look upon the tribulations of this transitory life! The astringent realism of Hegel's final solution is, however, precisely what renders it acceptable to many who find flights of transcendental otherworldliness nothing but a nauseous opiate.

Infinite teleology is therefore the central notion of the Hegelian Logic. How does it operate in the *Philosophy of Nature* and the *Philosophy of Spirit*, the remaining parts of the Hegelian system? Here it might seem that the transition from the Absolute Idea to the concrete sphere of Nature and Spirit was precisely *not* teleological, for does not Hegel say that the Absolute Idea freely releases its moment of particularity, thereby giving rise to the concrete, intuitive idea of Nature, and does not all this suggest the generation of the world by a ready-made, pre-existent perfection, which generation has all the purposeless gratuitousness of Thomistic creation, and is infinitely far from setting the 'truth' of the matter at the end rather than at the beginning? Hegel certainly tried hard in this passage and in some others to mislead his readers into believing that he held something like Christian theism, a doctrine that is not through and through teleological, that explains things by their origin rather than by their ultimate goal. He provides, however, the materials for his own demytholologization, and this can be abundantly found, e.g. in the treatment of the creation-story in the *Phenomenology* and in several passages in the *Philosophy of Nature*. He there makes perfectly plain that the transition at the end of the Logic really involves the breakdown of an abstraction rather than a creative advance to anything more comprehensive. We simply see that the idea of infinite teleology to which we have advanced, is so far a *mere* idea, an abstract *logical shadow*, rather than an actual concrete achievement, and that it is only in so far as it can *also* be a concrete achievement that it can be a *genuine* idea at all.

As Hegel puts it in the *Phenomenology*:

> The Spirit as declared in the element of pure thought is itself essentially this, not to be only in this element but also *actual*. . . . The merely eternal or abstract spirit therefore becomes an other to itself and enters existence, and immediately enters immediate existence. It therefore creates a world. This creation is an imaginative locution for the Notion in its absolute movement, for the fact that the thought asserted to be absolutely simple and pure is, because it is abstract, rather the negative and therefore the opposite and other to itself (*Phenomenology*, p. 336).

Or more explicitly in the *Philosophy of Nature*:

> How did God reach the point of creating a world. God as an abstractum is not the true God, but it is only as the living process of positing his Other, the world, and only in unity with his other, in Spirit, is God a subject (*Enc.* § 246).

Or

> the knowledge contained in the simple Logical Idea is only the concept of knowledge as thought of by us, not the knowledge which exists in its own right, not actual spirit, but merely its possibility (*Enc.* § 381).

Hegel tells us that the realm of logic is the realm of shadows, of thought-forms stripped of sensuous concretion. The Absolute

Idea may be the noblest shadow in the realm of shadows and for a shadow the most concrete. It is, however, nothing at all except as worked out in the realm of nature and man. In a sense, therefore, the Hegelian system *starts* with the *Philosophy of Nature*, and this gives a crucial central importance to some of the things said in this much neglected book. And the system is teleological in the sense that it starts with inert material objects in Space and Time, and only at the end yields us objects which have life and mind and spirit.

It is here instructive to stress how far the Philosophies of Nature and Spirit, the concrete part of Hegel's idealism, anticipate what is now called a philosophy of emergent evolution. Thus there is in Hegel no notion that Spirit and Mind lie at the origins of the world, or that they engineered the world by some exercise of creative imagination, both of them notions that dominate Kant and Fichte, and that one might expect to find in Hegel. Hegel the Aristotelian denies explicitly that Space and Time, the forms of the intuitive idea he calls Nature, are the projections of any sort of intuiting subjectivity. 'When we have said', he remarks,

> that our sensation receives the form of the spatial and temporal from the intuiting spirit, this proposition should not be understood as if Space and Time were merely subjective forms: the things themselves are in reality spatial and temporal. This two-fold form of mutual externality is not one-sidedly imposed on them by our intuition, but is imposed on them from the beginning by the infinite Spirit which has being in itself, by the creative, eternal Idea (*Enc.* § 448).

If anyone is tempted to construe this passage as teaching that the Idea is the infinite subject responsible for Space and Time, let him remember that the Idea is the mere possibility, not the reality of cognition, and that it is in beings like ourselves, and ourselves alone, that cognition becomes a reality. And we must note further that Hegel does not place his emergence of conscious life at the origin of the world: the facts of the geological record, which were becoming well known at that time, forced him to admit that the earth had a sort of life and a sort of history before what is properly organic and conscious arose on it. As Hegel expresses it in a passage dating from his Jena period but retained in his later exposition, the earth had 'a life which, fermenting in itself, possessed its own internal time'. It was a life in which 'the Earth-spirit, not yet risen to opposition' enjoyed 'the movement and dreams of a sleeper, until it awoke and reached consciousness in man, and was set before itself as a stable formation'.

Hegel imagines the emergence of various types of organism as taking place in the life of the Earth in a series of lightning changes: he lends his authority to the Mosaic creation story: 'Today the plants arose, today animals, today man.' The emergence is also compared to the sudden emergence of Minerva from the forehead of Jupiter (*Enc.* § 339). Whatever one may think of this strange mythology, it at least disposes of any notion that Hegel held a Berkeleyan or a Kantian view of the natural world in space and time. This natural world is spiritual in its ultimate destiny and purpose—it is only there to make the emergence of spiritual life possible—it is not spiritual in the sense of having covertly been manufactured by our spirit or by any spirit. If Spirit already existed in full reality there would be no need for Nature to exist at all. And the categories and forms and laws we find in Nature are present in Nature as organizing principles *before* we abstract them and think them: they exist there as a sort of frozen, petrified or alienated intelligence, but they are none the less really there.

If we now turn to the actual content of the *Philosophy of Nature*, it is through and through teleological. Nature exhibits what Hegel calls *die seiende Abstraktion*, the apparently separated, independent existence of aspects that cannot really exist separately and independently: its development is a steady elimination of this *seiende Abstraktion* until it acquires all the totality, the built-in unity of the Notion. From consisting of phases which lie outside of each other in space and time, and which have a merely inert, self-contained being and an indifference to each other's existence, it comes to consist of phases organically linked with one another and reflecting each other's existence. In other words it comes to embody the infinite immanent teleology of the Idea in the form of Life, and in this form it is ready to move inward to the form of Conscious Spirit. Hegel gives magnificent accounts of what he calls Nature's naïveté, its attempts to express various subtle logical entailments in the form of separately observable existences, like a child transforming abstractions into pictures. In so doing he seems to me to have done more to illuminate natural existence than any other philosopher. Nature we may say embodies Whitehead's fallacy of simple location even when it strives beyond it: thus the necessary unity of the two opposed poles of a magnet appears in a definitely located special indifference point between them (*Enc.* § 312), and the necessary presence of everything to everything else in the world is revealed in the special phenomenon of light. Like a child nature has made a category mistake, and turned a conceptual necessity into a quasi-material stuff (*Enc.* § 275–6). One may, however, very much regret that palaeontological study had not advanced far enough in Hegel's day for Hegel to give his Philosophy of Nature an explicitly evolutionary guise. For him spiritual phenomena evolve in time, but merely natural phenomena only involve a *logical* evolution, whose various stages and phases exist side by side in space. I do not think we can doubt that, if Hegel had lived a little later, he would have given us an evolutionary, teleological theory of Nature as he did of mind in history. He would have done with brilliant competence what Darwin, Spencer, and also Marx and Engels, did in an extremely incompetent manner.

I have neither the time nor the need to prove the teleological character of Hegel's Philosophy of Mind or Spirit. It starts with Mind immersed in Nature, and in the deepest rapport with its body and its environment, and shows us Mind gradually liberating itself from this bondage, and achieving the free universality of thought, which enables it to return to Nature and put *it* into chains, rendering it intelligible by science, and rendering it completely malleable to its purposes by the rational technology which springs from science. If Marx spoke of man overcoming the alienation of nature he was merely plagiarizing from Hegel, and plagiarizing without understanding the import of what he plagiarized. From the conquest of material nature man proceeds to the conquest of his own raw wants and needs, and to their organization in the rational aims of social living: a second rational Nature is reared in the open clearing made by the destruction of the first. Finally Spirit becomes absolute in Art, Religion and Philosophy, where rational conscious life realizes and enjoys itself as the final meaning, the accomplished end of everything in the world. Everything exists in order to promote rational conscious life, and the highest forms of rational conscious life are precisely the forms in which this is consciously realized: the life of the artist, the life of the religious devotee, and the life of the Hegelian philosopher. If the bringing in of religion in this connection still rouses some association of Kierkegardian otherness and transcendence, let us remember that for Hegel God is only self-conscious in man, and in man's consciousness of God (*Enc.* § 564). The religion recommended by Hegel is one in which it is good for God as a separately conceived being to die, and to be resurrected and live evermore as the shared spirit of the religious community.

I wish to conclude my inadequate treatment of Hegel's immensely complex teleological idealism by raising a few questions and sounding a few doubts. These are not the questions and doubts connected with most idealistic systems: Hegel does not believe in subsistent Platonic types, nor does he believe that *esse is percipi*, nor that all relation and unity in the world is the work of a constructive synthetic Mind, whether divine or human. What we have to ask in connection with Hegel is whether his queer brand of infinite teleology is acceptable. Is everything in the world explained by being shown to be a necessary condition for the emergence of self-conscious spiritual life? Does not the thesis readily permit of an inversion: that self-conscious spiritual life, far from being the explanatory focus of the world, is rather entirely dependent on that world for its existence and intelligibility, is perhaps only a negligible offshoot of it? That rationality depends on the irrational might be held to prove the irrationality of rationality, rather than the rationality of irrationality. Does not, we may further ask, the thesis prove too much? Could we not say of *every* phenomenon in the world that, since its necessary conditions are to be found in all reaches and levels of being, it too is the sense of the world, the thing for which the aeons laboured! Cannot Lawrence, Kansas or Chapel Hill, North Carolina[1] be regarded as the absolute end for whose realization everything is as it is, or was as it was? And what finally is the nature of the teleology which is not the work of a definite organizing agent—for that the Idea is no agent we have seen—but is somehow obscurely inherent in the constitution of things? Is such a teleology more than the regulative teleology of Kant, a particular way of reflectively regarding the facts of the world?

To these questions I am not able to give a finally satisfactory answer except to say that I think Hegel's infinite teleology will be an acceptable thought-scheme only to the extent that we really believe in a strong, increasingly dominant trend in the world towards enhanced self-consciousness and rationality. I do not myself think that it is enough to cherish Hegelian teleology as a sort of rational faith necessarily implied by our various higher

[1] This paper was given in both of these places.

enterprises: one must be willing to give that faith some sort of metaphysical, ontological justification. Hegel thought that the facts of nature and history evinced a steady progress towards liberated, self-conscious rationality, but some might feel that these facts can be given a different, less optimistic interpretation. I myself would accept something like Hegelianism only with a considerably wider sweep of knowledge, perhaps demanding penetration into spheres of being lying beyond the confines of this transitory life. But whether or not one accepts Hegel, the interest of his problems, of his solutions and of his methods remains unique. He has certainly set before us the richest intellectual feast in the world if it is perhaps also the most difficult of all to digest.

IX

THE DIREMPTIVE TENDENCIES OF WESTERN PHILOSOPHY[1]

Hegel, discussing some of the most beautiful passages in the *Bhagavad-gītā*, in which Kṛṣṇa declares his identity with the self of all beings, with sun, moon, the letter A, the syllable *Om*, with the delusive *māyā*, which men find so hard to transcend, makes the following characteristic remarks:

> The All which Krishna pronounces himself to be, is as little as the Eleatic One or the Spinozistic Substance, *everything*. This everything, the endlessly many sensuous plurality of the finite, is in all these ideas set down as the *accidental*, which has no being in and for itself, but has its truth in the substance, the One, which, in distinction from such accidental being, alone is divine, is God. Indian religion, however, goes on to the notion of Brahma, the pure unity of thought-in-itself, in which the empirical everything of the world, as well as the proximate substantialities called gods, vanish. . . . But the unity of God, of a spiritual God, is so little concrete in itself, so powerless— so to say—that the Indian religion, by an immense confusion, is also the maddest of polytheisms. . . . For that unity, in so far as it is intrinsically abstract and therefore empty, itself puts what is concrete outside of itself and gives it independence, whether as a multitude of gods or of empirical this-world singulars.[2]

In this passage, Hegel expresses one of the most characteristic urges of Western philosophy, the desire for 'true unities' which are not the mere product of abstraction or external colligation, but which are unities in and for themselves, which represent the genuine and not the fictitious furniture of the world. It is not enough in philosophy to have unities which arise because we

[1] Presented at the East-West Conference of Philosophy, University of Hawaii, July 1964.
[2] Georg Wilhelm Friedrich Hegel, *System der Philosophie, Dritter Teil, Die Philosophie des Geistes*, Sämtliche Werke, Jubiläumsausgabe, Bd. 10 (Stuttgart: Frommanns Verlag, 1929), pp. 463–6, 575.

ignore or blur essential differentiations, or because we link things together in some arbitrary personal manner, or because we treat gaps as if they were fillings, or names as if they were things named: what we want are unities which are in some sense solid and authentic. That this notion of solid authenticity is a clear one need not be maintained: it may itself prove to be the most vacuous of chimeras. It has dominated thought in the West, however, as only an idea can dominate when it is kept unquestioned in the margin, and seldom dragged into the light of day. And it is in terms of this idea that there is a tendency to see in such all-embracing unities of Oriental thought as have been put forth in the *Bhagavad-gītā* something merely abstract and empty, which may verbally unite and cement the world, but which leaves its disarrayed fragmentation unaltered, or which passes beyond it to an empty consummation which is nothing but a name. Whatever unity we desire, we do not desire that, the night in which every cow is black and is lost in the surrounding blackness.

It may further be said to be characteristic of Western philosophy —though not, of course, without important exceptions—that its unities tend to be many and small, rather than single (or few) and widely embracing. Such Western philosophers, for example, as have treated 'entities of reason' as 'true unities' have seen them less as cementing, than as divisive and dissolving, factors: they break up concrete things rather than link them together. The 'friends of the Ideas' are, as Plato says, κατὰ σμικρὰ διαθραύοντες[1], i.e. they chop ordinary things up into little bits, each a separate εἶδος or the copy of a separate εἶδος; they turn them into illusory combinations, where each εἶδος seems to be many by virtue of its association with other εἴδη in bodies and actions.[2] The εἴδη are, as Aristotle rightly maintained, ideal individuals, and the effect of their overpowering individuality is to deprive ordinary individuals of authenticity. If there is a Form for that embracing individual the cosmos and perhaps for the Soul, our actual world retains a looseness and disorder of structure that are absent from its εἶδος, and the Soul, at least in its earthly incarnation, is encrusted with as many barnacles as the sea-god Glaucus. If behind the fragmented forms there are vague unifying presences such as the One, the Good, the Great-and-small, etc. they play an enigmatic, equivocal part in the whole picture.

If we turn to that modern 'friend of the Forms', Bertrand Russell,

[1] Plato, *Sophistes*, 246c.   [2] Plato, *Republic*, 476a.

we see similar divisive forces at work, though they operate differently at different stages of his development. Common-or-garden things become 'collections of appearances'[1] or 'bundles of properties',[2] space resolves itself (at least in Russell's earliest, most interesting days) into a brilliant dust of variously distant points;[3] and the only genuine complex unities which have not the dubious status of mere aggregates are held to be 'propositions',[4] which in their turn become decimated by the departure of falsehoods and higher-order statements into the complex facts which are unities of simples.[5] These Russellian views are, of course, the original of Wittgenstein's later logical atomism, in which every statement about complexes is analysable without residue into a statement about their constituent parts, into those statements which completely describe such complexes.[6]

Western philosophy has, however, sought its authentic unities in the 'real' rather than in the ideal realm—they are individuals rather than universals—and there is the same tendency here as in the ideal case to restrict authenticity to fairly small rather than to widely spreading units. The 'true unities' are variously taken to be the eternal, indivisible, separate atoms—whether the void which separates them is unitary or divisible may be left undecided—or they are the 'natural' individuals of Academic and Aristotelian tradition, cows, trees, men, particles of earth, fire, etc. that we see or suppose. In the seventeenth century, Leibniz found the pattern of true unity in the individual conscious mind, the only thing that could embrace all its present and future modifications without breaking up into them as its parts, and so was superior to all mere colligations, and thus to extended things, which, despite a surface show of unity, really amounted to little more than such colligations.[7] Our own age has preferred the still smaller unit of the physical or sensible or somewhat mystically described 'event',

[1] Bertrand Russell, *The Analysis of Mind* (London: George Allen & Unwin, Ltd., 1921), p. 100.

[2] Bertrand Russell, *An Inquiry into Meaning and Truth* (London: George Allen & Unwin, Ltd., 1940), p. 128.

[3] Bertrand Russell, *Principles of Mathematics* (2nd ed., London: George Allen and Unwin, Ltd., 1951), pp. 423, 445.

[4] *Ibid.*, pp. 135–6, 138–41.

[5] Bertrand Russell (with Alfred North Whitehead), *Principia Mathematica* (2nd ed., Cambridge: Cambridge University Press, 1926), vol. I, pp. 43–4.

[6] Ludwig Wittgenstein, *Tractatus Logico-philosophicus* (London: Routledge & Kegan Paul, 1961), 2.0201, pp. 10–11.

[7] Gottfried Wilhelm Leibniz, *Lettres à Arnauld*.

with its unspecified spatial spread and its anthropomorphically specified duration of 'a few seconds'.

Even the philosopher whose logic least encourages fragmentation, who believes in 'totality', the built-in presence of everything in everything, as the essential characteristic of the highest, 'notional' thought, none the less gives a self-diremptive tendency an essential place in his Absolute, and is in some ways more anarchically individualistic, more concessive to strife and discontinuity, than almost any other philosopher. Hegel is a thinker who believes in real universals, which actively pervade and dominate their instances, but they are universals, unlike the Platonic, whose nature it is to be specified and individualized, inevitably in disjoined, dispersed incompatible, variously imperfect and contingent ways, and which are one only because they are one in such a many.[1] Hegel similarly believes in the eternal Idea of self-conscious Spirit, of Rational Mind conscious of itself as the be-all and end-all of everything, but this Idea remains an 'abstraction', not 'the true God', except as it involves itself in the living process of positing its 'other', the world, and in achieving union with its 'other' in the form of Spirit.[2] The rationality of self-conscious Spirit is certainly something shared by all men, something which binds them together into a single spiritual 'we', but this common rationality achieves its final, 'absolute' form only in the activities of individuals, in their aesthetic visions, their religious acts of worship, their moments of philosophical enlightenment. If our common rationality is divine or of God, 'God is God only so far as he knows himself: his self-knowledge is further his self-consciousness in man and man's knowledge of God which proceeds to man's self-knowledge in God'.[3] It is even arguable that Hegel believes in Absolute Spirit only as something as much contemporary as it is also eternal.

Philosophy, which for Hegel is Absolute Spirit, is also said to be 'its own time comprehended in thought', and the warning is added that 'it is just as silly to suppose that any philosophy goes beyond its contemporary world as that an individual can jump beyond his time'.[4] The overarching rational unity of Spirit is

[1] Hegel, *System der Philosophie, Die Logik*, Sämtliche Werke, Jubiläumausgabe, Bd. 8, pp. 163, 179, 358–61, 381–2.
[2] Hegel, *Die Phänomenologie des Geistes*, Jubiläumsausgabe, Bd. 2, pp. 584–7.
[3] Hegel, *System der Philosophie, Dritter Teil, Die Philosophie des Geistes*, pp. 454, 564.
[4] Hegel, *Grundlinien der Philosophie des Rechts*, Jubiläumsgabe, Bd. 7, p. 35.

therefore essentially dispersed among separate individual men who learn from one another in time—it has, says Hegel, 'impenetrable atomic subjectivity', which is as much *not* exclusive individuality[1] —and Hegel makes it plain that such personal dispersion is essential to its over-arching, connective functions. The life-and-death struggle leading to enslavement of class by class, for instance, is an essential stage in the development of those higher forms of self-consciousness in which men fully acknowledge one another and each other's rational claims. 'Each', says Hegel, 'is the means through which each mediately connects and closes with itself, and each . . . is self-existent only through such mediation. Minds acknowledge minds as mutually acknowledging one another.'[2] Even at the level of unconscious things, we find Hegel preferring a view of reality as a set of mutually provoking substances, each of which requires the other's solicitation to bring out its own peculiar contribution, and which is therefore profoundly free in being thus outwardly provoked and harried, rather than the view of reality as a single total thing or substance, of which finite things are the vanishing surface phases. We may say that Hegel follows the Leibnizian plan of concentrating the whole in each of its countless components rather than the Spinozistic plan of losing the parts in the whole.[3] It follows from all this that the philosopher who of all Western philosophers most stressed that 'the truth is the whole' is not to be looked on as one who disregarded the claims of individuality in general, or of multiplied and dispersed individuality in particular.

If one looks for a Western philosopher who really believes in one all-comprehensive unity rather than in many dispersed unities, then, apart from such great eccentrics as Erigena and Bruno, the only salient examples are to be found in Spinoza and in those relatively few minds that fell deeply under his influence: the most important of these are possibly Schelling and Bradley. It is gratuitous to say with Hegel[4] that Spinoza's subordination of the individual to the one Substance arises from his Jewish origin, for there is nothing radically unifying in the thought of the Jews: Jewish thought dwells on gulfs, peculiarities, exclusions, arbitrarinesses, special dispensations, and revelations,

[1] Hegel, *Die Wissenschaft der Logik*, Jubiläumsausgabe, Bd. 5, p. 327.
[2] Hegel, *Die Phänomenologie des Geistes*, p. 150.
[3] Hegel, *System der Philosophie, Die Logik*, pp. 150–6, 337–47.
[4] *Ibid.*, Sec. 151, *Zusatz*, p. 339.

rather than on what is all-inclusive, inescapable, and single. None the less, Spinozism represents a foreign element in Western thought, which is shown by the shock which his 'hideous hypothesis' excited in the seventeenth and eighteenth centuries. If that shock yielded to sympathy in the Romantic epoch and in the nineteenth century as a whole, this is due to the fact that that century was itself a unique century. In its later decades its tendencies toward monism were in part explained by the universal bulldozing onslaught of a simplifying deterministic, materialistic naturalism and of a similarly simplifying boundless free commercialism. In the writings of Bradley we have the supreme modern expression of Spinozism. Whatever is less than 'the whole' is a mutilated fragment torn from context: only when such 'mutilation' is wholly overcome have we anything that we can call 'reality'. Spinozism here achieved something like the position of a great tradition, for Bradley was also greatly influenced by Hegel, and, despite Bradley's disclaimers, it was to Hegel and Hegelianism that the 'mutilation doctrine' with its added stress on 'coherence', 'internal relations', and the honorific use of the non-Hegelian term 'universe' was attributed. And from Hegel this attribution was extended to Kant, Plato, and other Western philosophers. But, for Hegel, diremption and mutilation were an essential aspect of the life of the Absolute: it was only in so far as the world was torn apart into mutually exclusive elements that the healing of the diremption could be consciously carried out, in which healing the whole being of the Absolute consisted.[1]

It will now be worth while to stress the diremptive individualism of Western philosophy by considering the contributions of one very great, quite recent philosopher, Ludwig Wittgenstein. In him what we may call the fragmenting tendency of Western philosophy reaches a limit: it may, in fact, be said to over-reach itself and to take on the character of its opposite. For it is a consequence of fragmentation, of course, that, if it is so utter as to suppress all contrary wholeness, it ceases to be fragmentation at all: the fragment becomes the whole, all there is or possibly could be. The radical atomism of Wittgenstein's first work, the *Tractatus Logico-philosophicus*, has been commented on above: as the absolute contrary of Spinozism, which none the less has something of the Spinozistic method and emotional atmosphere, it fitly bears (in its English version) a Spinozistic title. The work has not the

[1] Hegel, *Die Phänomenologie des Geistes*, p. 23.

originality that its remarkable style suggests, since the roots of its
doctrine that there can be no genuine complex unities other than
'facts', whose constituents therefore must be utterly simple, is to
be found in Russell's 1903 *Principles of Mathematics*, one of the
few philosophical books that we know Wittgenstein thoroughly
read and disgested.[1] What is characteristic of Wittgenstein is the
inferred colourlessness[2] of his simple objects, their intrinsic
characterlessness, all their character presumably lying in their
connections with other objects, a simplicity so profound that it
quite empties of content the simples for whose simplicity it is so
concerned, and leaves us with nothing but termless connections.
What is likewise characteristic is the doctrine of the radical
independence, the mutual externality, of these ultimate factual
connections:[3] none of them entails or excludes any other, entailment or exclusion being the prerogative of propositional signs
covering wide overlapping or non-overlapping arrays of possible
facts, and involving only a seeming passage from one independent
fact or possible fact to another.[4] But such independence and
externality admit of just as much of what would ordinarily be
called 'internality' as one chooses, since one can simply strike
from 'logical space', from the range of allowable ultimate connections, any sort of connection one feels to be senseless, e.g. the
combination of blue and green, so that the independence of the
remaining possibilities remains as unfettered as before. It is,
in fact, impossible from reading the *Tractatus* to determine the
sort of world it prefigures: it might be as tightly restricted as
the colour-relations it sometimes mentions[5] or as ideally loose as a
set of mathematical permutations and combinations. Possibly
this lack of bias is a merit, but it does not accord with what it says
of itself.

In the later work of Wittgenstein the dogmatic atomism of the
Tractatus is subjected to severe criticism, and the notion is put
forward that it is entirely a matter of the language we use, and
of the particular purposes of that language, whether something
counts as simple or complex. The metaphysical argument that
there must be ultimate existent simples to guarantee the sense of
complex assertions is entirely abandoned. A broom, it is argued,

[1] Said by Ludwig Wittgenstein to me.
[2] Ludwig Wittgenstein, *Tractatus Logico-philosophicus*, 2.0232, pp. 10–11.
[3] *Ibid.*, 1.21, pp. 6–7.　　　　　　　　　　[4] *Ibid.*, 5.124, pp. 74–5.
[5] *Ibid.*, 2.0131, pp. 8–9; 2.0251, pp. 12–13; 4.123, 4.124, pp. 52–3.

is profoundly simple and unanalysable in the practical language of the kitchen, and it would be absurd to substitute for the intelligible order 'Bring me the broom' the unintelligible order 'Bring me the broomstick and the brush which is fitted to it'.[1] The atomism of the former theory still appears, however, in the notion of an indefinite multiplicity of uses of language, of language-games, games such as giving orders, describing, reporting, story-telling, joking, translating, even asking, thanking, cursing, greeting, praying.[2] Each of these was paradoxically thought of by Wittgenstein as capable of being a more or less self-contained performance, and as capable in such self-containedness of throwing light on the complex performance of actual speech. The notion of greeting or praying as capable of a self-contained linguistic existence without its respective immensely complex social and cognitive background is one of the curiosities of philosophy, a fit successor to the doctrine of simple objects simply connected as the sense-making underpinning of discourse. And with this diremption of speech into separate performances went the further denial of common and pervasive elements in thought and speech: all was a matter of 'family resemblances', of unnumbered distinct resemblances which overlap and run criss-cross like the fibres of a rope.[3] This strange view is also self destroying, since, if genuinely common and universal elements cannot be thought or spoken of, it makes no sense to deny their presence, nor to assert that what appears thus simply pervasive is really multiple and overlapping (if only because the overlapping strands of meaning set a new standard of simplicity). The so-called 'family resemblances' become in fact the norm of a new simplicity, and we are back where we were.

This particular *elenchus* was not one that Wittgenstein ever explicitly recognized, but there was another which he did explicitly recognize with extremely interesting consequences. Wittgenstein believed in the diremption of conscious persons far more completely and profoundly than any previous philosopher. He practised doubt in a region where even Descartes had never dreamed of it, the malign genius never having been a malign automaton, and he devoted an immense amount of thought and imaginative experiment to showing that no sense could be given to the possibility of

---

[1] Wittgenstein, *Philosophical Investigations* (Oxford: Basil Blackwell, 1953), Sec. 60, p. 29.

[2] *Ibid.*, Sec. 24, p. 12.   [3] *Ibid.*, Sec. 67, p. 32.

entering another's mind, sharing another's sensations, contemplating his images, etc.[1] Though he strangely held that the barrier which prevented such entry was linguistic or grammatical, he could not make the linguistic adjustment to surmount it, and the performances of entering other people's experiences which are reported to take place in *yoga* or in Buddhist *jhāna* (concentration) would be ruled out as internally self-contradictory. It follows that the world of one's discourse, if one dares to breathe such a consequence, is necessarily a solipsistic world, in which all data and objects and interlocutors are necessarily one's own familiars. But, even at the time of the *Tractatus*, Wittgenstein saw this solipsism to be self-destroying: if one can talk of nothing but what is one's own, the words 'one's own' lose all their meaning, since there is no other world or use of words with which they could be contrasted. Solipsism may show itself but it cannot be said. Or, as it is also put, solipsism, developed to the limit, swings over into pure realism: the self becomes an extensionless point, and all that remains over is a world of objects.[2] Solipsism becomes something which is so true, so basic, that it can no longer be uttered, except by employing a philosophically exaggerated use of language which can have merit only as countering other more misguided exaggerations.[3]

But this solipsism which has turned into pure realism now suffers a further transformation. The language which describes the world of objects can no longer be thought of as a private language, but is plainly the common language of the speaking beings who inhabit that world, who play descriptive, predictive, and other similar language-games with one another in regard to its contents. A purely private use of language in a world that no longer has a place for contrasted privacies is altogether excluded: it has no proper, testable connection with the world. It is one of the immense ironies of philosophy that what may be called Wittgenstein's refutation of solipsism and solipsistic language, at which so many British and American philosophers have grasped with such enthusiasm, is the invention of a philosopher who is probably the one absolute solipsist who has ever existed, who probably sincerely thought that his own experiences were all

---

[1] Wittgenstein, *The Blue and Brown Books* (Oxford: Basil Blackwell, 1960), pp. 48–54.

[2] Wittgenstein, *Tractatus Logico-philosophicus*, 5.64, pp. 116–17.

[3] Wittgenstein, *The Blue and Brown Books*, pp. 58–9.

there was or ever could be, and whose denial of private languages is a necessary, if tortuous, consequence of this solipsism. The things I have said no doubt require more justification, more textual and biographical documentation, than I can give them here: the change wrought by Wittgenstein in Western philosophy is, however, too important to be passed over. What I have said does not, of course, denigrate Wittgenstein's contribution. Great philosophers are those who by the sharpness with which they feel difficulties and distinctions promote the dialogue, the dialectic, of philosophy. Seen in this light, Wittgenstein's greatness is beyond all question.

It is time, however, to bring my historical excursus, dogmatic through the sheer impossibility of complete support, to a close. Western philosophical thought has been overwhelmingly diremptive and in some extreme cases such diremption has been self-destroying, has removed its own disunion through destroying the connections which alone make disunion significant. What, however, do we recommend on the matter? Are we to endorse our Western approaches, or are we to plead for that Spinozism which makes everything tight and seamless and single, or for the even more blanketing unification which makes all the baseless iridescence of a *Nirguna Brahman* or some similarly conceived negative ultimate? Or are we to be very modern and say that it is all a matter of language and linguistic emphasis, of the light in which we choose to look on the world and talk about it, and that it is 'altogether our affair' whether we speak of things diremptively and individualistically, or tightly and Spinozistically, or with the all-obliterating negativity of certain forms of Eastern thought?

I think that the proper answer to these questions—and here I am trying to speak on behalf of the Western tradition as a whole—is, first, that it does not do to be so very modern: some modes of conception certainly fit the world and are truer to it and our experience of it than others. It is not merely a question of linguistic advantage or of some special cognitive purpose whether we see things as apart and many or as welded together and single. And I shall show my hand at the outset by saying that I regard all utterly diremptive philosophies as distorted and self-destroying, just as I regard all wholly unifying philosophies as equally so. Differentiation on a background that connects and unifies seems to be, not only psychologically and epistemologically, but—dare I say it?—ontologically, necessary. Something even of the Hegelian

'built-inness' of one thing in another, of the Spinozistic rejection
of 'mutilation', of the impossibility of getting anything 'quite on
its own' and of making clear statements just about it and nothing
else, I should regard as essential to all sound and sensitive
philosophy, and as setting a limit to the exact formalization of any
subject-matter or the guillotine-like use of the Principle of Contradiction. The Principle of Contradiction is a flawless principle,
except that a significant notion or assertion seldom quite lives up
to the clear-cut use of negation that it presupposes. I should
regard it as equally essential, however, that we should meditate on
the schisms, gulfs, barriers, cleavages, oppositions, inconsequences,
and other divisive factors which are obvious in the world, which
are in fact the essential complement of its connectedness, and
which permit and encourage us to consider separate objects,
regions, levels, properties, alternatives, issues, etc. etc. without
dragging in what is irrelevant. To take but two examples from
very different fields, it is absurd, on the one hand, to consider
only the externalizing, divisive features of space and time, and to
ignore their connective features: if they set things apart, sometimes interject gulfs and barriers between them, they also link
them all by continuous routes in virtue of which they may literally
be said to pass over into one another and to be not fully separable
even for thought. It is in the same way absurd to fail to recognize
the gross ground-level impenetrability of our separate selves,
which is forced on us by a necessity deeper than grammar, but
it is just as absurd to fail to recognize that there is nothing whatever that we all more clearly and luminously understand than
precisely this impenetrability—even children recognize it in their
talk about their own and other people's thoughts—and that in
understanding it we also transcend it. Persons may not be pene-
trable to one another, but they acknowledge one another and
cannot, in fact, be without such acknowledgement. Sheer monisms
and splintered atomisms represent the two opposed poles of the
philosophically unacceptable, but to say this is not to say where the
bland equator really lies.

Here I am afraid I must come out in favour of the tradition I
represent: the world of our actual experience—of *samsāra*, if you
like—seems to be much more amenable to divisive, fragmenting
treatment than to unifying treatment: it is much more a place of
holes, bunkers, and loose earth than of smooth lawn-like continuities. And I am utterly against any attempt to escape from

these undoubted characteristics of our experience by any flight of abstraction, by simply disregarding what is most obvious in experience and the world. To say that the division of things is delusive is to grant reality to a delusion, and to add that this delusion is itself delusive is to return to a simple affirmation of the content of the first delusion. This much of rigorous applicability will I grant to the Law of Double Negation: I see no meaningful way of affirming the delusiveness of a delusion without reaffirming the content of the original delusion. And it is clear, moreover, that whatever sense, dignity, and worth attaches to ultimate unity and continuity, attaches to it only in virtue of its somehow preserving the rich variety of our dislocated existence, rather than merely eliminating it. I have once or twice amused classes by successively and slowly erasing the many words and diagrams I have put on the blackboard. While the erasure proceeds, there can be, if one suggests it, a marvellous sense of simplification, of liberation from confusion, of return to primal unity and emptiness: like a Buddhist *arhat*, one feels free as the air. When the erasure is completed the result is merely dull: the board's blankness is a blankness with no glorious contrasts within it.

But, though I am utterly against any flight of abstraction from our dirempted world, I am not at all against the possibility of a flight from it that represents a real state of experience, and one that does not obliterate, but somehow preserves, the rich variety that our dirempted world offers. I do not, in fact, find it inconceivable that our dirempted experience has a contrast in another much more profoundly unified type of experience in which mutual built-inness and interpenetration are more pervasive, and there are not as many things that permit one to treat them in isolation. Certain of our ordinary waking thoughts, as well as certain of the thoughts we have in dreams, manifest unparalleled concentrations of content without the slightest detailed, separate illustration, and it is not hard to conceive an experience that is almost totally of this type. It would be an experience which in a sense implied the dirempted dealings of this life, and was in a sense parasitic upon it—though I am not sure that the parasitism might not be conceived as mutual—but which presented them all in a totally new light or manner, possibly rather as Proust presented his personal history in his marvellous novel. I am ready to conceive that in that 'other life' we might encounter, for instance, types rather than individuals, not abstract Platonic Forms, but figures ready to pass into closely parallel figures with the fluidity we experience in dreams. The line between the publicly real and the private and imaginary might be much less rigid than it is in our present experience, and we might be 'disembodied' in the sense of being able to vary our bodily form at will. And it is a pleasing fantasy that the identity of angels may be less rigorously exclusive than the identity of men: meeting Gabriel may in effect mean meeting Ithuriel and Uriel, and the puzzles raised by Wittgenstein about feeling the pain and joy of others may simply be a laughable reflection of our present state. Certain fine passages in Plotinus, not his empty rhetoric about the One, but his descriptions of life in the 'intelligible world', similarly tend to persuade me that there may be kinds of experience much more profoundly interfused and unified than our own, and I sometimes faintly look forward to experiencing them, or of becoming part of something that experiences them, in the 'life to come'. I am also willing to entertain the hypothesis that the world might regularly alternate from some such unitary experience as I have indicated to the dirempted experience we now enjoy. Possibly Empedocles was right in thinking that the world regularly passed from a state in which all things were together to a state in which all things were divided and dispersed, and vice versa, and the Indian doctrine of world cycles points in a similar direction. But, whatever one believes, the unitive state must be a real experience, not an empty negation of experience, and it must be richly differentiated as is our present experience, though without its isolation and separation of elements. There may, in fact, be a state in which God or *Brahman* really enjoys in concentrated union the whole of what he has dispersedly undergone or been. But, if such a state is possible, which I am far from affirming, it is not our present state; we live in a world-age in which there may be gods, but in which there certainly is no God or none worth having. In our world the many and separate are more in evidence than the One, and the advantage goes to the sort of philosophy that more plainly recognizes this fact.

I may say, in conclusion, that I recognize many of my statements to be controversial: I have made them to arouse controversy. I also fully recognize the impossibility of saying anything wholly true about so indefinite and dispersed an entity as 'Western philosophy'. And I am not at all ignorant of the fact that there are Eastern schools of thought as subtly diremptive as the Western systems I have mentioned. I only doubt whether they ever achieve as fine a balance between unity and diremption as certain great Western systems. Let no one think, however, that, to the extent to which I know it, I do not greatly respect and admire Eastern thought.

L

X

THE LOGIC OF MYSTICISM[1]

I am both happy and honoured to have been asked to give this lecture on mysticism in memory of Leo Robertson, of whom I have many very pleasant memories. It was a delight to be wafted off to the Saville Club after a lecture here, and to discuss mysticism and philosophy on one of its many sofas. I am very sorry that this particular pleasure will not recur. Leo Robertson belonged to an old-fashioned climate of thought in which an interest in mysticism was respectable, and a long stay in the East had confirmed him in these leanings. I myself have always been constitutionally mystical, feeling that certain kinds of rapture, concerned with work, beauty, love and a few other things, are the only things absolutely worth having. I dropped my mysticism for a long period, partly on account of certain disillusioning experiences in my twenties, and partly out of deference to the dry methods and doctrine that prevailed in British philosophy. Latterly, however, increasing age has restored many of my illusions and made me generally more tender-minded; also, seeing the completely nugatory accomplishments of purely unmystical analysis, I have found myself reverting increasingly to my original mysticism. It was very refreshing to talk to a philosopher like Leo Robertson who took mysticism with the complete seriousness I think it deserves—as one of the truly fundamental human attitudes—but who also thought of it as supplementing and completing, rather than as undermining and nullifying, what other less rarefied thinkers do. It was also refreshing to hear all his talk about an earlier Cambridge, where he knew Wittgenstein in the full brilliance of his personal beauty as well as of his intelligence, and also knew Moore in the golden period of his dialectic, before he became so very preoccupied with the minutiae of the English language. Leo Robertson was a complete and rounded philosopher

[1] A lecture given in London at the Royal Institute of Philosophy on March 4, 1966, as a memorial to Leo Robertson, its late director, and published in *Religious Studies* 2, pp. 145–62.

rather than a hamstrung one, and knowing him has been a factor in strengthening my resolve to be a complete and rounded thinker too.

I am calling my present lecture 'The Logic of Mysticism' because I wish to study what is admittedly a very important and widespread form or set of forms of human experience from a predominantly logical point of view. I intend, that is, to study a whole range of notions and assertions and reasonings that could be called 'mystical', and the peculiar language in which they express themselves, rather than any highly specific, greatly prized experiences which lie behind these notions and assertions. And I wish to see whether there are not peculiar rules and guiding principles governing these mystical notions and assertions, and whether it is not possible to raise questions of the well-formed and the ill-formed, of validity and invalidity, in regard to them, as we can in other fields of discourse, e.g. of discourse on probability or on morals. I am approaching mysticism in this way because there is a widespread persuasion abroad that mysticism, so far from having a peculiar logic that can be studied and evaluated, has no trace of logic in its utterances at all, that it is in fact the very antithesis of the logical, and that the experiences it embraces, and which inspire its peculiar utterances, are not even experiences of which a satisfactory verbal expression is possible. They are intrinsically ineffable experiences, as the mystics themselves often allege, while expressing them so richly and so eloquently as to demonstrate their extraordinary effability. They are also experiences whose expression delights to flout all logical rules rather than to obey them, and which accordingly admit of no logical treatment whatever. The experiences which lie behind mystical assertions are often thought, further, to be experiences of a very peculiar class of persons called mystics, people liable to trances, seizures, illuminations and unmotivated convictions: if we value them, we value them as we do clairvoyants or people gifted with extra-sensory perception, and if we do not value them, we think of them as physically and psychologically abnormal beings who must certainly not be encouraged. In neither case is there anything of profound philosophical importance in what they say, let alone anything of *logical* significance. Whereas what I want to hold is that mystical utterances reflect a very peculiar and important way of looking at things which is as definite and characteristic as any other, which, while it may override and sublate ordinary ways of looking at things, and so have an appearance of senselessness and inconsistency, none the less has its own characteristic, higher-order consistency, and I wish further to suggest that this mystical way of looking at things, so far from being the special possession of peculiar people called mystics, rather enters into the experience of most men at many times, just as views of the horizon and the open sky enter into most ordinary views of the world. At the horizon things become confused or vastly extended, parallel lines meet and so on; just so, in the mystical sectors of experience, some things behave and appear quite differently from things in the near or middle distances of experience. Some people refuse to cultivate mystical ways of looking at things, and in fact resolutely exclude them. In the same way some people never look beyond the physical situation in which they immediately find themselves. This kind of experiential and logical myopia only shows that there are many myopic people, and that some are deliberately myopic: it shows nothing about the logical or illogical character of mystical utterances and experiences. On the view to which I adhere the so-called great mystics, people like Plotinus, Jalalud'in Rumi, St Teresa and so on, are merely people who carry to the point of genius an absolutely normal, ordinary, indispensable side of human experience and attitude, just as some other people carry to the point of genius the numerical, additive way of looking at things which all men possess in some degree. There are people whose incapacity for mathematics leads them to form an aversion from the whole subject, and there are people whose incapacity for mysticism leads them to form a similar aversion, yet it does not follow that either capacity is not a form of normal human endowment, expressing itself in a peculiar type of utterance and discourse, in fact with such regularity as to merit the title of a 'logic'. Such, at least, will be the assumption on which the present lecture will proceed.

In the lecture I am about to give I have been greatly assisted by W. T. Stace's excellent book *Mysticism and Philosophy*, published in 1961. This book is valuable because it deals with the essential questions which concern mysticism, and deals with them in what I consider a reasonably adequate manner. Stace starts, not by attempting to define mysticism or the mystical, which would *assume* that there was one uniform phenomenon called 'mysticism' in all the experiences and utterances that we cover by this name, but by asking whether there is not what he calls a 'common core' to all the experiences and utterances in question. Stace is quite well aware of the Wittgensteinian view that our general terms cover a large spreading *family* of cases rather than have as their scope a single uniform meaning: he understands that we cannot assume, with Socrates, that one word always points to one idea, that we cannot always ask 'What is being so-and-so itself?', and expect a clear and uniform answer. But he also perfectly sees that Wittgenstein's view of the meaning of general terms is as rashly dogmatic as the Socratic view—we may in fact contrast the Wittgensteinian with the Socratic *dogma*—and that only a detailed examination of cases can show whether a word covers a fairly uniform swath of significance or whether it varies so widely as to retain nothing in common over its whole range of application. Stace then elaborately shows, by quoting a wealth of material, that there are immense similarities of approach in utterances called 'mystical', which stem from the most varied sources, and have few or no historical links: a Christian saint uses much the same astounding language as a Moslem devotee or a Hindu Yogi, without being aware of the wide community he exemplifies. Profound differences there certainly are between varied styles of mysticism, but the resemblances are much more striking, even oppressively so, and they are not at all like the loose family resemblance embodied in, say, the Hapsburg features or coun- tenance. Stace arrives at the view, after considering all the material, that there is something like a uniform core to the many cases that we unhesitatingly class as instances of 'mysticism', and he further arrives at the view that this core diverges into two main specifications which he calls 'extrovertive' and 'introvertive' mysticism respectively. Of each of these varieties he gives a careful and well-documented characterization, and he does so without claiming for it either exhaustiveness or definitory exact- ness, and without rejecting the possibility of isolated cases which deviate from it. Some performances and utterances may have *some* of the marks of the mystical without the others, but the marks cluster together in a great number of cases, and have moreover, a character of mutual 'belongingness' which makes such a cluster- ing seem natural and appropriate.

Having thus pinned mysticism down as a more or less treatable, uniform phenomenon, Stace considers the question of the validity of mystical utterances: he deals with this under the heading of

'The Problem of Objective Reference'. Is mysticism, in other words, a merely personal, subjective way of looking at things, or does it really contribute to our vision of the world? I do not myself at all agree with Stace's interpretation of this question, nor with the answer he gives to it. For he practically identifies objectivity with membership of a law-governed causal system, and, while mysticism as an *attitude* may fit in with such a system, and so be 'objective', the matters it claims to reveal, that it takes a stance towards, certainly lie quite outside any such system. Mysticism does not profess to acquaint us with something like high entropy or the Aurora Borealis, and it is in this obvious sense not objective. But, since it makes no claim to be filling in a particular gap in a law-governed cosmic picture, mysticism is not, in Stace's view, subjective either. What it reveals is not hallucinatory or delusive like, say, ectoplasm or the canals on Mars. Mysticism, says Stace, is neither subjective nor objective, but trans-subjective: it is a community of attitude that many people share. Now I am not in the least satisfied with all this, for mystical moods and persons, are, above all, assertive, and they put something before us as *true*, as *real*, whether anyone thinks so or not. Mysticism is characterized throughout by the noetic quality on which William James laid such stress in his account of religious experience. If mysticism tells us nothing about the world, then it is, in a deep sense, very false indeed, since it certainly professes to tell us something about it. I certainly therefore wish to answer this question as to the validity of mysticism in a manner different from Stace, and I do not wish to assume that whatever validates a mystical utterance is also what validates a scientific utterance. The truth of mysticism may be deeper than the truth of science, and it may only be in the light of mystical truth that scientific truth is fully intelligible. But Stace has proceeded usefully in separating the question of validity from the question of phenomenological description, and in showing the peculiar difficulty of the questions 'Is mysticism true?', 'Are mystical assertions valid?'.

Stace then goes on to consider a number of questions which illuminate the value and validity of mysticism. Is mysticism dualistic and theistic, is it pantheistic, is it inveterately monistic? What is the relation of mysticism to various historical forms of religion? What is the relation of mysticism to supernatural and visionary phenomena, and to the survival by the person of bodily death? What is its relation to ethics? What is its relation to science? What, above all, is its relation to logic? On all these points I am only in partial agreement with Stace, since I do not have the faith in science that he has, and since I take mysticism far more seriously than he does. My own views will, however, become plain at a later stage in this lecture.

I now wish to follow Stace's method by documenting mysticism with quotation. I could quote from the Upanishads or the Buddhist Sutras, or the Tao-teh-King or St Teresa or Ruysbroeck, etc. but, since we are all philosophers, and our purpose philosophical, I shall mainly cite from one who is as great a philosopher as he is a mystic, namely Plotinus. He certainly practised mysticism to the limit, since he achieved the uttermost ecstasy or union with the Absolute on at least four occasions, as his biographer Porphyry relates. My first quotation is from *Ennead* V, Treatise viii, paragraphs three and four, *On Intelligible Beauty*; it describes the manner of existence in the true, the intelligible world. 'For all there is heaven: earth is heaven and the sea is heaven, and so are animals and plants and men, all heavenly things in that heaven. . . . And life is easy yonder, and truth is their parent and nurse, their substance and sustenance, and they see all things, not such as are in flux but as have true being, and they see themselves in others: for all things are transparent, and nothing is dark and resistant: everything is inwardly clear to everything and in all respects: light is made manifest to light. And each thing holds all within itself, and again sees all in each other thing, so that everything is everywhere, and all is all, and each all, and the glory infinite. Each of those things is great, since even the small is great, and the sun yonder is all the stars, and each star the sun, and again all the stars. One thing stands forth in each, though it also displays all. . . . Each there walks, as it were, on no alien earth, but is itself always in its own place; its starting-point accompanies it as it hastens aloft, and it is not one thing and its region another.'[1] In this passage we have the mystical doctrine of interpenetration, of seeing the diverse things in the world as in some deep sense one and the same. This doctrine is put forward by Meister Eckhart when he says: 'All that a man has here externally in multiplicity is intrinsically one. Here all blades of grass, wood, and stone, all things are one. This is the deepest depth.' And again: 'Say, Lord, when is a man in mere understanding? I say

[1] It is interesting to report that Leo Robertson wrote a poem on this passage.

to you, when a man sees one thing separated from another. And when is he above mere understanding? That I can tell you. When he sees all in all, then a man stands above mere understanding.'[1] I could also quote famous utterances from Mahayanist Buddhist Sutras in which the same doctrine of mystical interpenetration is put forward.

I return, however, to a second quotation from Plotinus of a somewhat different tenor: it comes from *Ennead* VI, Treatise ix, paras. 5, 6, 11. 'This is the point of the rule which governs our mysteries, that they should not be divulged to outsiders: one is forbidden to reveal the divine to one who has not enjoyed the vision of it. Since seer and seen were then not twain, and the seen was united with the seer rather than seen by it, the seer retains an image of the Supreme when he remembers his union with it. He himself was the One, having no difference towards anything in himself, nor towards other things. All then was still with him, no stirring, no desire was with him when he rose to that state, nor any notion nor act of thinking, nor if one may so put it, himself. But as if caught up, rapt, he has passed in quiet to an unshaken state of solitude, completely at rest, and become as it were, rest itself.' (The last phrase 'rest itself' is a typical piece of mystical syntax.) 'He no longer moves among beauties and has outstripped beauty itself, has outstripped the choir of the virtues also, and is like one who, entering an inner sanctuary, leaves behind the statues in the temple that will again be the first to greet him, as secondary spectacles, after the spectacle and the communion within, a communion not with a statue or an image, but with the thing itself. Perhaps however, there was no spectacle there, but an approach other than sight, an ecstasy, a simplification, a surrender of self, a reaching towards contact, a peace, a contrivance of harmony that brings what is in the sanctuary into view. To look otherwise is to find nothing there.' This extraordinary passage can be paralleled by many passages from St Teresa where she speaks of a beam of light being temporarily lost in a larger light, or of the water in a bucket being temporarily lost in a larger body of water in which it is immersed. Or one can quote from the *Brihadaranyakopanishat*, VI, iii, 21, 23, 32, where it says that 'Now as a man, when embraced by a beloved wife, knows nothing that is without, nothing that is within, thus this person, when embraced by the intelligent self, knows nothing that is without,

---

[1] See Otto, *Mysticism, East and West*, p. 61, quoted by Stace, *loc. cit.* pp. 63–4.

nothing that is within. . . . And when he does not see, yet he is seeing, though he does not see. For sight is inseparable from the seer, because it cannot perish. But there is then no second, nothing else different from him that he could see.' One is not operating very differently if one turns to Wittgenstein's *Tractatus*: 'The world and life are one' (5.621); 'I am my world' (5.632); 'The subject does not belong to the world, but it is a limit of the world' (5.632); 'The philosophical I is not the man, not the human body or the human soul of which psychology treats, but the metaphysical subject, the limit, not a part of the world' (5.641); 'The contemplation of the world *sub specie aeterni* is its contemplation as a limited whole. The feeling of the world as a limited whole is the mystical feeling' (6.45); 'There is certainly something ineffable: this shows itself, it is the mystical' (6.522); 'My propositions are elucidatory in this way: he who understands me finally recognizes them as senseless when he has climbed out through them, on them, over them: he must so to speak throw away the ladder after he has climbed up on it' (6.54). This last proposition is paralleled by an aphorism from the founder of Zen Buddhism about throwing away a raft once it has taken one to the further shore.

I shall now consider the enumeration of the basic traits of mysticism, its 'universal core', which occurs in Stace's book. Stace, as I have said, distinguishes two varieties of mysticism, an extrovertive and an introvertive, and for the extrovertive he enumerates the following. (I rephrase his words a little.)

1. The unifying vision, expressed by the formula 'All is one'. The one is perceived in and through the multiplicity of objects.
2. The more concrete apprehension of One as an inner subjectivity, a life, a consciousness, a living presence in all things. 'Nothing is really dead'.
3. The sense of objectivity or reality: what is apprehended is absolutely real.
4. The feeling of extreme blessedness, joy, happiness, satisfaction, etc.
5. The feeling that what is apprehended is holy or sacred.
6. The feeling that what is apprehended is paradoxical.

And with reservations he adds:

7. The allegation that what is apprehended is 'ineffable'. 'Such

phrases as "inexpressible", "unutterable" bespatter the writings of mystics all over the world.'

For introvertive mysticism Stace gives the same list of features, except that its first two members are different. In introvertive mysticism we have, instead of a unifying vision connected with all empirical contents and objects, 'a unifying consciousness from which all the multiplicity of sensuous or conceptual or other empirical content has been excluded, so that there remains only a void and empty unity'. Instead of the One which is All, one has, in short, the One which is Nothing. And instead of (2), the sense of a universal life and consciousness in things, one has the idea of something essentially non-spatial and non-temporal, and otherwise uninvolved. Stace here quotes from a Buddhist Sutra: 'There is, monks, an unborn, not become, not made, uncompounded, and were it not, monks, for this unborn, not become, not made, uncompounded, no escape could be shown for what is born, has become, is made, is compounded.'[1]

I think Stace's account of mysticism has deep faults which reflect its method. It is an external, empirical account based on mere examination of single cases, and an attempt to find common traits which occur in them all. Its outcome is a rag-bag of empirical features, having no plain philosophical significance. Some people, it seems, like to speak in terms of an absolute unity present in all things, or utterly separate from them all, they like to say that this unity is objective or real, they feel bliss and awe in its contemplation, they like to say paradoxical things about it, they profess to find it indescribable, etc. Such people, it seems, are also liable to appear all over the world and at any point of time, like mongols or cretins, and the things they say are always remarkably uniform. But all this is a mere fact of human experience and behaviour like, for example, the basic characters and the many mutations of the sexual instinct. I myself am a philosopher who is utterly uninterested in anything which is a mere matter of fact, externally observed, even if it is a fact connected with what people think and say, and I do not regard any mere decanting and classification of empirical fact as genuine philosophical investigation. Philosophy is to me the bringing forth, not the mere registration or discovery, of conceptions which are what I should call intelligible unities, whose various components hang together necessarily, or with some

[1] *Loc. cit.* p. 126.

approach to rational necessity, and which alone can illuminate the complex windings of fact. Philosophy I regard as the overcoming of notional contingency, of the kind of loose combination of traits into a concept because such traits often occur together in actual cases, or are combined together in people's actual usage. If mysticism or the mystical is to be a worthwhile theme for philosophical study, it must be a coherent, notional unit, and a coherent notional unit which is necessary for the understanding of man and the world, and so rightly reckoned as fundamental. I am not at all interested in mysticism if it is a mere natural fact, or body of natural facts, about man, or if its concept is a mere natural fact, or body of natural facts, about human language. I think there is such a thing as belongingness or mutual affinity among conceptual features which moves us to combine them into a single concept, and to use a single term more or less to cover them all, and that their analytic discoverability in the meaning or use of that term is a consequence of this affinity. And I think the business of philosophers is to make concepts more of a notional unity, involving a deeper belongingness, than do the concepts which occur in ordinary usage. Philosophical analyses that profess to concern themselves with mere facts of usage in fact do not do so. The usages they select and consider together, always have a notional unity and importance, and the concepts they use to illuminate them, even when geared to what the ordinary man thinks or says, always depart far from the ordinary man's style of thinking. The immense merit of Austin is to have shown how fantastically far ordinary usage is from philosophy, but the concepts he himself elaborates, to *deal* with ordinary usage, the illocutionary, perlocutionary, etc. suggest that philosophers like himself do well to depart from ordinary usage. The notion of the perlocutionary, for example, is not one that ordinary speakers ever have framed or could frame.

Leaving these methodological issues aside, I proceed to sketch the mystical in what I feel to be a more satisfactory manner, and I am led to say, first of all, that mysticism is essentially a frame of mind connected with an *absolute* of some sort, meaning by an absolute an object of very peculiar type having very peculiar logical properties. By an absolute I mean something which, on the one hand, is irremovable and necessarily existent and self-existent, which could not meaningfully be supposed absent, nor dependent for its existence on anything else, and on which all contingencies of existence, whether within or without itself, are wholly dependent, and which further has the uniqueness and singleness which goes with its absolute status. I also wish to mean by it something which shows forth absolutely *every* recognized type of excellence or value in a fashion so transcendent that it can perhaps be rather said to *be* all these types of excellence than merely to embody or exemplify them, which *is* them all of necessity and is them all *together*, and which is certainly the sole cause for their presence in any finite case or contingent manifestation. I do not doubt that you will see what I mean by saying that the features of an absolute have logical affinity, that, while it is logically significant to conceive of them apart from each other, and so to build up the notion of a quasi-absolute which has some of these traits and not others—value-free quasi-absolutes are certainly constructed by many—the features in question do belong together and do complete each other, and that what they furnish is an integrated whole, the conception of something superlative, self-explanatory and all-explanatory, which rounds off all our concepts and valuations, and provides the necessary background for all of them. The various features which Stace laboriously discovers all arise because mysticism is oriented towards an absolute: the feature of absolute unity because an absolute is necessarily single and unique, the feature of reality because an absolute can only be thought of as inescapable, necessarily existent, the emotional colouring of bliss and awe, because an absolute is thought of as embodying all values and embodying them necessarily, the features of paradoxicality and ineffability, because an absolute necessarily differs in category, we may say, from any ordinary, finite object, being necessarily self-existent while ordinary objects exist contingently and dependently, and being all excellences whereas an ordinary object cannot have one excellence without inevitably failing to have another, and so on. Many would say that what I have called an absolute is a deeply contradictory or senseless notion, since the notions of necessary existence and unsurpassable excellence are either meaningless or self-contradictory. But whether this is true or not, self-contradictory and empty notions play a vast part in human experience and attitude, and this is certainly true of man's limiting notions of absolutes. Even philosophies which repudiate absolutes in their logic, and have professedly built up radically contingent, value-free systems, generally smuggle in absolutes of some sort, matter, logical space, the totality of atomic states of affairs, etc. etc. The paradoxicality and ineffability of mystical absolutes is simply a logical consequence of their being absolutes at all: every absolute differs *toto caelo* from any ordinary, empirical existent.

The traits of absolutes we have so far mentioned would, however, be found in purely intellectual approaches of various sorts that are anything but mystical. Much orthodox theology, for instance, is concerned with the unique properties of a transcendent deity, without there being the slightest spice of mysticism in its approaches to this being. It may even be held that strict theism is essentially unmystical, and this is why mysticism is frequently condemned in a theistic period of orthodoxy. Meister Eckhart, perhaps the greatest of Christian mystical philosophers, was condemned as a heretic by John XXII, the worst of the Popes. Mysticism may in fact be said to arise when an absolute is treated with extreme seriousness, both in theoretical vision and in practice: it is the sort of absolute we get when the logic of absoluteness is pursued to its furthest limit. Above all, what characterizes mysticism is a refusal to accept and use the notions of identity and diversity which the ordinary logic applies so confidently, whether in the relation of finite objects to the absolute, or of finite objects to one another. Ordinary logic assumes confidently that we can always pick out a number of separate items, *a, b, c, d, e*, etc. which, however much alike and intimately related, have each their own numerically distinct individuality, and can maintain it for a considerable period, during which they have absolutely no tendency to pass over into other things, or coalesce with them, or lose themselves in them. Whereas, if the uniqueness and omniresponsibility of an absolute is taken seriously, and there is not thought to be anything that is not an extension or expression of itself, then there can be no *a, b, c, d, e*, etc. which are not simply different names and guises of the same absolute, and which do not really differ from each other otherwise than as the morning star differs from the evening star. To take the notion of an absolute quite seriously is in fact to put the ordinary notion of diversity, and with it the ordinary notion of identity, out of action. Both can be only notions of the surface, of the first regard, which can be given an immediate, but not an ultimate, application. Mystics do not believe that the effective use of a notion in ordinary situations is sufficient to establish its ultimate legitimacy. The only sort of identity that can be ultimately admitted is one that can be stretched in varying degrees, which can come nearer and nearer to the limit of sheer diversity, otherness, without ever reaching it. We may say, if we like, that the absolute may be *alienated* from itself in different degrees in different forms or phases, and these in different degrees from one another, without ever reaching the breaking-point of sheer diversity. What we ordinarily wish to say will appear in a new form in a fully developed mystical logic, in which all absurdity will be carefully circumvented. But a mystical logic, like any other logic, takes a long time in construction, and, before it is fully developed, there will be phases in which we shall seem merely to be subverting ordinary forms of expression, without putting anything effective and lucid in their place. We can understand how, plagued by the seeming absurdity of two conflicting schemes of diction, there should be a desire to say of an absolute that it has *none* of the mutually exclusive characters of its forms and phases, that it is, in some quite non-ordinary sense, wholly *other* than them, or beyond them, that it is not to be called a *thing* or an *entity*, and that it is in some very deep sense Nothing at all. Most Japanese tea-houses have a symbol for the ultimate Nothingness which blessedly underlies tea-drinking like all finite objects, but it is plain that this Nothingness is only a step removed from the Everythingness and All-pervadingness of more positive mystical characterizations. Even of some of our packed thoughts it is as proper to say that they are very rich in distinct items as that they are wholly void of any distinct items at all, and such seemingly contradictory characterizations, which are certainly only analogical, are *a fortiori* no objection when applied to so remote and difficult an object as a mystical absolute.

To take this notion of an absolute seriously is further to treat the identity of everything, including oneself, with the absolute, as no mere remote intellectual conviction, but as something that ought to be capable of being realized so vividly and compellingly that it becomes a direct personal experience. Mystical experiences are not to be assimilated to queer extra-sensory perceptions. They are the understandings of an identity as logically perspicuous as 'If p then p' or 'If $p.q.$ then $q.p.$'. Only, while the theorems of the propositional calculus can be understood without passion, being adjusted to our normal state of alienation, the theorems of mysticism can only be understood with passion; one must oneself live through, consummate the identity which they postulate. All mysticism involves a doctrine and a practice and an experience of ecstasy, and the experiential character of mysticism is simply a consequence of the meaning of the identity it posits, an identity in which the ordinary person is taken out of his alienation, and taken up, or partially taken up, into the ultimate mystical unity.

Some of you will perhaps have been charitable enough to concede that what I have so far said may be quite all right as describing what mystics *think* is the logic of their utterances, but will none the less doubt whether there is any serious logic of this putative sort. The notion of an identity underlying plainly incompatible specifications is, they would say, a purely self-contradictory notion, especially when the absolute is not thought of as broken up into parts, and as admitting incompatible characterizations of its several parts. The notion of an identity underlying separable entities is likewise a wholly empty conception: it points to nothing and tells us nothing about anything. The notion that sheer diversity and complete independence are impossible is likewise inadmissible: they are perfectly possible, and should be recognized as such in any sound logic. And the notion of what exists of necessity is purely meaningless: necessity only connects characterizations of possible existents with one another, and existence always involves the connection of characterizations and descriptions with extra-linguistic reality. A necessary existent, were it admissible, would, moreover, be there whatever were the case, like the number Two or the ideal of Chastity, and this would make its so-called existence a wholly empty, abstract case of subsistence. Only what could be absent from the world could also contribute to its content, could exist in an ordinary sense, and could exercise all those saving, illuminative virtues which mystical thinkers have always been ready to attribute to their absolute. There is, finally, no meaning in the notion of perfection, in the joint embodiment of all excellence in an unsurpassable form: it is the nature of valuable qualities to conflict with other valuable qualities, and to be such as to have no maximum, but to permit always of being surpassed.

The answer to these and to many other similar objections is difficult: all that I here have to say is that the difficulties raised are to a large extent question-begging; they rest on a metaphysic or ontology which lies securely ensconced behind the very forms of our common utterances, of our ordinary logic, and which so absolutely commits us to a certain way of regarding the world and anticipating its contents, that it seems to commit us to nothing at all. The forms of our common utterance are by no means vacuous and innocuous: though they may not *say* that the world consists of certain types and ranges of elements and no others, or that it permits of certain sorts of treatment and no others, they may be said to *imply* that this is the case, and what they imply may be open to question, it may not, on reflection, be the only nor the truest way of viewing the facts in the world. The forms of our common utterance imply the existence or the possibility of an independent array of logical subjects, a, b, c, d, e, etc., each capable of existing or not existing separately without others, and permitting the attribution of characters, the possession of which by one logical subject tells us nothing as to the possession of the same character by another logical subject. They also imply the presence of relations among subjects which are external and indifferent to their existence and their character. The forms of this type of utterance readily lead to the development of a metaphysical atomism even more drastic than that worked out by Wittgenstein in the *Tractatus Logico-philosophicus*, an atomism of wholly independent existences, quite contingently characterized and related. But there is nothing to prevent us from holding this metaphysic to be merely an abstract or surface way of regarding the world, completely absurd if regarded as setting forth in completeness what a world conceivably could be, unable to make sense of the rational procedures which enable us comprehensively to understand the world and the beings who share it with us, and yet presupposing these procedures in the comprehensive, *soi-disant* intelligible view it sets forth of what is. Faced by deep reflection on what I may call the unitive aspects of our experience, we may well move towards a Spinozistic logic in which, instead of saying things about separate finite logical subjects, we say them in a somewhat transformed guise of a single logical subject *in so far* as it is expressed in this or that modification. Instead of saying that John is tall, and Paul fat, we may say that the absolute substance is tall in its Johannine aspect, fat in its Pauline one. We may then, taking into account certain deeper strands of experience, progress to Meister Eckhart's statement that this blade of grass is this wood and this stone: properly understood, this is no more illogical and no more destructive of ordinary beliefs suitably expressed, than saying that the morning star is the evening star. If certain philosophers here object that we are merely talking about ordinary facts in an extravagant and un-enlightening way, we may question the whole metaphysics of hard facts indifferent to the conventions of our language, and we may say that the whole structure of the world and thinking subjects, and the structure of any world and any thinking subjects, makes certain ways of talking about the world more deeply revelatory of its being, truer to its deep structure, than others.

In much the same way, though we can frame a scheme of utterance in which it is as possible that nothing exists, as that something does, and in which, if something exists, there are absolutely no restrictions put upon its character, there is nothing to exclude our arguing that such a scheme is absurd if treated as more than a convenient abstraction, and that there are things or a thing in the world which could not have been absent from it, or from any conceivable world or non-world, in other words a being that exists of necessity and whose essence involves exist-ence. While we cannot use the concept of such a being to prove its existence, as is done in fallacious forms of the ontological argument, there is no reason why we should not axiomatically postulate that some such being is actual: it is even sufficient to postulate that it is possible, for, if we do this, it is not very hard to prove that such a being exists actually and necessarily. Since it cannot exist or be non-existent contingently, it is either quite necessary or quite impossible that it should exist; which means that if it exists possibly, it also exists necessarily and therefore actually. And in favour of the possibility of such a necessary existent, it is sufficient to point out how readily people believe in something which cannot be eliminated from existence, while its detailed expressions or contents may: most people think of space and time in this manner, many conceive matter in this fashion, many think abstract essences or features have this sort of necessary being, and so on. Even a man like Wittgenstein, who makes all facts contingent, still believes in the ineliminable character of something that he calls 'logical space'. If it be argued that a necessary existent, not being conceivably absent from the world, really contributes nothing to that world, it may be argued that some cases of existence make themselves known to us, not by the startling fact that something is there and need not be there, but by the deep realization that, however much we try to think something away or get rid of it, theoretically or emotionally

M

or practically, we cannot succeed in doing so. The absoluteness of the one necessary subject shows itself in the fact that if we take the wings of the morning we do not successfully evade it. Of course, all this presupposes that necessity in general, and necessity of being in particular, is not a mere consequence or reflection of linguistic rules, but the view that it *is* a mere consequence or reflection of linguistic rules itself involves a metaphysic that we may well repudiate as inept and superficial.

The notion of unsurpassable, all-inclusive excellence or perfection likewise raises considerable difficulties, but these can perhaps best be met by holding, as mystical people in fact frequently hold, that the absolute does not so much *have* all excellences as *is* them all: that is, the absolute is not beautiful but beauty itself, not just but justice itself, etc. etc. In the case of the absolute, in short, the distinction of type and instance falls away: it is not a case of goodness, nor an abstract character of such cases, but it is, if you like, a character which is also a unique case, and a unique case which is also a character. I am not sure that this is not exactly what was present in the mind of Plato when he talked about the causality of the Forms and of the Form of the Good which engendered them all. If there is difficulty in the notion of a subsistent perfection, or set of subsistent perfections, there is certainly no difficulty in a mind which contemplates and desires them all, and which only contingently contemplates or desires particular instances of them, and which is so intrinsically one with what it desires and contemplates as to be rightly said to *be* them all, and to be them all in unity. I do not think it is at all difficult to conceive a profound spiritual simplicity in which all possibilities of being and goodness will be enjoyed together in a single vision, and which is such that any instantiation of such a comprehensive unity will necessarily be one-sided and partial and piecemeal, or in other words creaturely. Nor is it hard to imagine that the relation of finite instantial beings to the all-embracing seminal absolute is neither one of mere otherness nor of simple identity, but a unique variable relation of logical remoteness or alienation. It is not one of mere otherness, since it is arguably of the essence of a mystical absolute that its ideal perfections should be variously forthshadowed in actual instances, and, since each of those instances embodies an aspect, a side of its eternal essence, and can be mystically seen as embodying precisely this, but it is also not one of mere identity, since any realized instance differs categorially from a spiritual simplicity which involves the thought of all realizable instances, and sorts of instances, whatever.

This is not the time nor the place to develop a complete mystical logic and mystical theology, nor do I think that more than the rudiments of it exist in such works as the *Summae* of Thomas Aquinas, or the Commentaries on the *Vedanta Sutras* of Shankaracharya and Ramanujacharya. Suffice it to say that I think that, while mysticism and its logic can be developed in an undisciplined, chaotic or poetic way, in which no attempt is made to achieve genuine consistency, and contradictions are even reverenced as stigmata of higher truth, mysticism can also be developed in a manner which has complete logical viability, even if it involves many concepts strange to ordinary thought and reflection. The logic of a mystical absolute is the logic of a limiting case, and we must not expect a limiting case to behave in the same logical manner as a case which does not fall at the limit. If even in mathematics we can regard a straight line as a queer limiting case of an ellipse, we must not steer clear of similar queernesses in the construction of a viable mystical absolute. The outcome of my statements is clear: the forms of utterance that we adopt in our ultimate view of the world should not be arbitrary, but should reflect our profound reflections on what, considered most carefully, is really necessary and possible, and the fact that our ordinary, unconsidered forms of utterances have little or nothing that is mystical about them, does not prove that the forms of utterance which will survive in the deepest and most careful reflection will not be entirely mystical. It is not a question of being inconsistent or illogical, but of deciding what form one's consistency or logicality may take. Ultimately there may prove to be only one such wholly satisfactory pattern of consistency or logicality, and that a mystical one.

It is, however, one thing to remove the main sources of objection to mysticism, and quite another thing to recommend it strongly and positively. And it is here, of course, that a lot of persuasive argument is necessary, for most men at most times, and some men at all times, feel no impulse to pass beyond the sundered, dismembered, sorry world of our common experience, and see nothing but an irrelevant expression of temperament in the utterances of mystics. Even if they at times see the world in a mystical light, as involving 'something far more deeply interfused' and Wordsworthian, they are at other times no more inclined to see anything more deeply revealing in their vision than is seen in the euphoria of drunkenness, the ecstasy of sex or the dead sea dryness of jaundice. Mysticism, they think, is an attitude, deeply and widely human, which paints the world in peculiar, transcendental colours: these colours are an insubstantial pageant which reflects nothing deeply rooted in the nature of things.

To counter this line of attack, I shall first argue that mystical unity at the limit or centre of things alone guarantees that coherence and continuity at the periphery which is involved in all our basic rational enterprises. Unmystical ways of viewing the world would see it as composed of a vast number of wholly independent entities and features, and this, as is well known, raises a whole host of notional quandaries, of ontological and epistemological problems. How can we form a valid conception of the structure of all space and time from the small specimens given to us? How can we extrapolate the character and behaviour of an individual from the small segment known to us? How can we generalize from the character and behaviour of one individual to the character and behaviour of a whole infinite class of individuals, wherever it may be distributed in the infinite reaches of space and time? Why, finally, do we think experienced things will have that affinity with our minds and our concepts that will enable us to plumb their secrets? It is well known that, on a metaphysic of radical independence and atomism, all these questions admit of no satisfactory answer. Whereas, on a mystical basis, the profound fit and mutual accommodation of alienated, peripheral things is precisely what is to be expected: it is the alienated expression of a mystical unity which, however much strained to breaking point, never ceases to be real and effective.

Much the same holds if we turn to that deep understanding of the interior life of others which arguably underlies all our interpretation and prediction of other people's behaviour, all acts of communication and co-operation, and all the ethical experiences and endeavours which arise in our relations with them. It is surely clear that unmystical views have the greatest difficulty in rendering these matters intelligible. They cannot make plain why we should be clear that others feel as we do in similar circumstances, and even how we attach meaning to such a presumption. They are forced to give unsatisfactory, behaviouristic analyses of what we are so sure of, or justify our certainty in strange left-handed ways.

Whereas, on a mystical basis, our understanding of others rests on the fact that they are not absolutely others, but only variously alienated forms of the same ultimate, pervasive unity, which expresses itself in the inkling, whether clear or remote, of what may be present in the experience of others. And alienation, however profound, is something that could be surmounted at a sufficiently high degree of mystical *approfondissement*, at which levels the puzzles of the *Blue Book* or the *Philosophical Investigations* would be not so much solved as dissolved. All our higher valuations of impersonal benevolence, of justice, of knowledge, of beauty, of virtue are, further, attitudes having their roots in a transcendence of the separate individual and his contingent interests, and in a rise to higher-order interests which make an appeal to everyone and consider the state of everyone. The supreme dignity and authority of these valuations is much more understandable on a mystical than on an unmystical basis: a moralist like Schopenhauer, for example, bases all morality on a profound suprapersonal identity. The attempts of unmystical people like Hare or even Ross to write books on the foundations of ethics is not anything that encourages imitation. I should say, lastly, that the deep meaning and also the absurdities of various religious systems are best understood on a mystical basis, and totally unintelligible on an unmystical basis. This applies particularly to our own family of Semitic religions. What readily appears as an unedifying series of myths about the arbitrary acts of an external being, involving much ritual effusion of blood and legalistic substitution, becomes understandable when seen as expressing the profound unity, despite alienation, of the finite human person with the principle of all being and all excellence.

I should, however, be misrepresenting the difficulty of all that I have been saying if I did not indicate further presumptions and tasks which I think the acceptance of a mystical logic would certainly involve. A mystical system must not only explain and justify what I may call the unitive aspects of our experience, but also the patent disunity, confusion, imperfection and badness which the world at its surface exhibits. It must, to be a satisfactory logic, integrate the surface of the world with its centre, show each to be necessary to the other. This it is plain is what many mystical ways of regarding things certainly have not done, and they have accordingly become largely an empty form of words, inflated with an emotional inspiration which meaninglessly babbles of a profound unity, embodying and unifying all value, behind the job-lot which actually confronts us. There are, however, forms of mysticism which make alienation and deep-identity mutually dependent: the absolute must alienate itself in limited, instantial forms so that it may steadily reduce and overcome their alienation, and in so doing truly possess and enjoy and recognize itself. This is more or less the creed of some of the great Christian mystics, mainly Germans, who include Meister Eckhart; it is a view which also runs through the whole philosophy of Hegel, and so may fitly be called the 'Germanic Theology'. Some form of the Germanic Theology is, I think, necessary to giving a viable sense to mystical utterances. And I should go further in thinking that a fully developed working mysticism demands a developed other-worldly cosmology, in which numerous states of being are postulated which mediate between the extreme of alienation characteristic of this world and the extreme of unity characteristic of a mystical ecstasy. There must be levels of experience and being achieved either in or after this life, in which things become steadily more manageable and dreamlike, more fluid and interpenetrating, more general, more marked by personal attitude and communion, more dominated by values than things in this life, until in the end the extreme of mystical unity is reached. Competent mystics like Plotinus, Dante, Swedenborg, the Buddhists, have described such transitional states, and it is my conviction that this world and this experience only makes sense if it is linked, not only to an ultimate mystical unity, but also to the transitional states in question. Mysticism is a logical matter, but a logic is only acceptable if it finds the right sort of empirical material to fit it, and the right sort of material must include worlds and lives stricken with less dispersion and diversity than our present life.

In concluding this lecture on mysticism I shall not apologize for the way in which I have dealt with the subject, that is as a committed partisan, concerned to put on mystical phenomena a very special logical slant of my own. The subject is so vast, difficult and complex that without a strong, simplifying, personal line, one cannot hope to get anywhere among its intricacies. I believe that mysticism enters into almost everyone's attitudes, and that it is as much a universal background to experience as the open sky is to vision: to ignore it is to be drearily myopic, and to take the element of splendour and depth out of everything, and certainly out of philosophy. That element of splendour and depth is certainly present in Plato and Aristotle, in Plotinus, Aquinas, Spinoza, Hegel, and let me finally say in Wittgenstein. And there is no reason why we should let it be squeezed out of philosophy by any form of logic-chopping or minute analysis.

XI

ESSENTIAL PROBABILITIES[1]

The aim of the present paper is to mull generally over the eidetic method in philosophy and to connect it with the theme of modalities in general and probability in particular. I wish to suggest that phenomenological insight into intrinsic probabilities represents an indispensable philosophical task, which the general atmosphere of phenomenological investigation, with its stress on the absolutely necessary, has tended to make people pass over. Yet the probabilistic *a priori* can claim to be an inevitable extension of the strictly necessary *a priori*, and to be in fact the most living and interesting part of the whole *a priori* field. To those to whom these notions and methods represent genuine intellectual options, not faded traditional rubrics to which no contemporary sense or use can be given, the points I am about to stress cannot seem unimportant.

The eidetic method in philosophy can be said to be an analytic method, also a synthetic method, which throughout employs the 'seeing eye'. Scanning ranges of things and cases roughly assembled under certain more or less interchangeable or cognate expressions, and noting the way in which such expressions are used or modified in relation to such cases, it tries to distill from the whole examination the sense of certain salient, dominant universals, some so generic as to rate as categories, others so specific as to have almost an air of chance about them, but all such as to specify themselves divergently without loss of unity, and such as to suggest and permit an interesting analysis into traits which genuinely 'hang' or 'belong' together and are not merely empirically associated. Further, these traits show themselves as having certain indispensable or nigh-indispensable 'roles', in connection with other widely different generic and specific patterns, in building up a picture of a total viable world or of a total viable experience.

This 'seeing eye' method is certainly the one described by the author of the VIIth Platonic Epistle in a sentence (344b) which many are foolish enough to think was not Plato's, and which I

[1] Published in *Phenomenology in America*, Quadrangle Books, 1967.

shall translate as: 'When all of these, names, definitions, sights and percepts are with difficulty rubbed together and are probed in questions and answers in friendly fashion and without jealousies, a wisdom and insight into each flashes forth, which reaches to the bounds of human capacity.' This 'seeing-eye' method is the one which is ostentatiously discouraged by certain modern philosophers of language, who see in it all the false philosophical passion for generality which prevents men from seeing the blessed loosenesses, the happy opennesses, the shifts, stretches, arrests, and hesitations that make ordinary concepts so different from, and so superior to, the stale stereotypes of philosophers, which create many more problems than they resolve. The discovery of the real character and merits of what we may call 'unphilosophy' certainly represents a major philosophical breakthrough, but the superiority of unphilosophy, as regards the *special* sort of insight or conception that philosophy seeks to achieve, would not seem to have been convincingly made out. The linguistic philosophers, we may note, themselves use the 'seeing-eye' method—there is no other *to* use in an unexplored field—in their own analyses of human diction. The notion of 'family relations', for example, is not itself a 'family-relations' notion. And Moore and others like him, who tested analyses by comparing them with concepts they had 'before their minds', did much the same. Moore remained magisterial in relation to ordinary diction and used it to trap concepts rather than to delimit them. The 'seeing-eye' method is, moreover, the method followed by Husserl, who, however, uses it in a comprehensive, non-piecemeal way, which in general gives his treatments, though at times a little dogmatic, a greater nearness to the appearances, to the matters on hand, than those of the analysts. Different notional regions and strata, the logico-mathematical, the natural-scientific, the psychological, the intersubjective, and so on, are each seen not only for what they separately are but also as making their characteristic contribution to the total pattern of a world as such, as constituted in or before a pure or transcendental consciousness.

The 'seeing-eye' method is often called 'descriptive' by those who practise it, but the term is dangerous and has in fact led to the most unfortunate consequences. It is quite properly used to enlist on behalf of what we may call real background- and framework-features of our empirical world, the interest and respect aroused in our culture by what is matter of observation, by what will come before us if we will but train our eyes firmly in the right direction. As an antidote to a view which regards necessities as not being *also* genuine matters of fact but mere reflections of the ways in which we have decided to interchange or not to interchange our expressions, such a way of speaking may be useful: necessities, when we recognize them, are certainly 'part of the phenomena', are certainly written into the structure of the world. But the term 'description' suggests that the investigation of the categorial or sub-categorial patterns of things and their relations is not unlike being shown round someone's farmyard, and seeing how its various sheds, runs, enclosures, and paddocks stand to one another. The term 'logical geography' has the same descriptive suggestions. Many of Husserl's transcendental constitutions, immense in their subtlety, do in fact read like a mere re-description, in eidetic terms, of familiar empirical matters of fact. If I may cite an instance at random (*Ideen*, Book II, p. 56), Husserl writes: 'The body is in the first place the instrument in all perception; it is the organ of perception, and is necessarily present in all perception. The eye in seeing is directed to the seen, and runs over corners, surfaces, etc. The hand glides in touch over objects. I move to bring my ear nearer to hear.' These descriptions might have come, if not from Christian Wolff, then from a rather sententious textbook of physiology or psychology: there is nothing very transcendental about them. Many like such treatments, not because they bring out essential connections but because they read so much like empirical commonplaces given new excitement by eidetic language.

What is missing here is the clear realization that the sort of experience which could reveal εἴδη and their connections is not the sort of experience that with astonishment records something that it could not at all have expected, but the sort of experience which, after many attempts to *evade* the closing elenchus of a conceptual linkage, finds that it is up against the inescapable, that if it makes its bed in Sheol or takes to the wings of the morning, it will still be faced by the same connection. The experience of the necessary has not been sufficiently written up by phenomenologists or existentialists but it remains one of the most unique and astonishing we can have, an experience in which our own impotence and unsuccess mediates the understanding acceptance of something as impossible in itself. In other words, as the Platonic Epistle tells us, the experience of εἴδη and their necessary relations must be dialectical: it must arise in the active rubbing together of words, illustrations, and rough ideas, and not through any merely passive glance.

We may say, further, that the experience of the necessary is dialectical in the further sense of always involving revision: what we at first find readily formulable and entertainable, a possibility in short, has, on a deeper examination, been found incapable of a genuine carrying-out—it is an empty, an unfulfillable assignment. But we can only discover it to be unfulfillable by first attempting to fulfil it, and by then being frustrated in that peculiar positive manner which we say mediates understanding. Of course, once we have gone through the experience, it can leave its painless trace in linguistic usage: what we painfully found to be impossible comes to be avoided as a mere solecism. It goes without saying, of course, that the necessities of which I am speaking are all 'synthetic'—though some often called 'analytic' would be reckoned among them—a class that for me does not consist of a few, queer borderline cases requiring special justification, but is strewn as thick as autumnal leaves over every field of inquiry, so that it is in fact hard to isolate anything that is not overlaid with it. Facts that are quite purely 'mere', like individuals that are quite definitely individuals, are things that many people claim to have encountered on their wanderings, but which are for me at best objects of devout faith rather than immediate acquaintance.

This dialectical character of modal terms means, further, that we cannot rest in any one secure use of them: what is perfectly possible on an examination which ignores certain vital relations of εἴδη to other εἴδη, may be impossible once these relations have been considered: what is mere matter of fact on one limited survey of a notional field may be wholly necessary when seen in a wider context. Philosophers of ordinary language have in fact long used this particular elenchus against those who attempt to be linguistically extraordinary. We may, in fact, require not one phenomenology like that of Husserl, achieved by a single ἐποχή or suspense of naïve conviction, but a whole series of phenomenologies as numerous as the Hegelian categories or 'shapes' of spirit, and separated from one another by as many suspensions and transformations. But it is not my purpose in this paper to develop any such interesting thesis. It is rather to recall that modals vary systematically in sense, or rather in use, according as one considers matters more or less abstractly. What is quite possible as a matter of mere logical form may not be so if special contents are brought in, and what seems quite possible if certain contents are abstractly considered may not be so if their necessary bearings on other contents are dwelt upon. (I am not here considering any merely *ex hypothesi* modalities which are only *relative* to situations having no necessary character.) It is never easy to be sure that any given connection or existence is really possible or contingent, even if it plainly seems so in a given language, or even seems so for our surface imagination. The language may need to be adjusted, whether Spinoza-wise or Russell-wise, and the imagination may need to be declared out of bounds and wild. We can have haunting doubts that temper necessitarian dogmas, or that question a boundless atomism of possibilities, but where the decision will lie is a matter for insight in the given case.

It may, however, quite generally be emphasized that, whatever the encroachments of the necessary, and the impossible, there must necessarily be a residual sphere, difficult no doubt to delimit, for the possible and contingent without qualification. (*Ex hypothesi* modalities are again not here in question, nor do they offer points of interest.) Even if reflection should not support—as it very well might not—the now current dogma that all existence is necessarily contingent, it could hardly verge towards the opposite dogma of holding all being to be necessary and none of the instantiations of universal types, their number and order, as well as the particular ways in which they run across one another, to be irreducibly contingent, the sort of thing that could only be known through that sheer encountering or stumbling upon them which for some counts as the sole paradigm of 'experience'. This need for the contingently empirical may be justified—few would feel that it needed justification—on mere grounds of contrast: if there were no merely factual element in things, there could also be no such thing as a necessity. The necessary is what you cannot get away from, no matter what you may do, and no matter what may be the case: it presupposes a variable field of alternatives, in respect of which, as Husserl says, it remains invariant. If whatever you do and whatever is the case are one thing only, then there is nothing to put necessity through its paces or to show up its form. We are really in a state where modality has become inoperative, where only simple assertion and denial are in place. The regionally or stratigraphically or otherwise necessary therefore presupposes a filling, a detailed content that is not necessary but merely factual:

the merely factual or existential is, therefore, both a foil and a complement to the necessary, which latter has not the merely hypothetical status, the indifference to fact and existence with which it is often credited. (Even universal non-existence or absence of all positive character or connection, if genuinely conceivable, would itself be a mere matter of fact and existence, a limiting member to a whole series of contingent combinations.)

But I maintain that the converse entailment also holds, and that the merely factual must always specify a framework which is constraining, necessary in a more than empty sense. This is a very shocking contention which runs straight athwart much contemporary dogma, according to which there is and can be no genuine limit to the factual, such limitations as there seem to be being merely guards against certain symbolic abuses which seem to say something contentful about the world but in effect say nothing at all. I am, however, saying that, wherever there are mere facts or a merely factual element, they must necessarily fall within and give content to a definite regional mould which prescribes definite external and internal contrasts, definite external and internal dependences and independences, as well as pervasive communities and continuities characteristic of the whole region. Facts, whatever their complexity and intricacy, must ultimately concern and radiate from thematic centres or subjects, limited in type-number and simple in type-character; it is necessary that, whatever their degree of independence, it should also have the interdependence characteristic of a single theme or story. Everywhere there must be variety, not mere monotony; but such variety must stem from a smallish number of ultimate bases: mere number is everywhere welcome, even if it swells to the transfinite, but it must, except in interstitial cases, observe strict denumerability and pervasive community. These requirements hold not merely for the specifications of categories but for categories themselves and for the diversified unity they form. All these are not mere subjective requirements, geared to the limitations of understanding or language. Characters or types, we may say, would not be characters or types if they ran to unprincipled diversity or mere monotony; facts would not be facts if they illuminated infinitely numerous, unrelated topics or themes; there could be no cases of number if there were no deep gulfs and communities, and not much more of continuous connection than we postulate for sets or classes. Because there is an elastic stretch within which mere variety or diversity or discontinuity can be varied without let or hindrance, it seems abstractly evident that we could go on doing the same indefinitely, not seeing that what is possible then veers round into what is in a deep sense impossible. The Limit, τὸ πέρας, we may say, is no mere Platonic or Pythagorean superstition but a necessary property of all being, which is not to say that τὸ ἄπειρον, if duly contained and curbed, may not also have an honoured place in being. Or, in other words, to be is to be a value, not of *any* variable, but of a *few*, ultimate, contrasting, interrelated variables. The *a priori* necessity of *measures* which we can none the less only vaguely characterize as *not being too great or too small*, also shows, at this early stage of our discussion, how thoroughly probability enters into ontology, and how we can often not so much state something to be quite necessary or quite impossible, as to have this or that relative place on a vague scale of absolute likelihood. If the foundations of things are thus indefeasibly nebulous, it is not I who have made them so.

All this will of course sound less absurd and less arrogant if I state my point in terms of intelligence and intelligibility. Experience of detailed fact and existence, one may say, is impossible in a framework which is really no framework—the familiar framework of modern radical empiricism, which is always prepared for a bad infinity of what it calls 'logical possibilities', and which only feels able to guess desperately and quite foolishly regarding them. To experience things and to learn from one's experience is to do so in a demarcated region, and it is logically necessary to have an advance knowledge of the general mould of this region and the sorts of things encounterable in it. One can, in other words, only find out in detail what one already knows or conceives in principle, though of course what one finds out in detail may react upon and modify what one has conceived in principle. A strong, positive *a priori*, holding at bay the mere insolence of number and variety, is in short the logically necessary condition of there being any *a posteriori*, of there being anything that one could study or probe or learn about or learn from. And it is supremely strange that Kant, who was the first to discover the necessity of such an *a priori*, also thought that there was something puzzling and requiring explanation about it, as if radical contingency was not much more unintelligible and requiring of explanation. The need of a generic *a priori* for any detailed instantial experience may therefore be accepted, and it is what Husserl accepts when he says that whatever comes before us must embody an εἶδος, though he says little or nothing of the hard, insightful work required for distinguishing a true εἶδος from a merely factitious, interstitial type. I must, however, myself deprecate any reformulation of what I have been saying in terms of mere 'intelligibility'. For even if we do not follow Husserl and other idealists in conceiving the world as constituted in and for consciousness, we must none the less avoid that most perilous and malign of surds which makes the relation of the natural world to mind external and fortuitous; the world may, at many points, exceed our grasp by its difficulty, but it cannot exceed any positive grasp whatsoever without ceasing to be a world at all.

The aim of this essay is not, however, to remain lost among all these difficult generalities but to consider the role of probabilities in this whole *a priori* set-up. As long as the contingently factual is supposed alien to the necessary, a sort of verminous growth that multiplies in its precincts, there seems no reason why the necessary should have as its offshoots various necessary or *a priori* probabilities. Whereas, if we see the contingently factual as what gives full concreteness and specific form to the necessary, we shall expect each regional *a priori* to extend far down into the detailed depth of things, and not only to set bounds to what it may contain but to 'bias' it preferentially in one direction rather than another, or in certain degrees rather than others. And to exercise a 'seeing eye' in the region in question is to become aware of all these biasing tendencies as well as of the inescapable principles they specify. It is a strange fact that a culture, one of whose earliest and most magnificent triumphs was the Platonic *Timaeus*, should have so far forgotten the doctrine of εἰκοτά, of rational probabilities, which throughout characterizes that work, as to have limited the probable to an unsatisfactory theory of chance encounter. The real domain of reason is in the field of the inherently plausible and the analogically coherent, not in the barren, interstitial play of dirempted possibilities.

I shall, however, beat about the bush no longer, but come down to specific examples. And here I shall choose not examples culled from the field of nature and natural science but from the field of mind, in which Husserl too plied his phenomenological arts and which almost seems, though he wholly failed to see it, the native territory of the probable. I shall first deal with a number of basic psycho-physical εἰκοτά which certainly govern us in our personal dealings, even if they may have seemed strange to ultra-empiricist philosophers, who not only believe the old view that all facts are learned from individual encounter but also the new view that all meanings are taught by acts of individual ostension. The first is the inherent likelihood of there being minds around—a likelihood recognized in the 'animism' of the textbooks—and, by there being minds around, I of course do not mean there merely being reacting organisms around, but organisms whose reactions are given as problematically reaching out into a hidden dimension, a dimension *given as hidden* and also *given* as an object of permanent conjecture, but also given as capable of being appresented (to use Husserl's fine term) *through* a creature's reactions, much but not quite as a body can be seen through a cloth, all these being possibilities that we perfectly understand and can introduce to others, even though every showable instance of them exhibits the 'through-ness', the intrinsic indirectness which the phenomenon itself involves and requires. The world is not and cannot be the day-light world of the Wittgensteinian language-games: it is a world where the hidden and intrinsically problematic is everywhere lurking *qua* hidden and *qua* problematic, as a dimension towards which we may gesture and which is also capable of an inherently uncertain disclosure which never deprives it of its essential hiddenness. All these are not secondary growths upon primary daylight acts but the penumbra in which those daylight acts alone are possible. One cannot say, 'There's a red apple' for the hearing of others without being penumbrally conscious of the intentional *sense* which this statement implies, as well as of the countless possible conscious centres in which that intentional sense could possibly be enjoyed.

But of course not merely the existence of this interior dimension is always intrinsically likely, but also, indirectly, the character of its contents. For the interior life of anything is always intrinsically, if probabilistically, geared to its outer life, much as the inner contours of a sheet of metal tend to be geared to its outer contours, concavity matching convexity and convexity concavity. For the relation of inner states of feeling, sensation, thought, attitude, and so forth to outward situations and actions is not, and cannot be, that of two disparate things empirically associated: the one repre-sents the concentration into unity of which the other represents the dispersion into separateness, it being intrinsically likely, *ceteris paribus*, that the former will issue in the latter, and vice versa. No one who trains his 'seeing eye' on his own condensed moods of feeling and thought, on the one hand, and their explication in behaviour or objective situation, on the other, can doubt that we have here a connection of essence, if only an intrinsically likely connection. The one completes and fits the other. The same holds if anyone will study the language of physical analogy in which we talk of the interior life of mind, an analogy by some thought to be idle and personal and by Wittgenstein to be wholly constitutive of inner-life meanings. The truth is that it is neither: the analogies in question express the real, *a priori* affinities through which inner-life facts sometimes enter our common language.

What I have said will be even more plain if we consider the different modes of minding objects which have so exercised philosophers: the believing or disbelieving mode, the attentive or inattentive mode, the acquiescent or objecting mode, and so on. Here each mode points to a host of manifestations, interior or overt, into which it is *likely* to expand, which a too zealous interest in 'necessary and sufficient conditions' too readily banishes from our 'analyses'. Thus belief not only has its inner core of acquiescent acceptance, and its placing of contents somewhere in an unbracketed total picture; it also has highly probable overtones of assertion, of the willingness to persuade, of the expectation that others will see things as we do, and so on. And it also involves all those probable modifications of our goal-directed behaviour, removed only in the incurably abouliac or schizophrenic, in which some have seen the whole essence of believing. All these are *a priori* connections, rooted in the content of the phenomenon before us, but they are also all probabilistic connections which might not be manifest in the particular case. Husserl, with his naïvely simple, Brentanesque view of belief as simply a *thetic* state of mind, characterized also by an 'activity which the 'seeing eye' should have told him is not always present, missed all this vivid field of probabilities, which yield up their wealth to *reine Wesensschau* as to nothing else. Obviously Brentano and Husserl would have constructed a much more brilliant, complete psychognosy or phenomenology had behaviour-analysis and language-analysis been pushed as far in their time as they have been in ours. We who wish to preserve and to extend their invaluable doctrines must take account of these fundamental disciplines and their findings. But we must develop them in *a priori* fashion and not merely by borrowing pages from empirical studies.

N

(Though what *is* the case certainly may stimulate our vision of what *must* be the case.)

I shall not make further excussions into special fields. The *a priori* probabilities of nature and of natural science are a subject of absorbing interest and almost complete non-cultivation. Husserl, in his elaborate constitution of nature, says extremely little about them. Some inductive logicians—Keynes, for example —have made timid forays into these regions, but always the noise raised by the positivists and the radical empiricists has driven them shamefacedly from the field. It is, in fact, impossible to state any genuine *metaphysische Anfangsgründe der Naturwissenschaft* in the atmosphere of our time, for they would emphasize notions like that of simplicity and analogy, 'good form', and inherent probability, which now seem inherently ridiculous. I have no wish to burden this essay with further occasions for ridicule. I should like, however, to conclude by saying that I think that a treatment of intrinsic necessities and probabilities cannot end without treating the intrinsic necessities and probabilities of *being* or *existence*: it cannot be limited to the merely hypothetical study of the necessities and probabilities conditional upon the existence of this or that sort of thing. We must, in short, invade the citadel which Kant and others have sought to barricade completely and shut off finally.

XII

THE LOGIC OF ULTIMATES[1]

The present paper continues and develops a symposium contribution on 'Alternative Absolutes' given at the Chicago meeting of the Western Division of the APA last May: it was ably if somewhat destructively criticized by Professors William Alston and David Rynin. Neither of these commentators had much taste for my enterprise of 'Absolute-hunting', though they went some distance in trying to make sense of it: they admitted that much of the past history of philosophy could fitly be described as the setting up and knocking down of one Absolute after another, but this did not make them think more kindly of the enterprise nor wish to recommend its continuance. And my attempts to hunt down Absolutes in a logical rather than a metaphysical or inspirational manner, were taken by them to be attempts to argue rigorously and cogently according to the rules of some pre-existent logic. Whereas what I was doing was precisely not to operate on some pre-existent logical system, but to consider with great tentativeness what sort of logical system we *should* adopt if we were to find lodgment in it for that ancient, odd, nebulous, unfashionable, but not genuinely discredited, and highly interesting logical object called an 'Absolute', how we were to fix and fill in its logical shape more precisely, and to put it to work in various contexts of our discourse. And although a few of my arguments intended rigour, most of them were meant only to be highly persuasive, like the arguments written in English in the interstices of *Principia Mathematica*.

I of course rejected in my paper all notion of a presupposition-less, uncommitted, unmodifiable, topic-neutral set of forms and principles which is the logical mould of discourse on all matters whatsoever: I took it that we should require all our insight and all our reflection, constantly revising and deepening previous stances and positions, and constantly immersing ourselves in the

[1] Presented in an American Philosophical Association Symposium on the Logic of Finalities, December 28, 1967. Published in the *Journal of Philosophy*, October 5, 1967.

particular matters on hand, to decide how we might legitimately and intelligibly talk about the world. The assumption, e.g. of a boundless logical independence of elementary facts and existences, such as is made, rather than asserted, in many logical systems, and which Wittgenstein's *Tractatus* tried to state clearly, might yield an acceptable background for descriptive discourse about the objects lying at random on a table or the images coursing confusedly through a mind, but from the standpoint of a more deep-cutting, explanation-seeking discourse, it may count as the very paradigm of the self-contradictory and absurd, bringing together what has no conceivable business to be brought together and affirming a reality and a truth that has no meaning except in a more profoundly integrated system. Logic, in my view, required to be developed in levels or stages, and at each level new types of logical object and connective might make their appearance; things previously unsayable, but implicit, might become sayable; necessities might emerge where previously all had been matters of truth and falsehood; matters of fact might be transformed into necessities and even seeming impossibilities become necessities and so on. What is self-contradictory must indeed always be avoided, but our notion of what *is* self-contradictory may profoundly alter its face as we adventure further. In such deepening of discourse there is never a line of ordinary proof leading from lower and poorer to higher and richer patterns of discourse. Only our deep sense that there is something we burningly want to say, which yet cannot be said in a certain mould of discourse, can force us on to adopt a new pattern. The notion of an Absolute or self-explanatory existent may be a notion unneeded and of doubtful construction at the descriptive, causal-generic, and intentional levels of discourse, but it may precisely be our deep feeling that we cannot say all we want to say at those levels that pushes us on to talk in terms of such an Absolute. That it is difficult to talk clearly and consistently at this level does not prove that it is impossible to do so, nor that we may not find, in the development of such talk, not the destruction, but the culmination of all logic.

The justification of attempts to work out a logic of Absolutes lies further in the fact that there *is* such a logic in the thought of most persons and that this logic has been further refined and extended by many major philosophers. The ordinary notion of space, as I pointed out in my previous paper, affords us a good example of an Absolute, or something we feel could not be 'imagined away' (whether or not we are right in this feeling) and which seems the irremovable, underlying basis of all bodies and all motions. And philosophers have had as their Absolutes Water, Fire, Air, Matter, the Conscious Mind, the Cosmos, God, the Forms, Logical Space, Moral Standards, and so on, making these things unalterable and not dependent on the transient things of this world, which in their turn depend (at least in part) on them. The game of Absolutes is not merely played; it has been played by practically everyone except (in intention) by a very few philosophers, and even these have in fact sometimes played it *sub rosa* (e.g. Russell in PM 22.351). Logicians have introduced special branches of logic, e.g. the logics of tenses, of modality, etc. to formalize well-established branches of discourse; the same justification would apply to a well worked-out logic of Absolutes, many of whose initial gambits are to be found in Spinoza, Aquinas, and others.

It will, however, be best at this point not to talk generally but to resume some of the 'theorems' or theoretical stances, arrived at in my former paper. Here the first was the extremely interesting theorem that Absolutes permit of a valid inference from mere conceivability—if we are sure of such conceivability—to certain reality, a property first discovered by Anselm which certainly gives Absolutes a unique place among logical notions. An Absolute being something that exists, if indeed it does exist, self-explanatorily or 'of necessity', we cannot treat the question of its existence as an ordinary sort of open question, decided by 'finding', in some ordinary or unusual sense of 'finding', that the thing in question is there or is not there. The sort of thing whose existence or nonexistence can be established by this sort of 'finding' is certainly not an Absolute, and, if all things are of this sort, then there certainly are no Absolutes. If we can even conceive of an Absolute as absent, not of course in a superficial and abstract, but in some sufficiently deep sense of 'conceiving', then that Absolute certainly fails of reality, must in fact fail of reality, since something that can, on the fullest consideration, be conceived absent is certainly not an Absolute. This is the basis of my disproof of the Divine Existence, which was put forward in 1948 and had much acclaim in certain quarters. What I did not, however, clearly see when I put forward that proof is that it can be made to work both ways and that if, in the case of an Absolute, a sufficiently deep doubtfulness or possible falsehood entails a falsehood that co-incides with impossibility, then also, *per contra*, a sufficiently deep conceivability or possibility entails a certain truth which coincides with necessity. An Absolute plainly and obviously will not admit of the ambiguity of status characteristic of contingent things; it is nonsense to suppose that it may either be or not be: either there is no coherent conceivability of there being any such thing, or, if there is, it covers the whole range of conceivability and amounts, therefore, to certain and necessary truth. Research in the region of Absolutes involves, therefore, only the initial charity of assuming that it is not absurd to suppose that there is some such thing, and then keeping on the watch for incoherences, logical flaws in the conceptions that we form. At no point would it be relevant to submit our assertions to an empirical or other external test. But we of course always face a possibility of falsification, since our insight into modality never can be guaranteed perfect: though what it is incoherent to conceive can certainly not coherently be conceived coherent, this may not be true epistemically or 'for us', and we may genuinely be in doubt about, and in a sense able to conceive, both the logically flawed and the logically flawless character of some conception. The existence of an Absolute will, of course, be highly peculiar, since it involves no contrast with possible nonexistence, but contrasts rather with those things to which the latter contrast applies. But Absolutes, if there are any, are precisely those residual, fundamental, categorial elements which resist all our conceptual attempts to shift them from the scene, which resistance, combined with and correcting our defec-tive insight into modality, can at times give rise to the most poignant and most positive experience.

The next important theorem in absolutist logic is that an Absolute can have no ultimately conceivable alternatives: if there were two ultimately conceivable Absolutes, there would, *per impossibile*, be none at all. For otherwise something would exist of necessity which also might not have existed and whose place might have been taken by something else. But of course this does not mean, as said before, that there may not be alternative Abso-lutes *for us*, and also the alternative of there being no Absolute at all.

I then went on to assert, as a more or less obvious theorem, that being an Absolute must be consequent upon being something *else* as well: an Absolute could not be *merely* necessarily existent and no more, nor could one be necessarily existent if it were not so *in virtue of* some other feature or features; and the phrase 'in virtue of which' means that these other features must be such that showing them forth *entails* being a necessary existent and vice versa. So much may be saved out of the wreck of the ontological proof. Whatever is said to *be* must in each case exemplify, or perhaps in some cases simply *be*, a certain nature, in default of which its existence could not be meaningfully propounded; and whatever necessarily exists must likewise have or be a specifiable nature, which its being, however, must entail and which must entail its being, and which must be such, moreover, as to differ in kind from the sort of variable thing one must be in order to exist non-necessarily. One cannot in particular exist necessarily in virtue of exemplifying one side of an empirical opposition or contrast and not the other: one could not, e.g. be an Absolute in virtue of being red and here and a cushion but not in virtue of being blue and there and a tablecloth. And since the really specific content of our notions consists mainly of features belonging to one side of an empirical contrast, it is plain that what makes an Absolute an Absolute cannot be any such specific content. Absolutes, we may say, cannot be Absolutes in virtue of being some highly special sort of thing (though they are, of course, in a higher sense, a very special sort of thing): there is something necessarily unspecific in their essential features, which explains why, when people have constructed them, they have done so in terms of quantifiers of unlimited generality, such as 'all' or 'none' or for some purposes 'some'. Thus Absolute Space is the substrate of *all* possible types of occupancy, or is what would remain if *no* bodies existed, or is what must have *some* scheme of occupancy but no definite one, etc. The puzzling character of Absolutes, for many persons, particularly in accounts of mystical experience, is precisely their lack, apart from metaphor, of all essential empirical content: they seem the merest constructs of pure logic. (The one without a second, the all-container, the unsurpassably real, etc. etc.)

But though an Absolute cannot be an Absolute in virtue of some specific content, we must not infer from this that an Absolute can be *without* specific one-sided content. It *must* have contingent, non-essential as well as essential, Absolute-making features, though it could always have had *other* contingent features than those which it actually has. An Absolute of any category must be thought to be an accomplished, fully worked-out entity, and its characterization in terms of 'all' or 'none' or 'some' would be totally unmeaning were there no concrete, in some cases empirical values, over which its defining generalities could play. Thus Absolute Space, while involving the possibility of *all* types of occupancy or non-occupancy, is also contingently characterized by the pattern of occupancies that obtains; a Creator-God, though able to create or not create any possible state of things, is contingently characterized in terms of what he does create (the God of Israel, etc.); a Platonic Form, though timeless and irremovable, is contingently characterized by the things that participate in it. Even empty Space or an uncreative God or a Form-world without instances would not evade contingency: its negations would be as contingent as the contrary affirmations. Contingency is in fact the necessary foil and the raw material for the necessary, and even an Absolute must involve contingencies, not merely extrinsically but in and for itself. Spinoza's attempt to remove contingency by pushing it back indefinitely not only failed of its purpose; had it been a success, it would have robbed necessity of its meaning and of its place in discourse.

Several important theorems remain over from my former treatment. The first is that an Absolute must be unitary *at least* to the extent that, if it involved a number of distinct elements, each of which existed necessarily, it would at least be necessary that they all should exist *together* and that no quasi-scientific technique should be able to pry any of them apart from the others. We should have in fact a corporate Absolute, of which the Trinity or the Communion of Saints or the spiritual society of McTaggart are perhaps plausible examples. But, once embarked on this line of thought, we seem to see that there could be differences of the close-knit and the loose-knit even among such Absolutes: in some the description of each member would entail, and in a manner include, the description of all the others, they would be essentially *of* one another; whereas in others they would be necessarily related only *in so far* as they were all necessarily existent. There would in fact be something like a higher-order accident in their all being 'thrown together', like passengers on a voyage, in the same plight of necessary existence. A series of Absolutes, from the most close-knit to the most loosely knit, is, however, impossible, since there can be no alternative Absolutes. And we have the further absurdity that a close-knit Absolute would be *more* explanatory of its elements, and so *more* of an Absolute, than a loosely knit one. We can eliminate this competition among Absolutes only by ruling, and ruling with insight, that a conception that thus introduces accident into the very citadel of the self-explanatory, destroys itself rather than the latter notion. There can, on this insight, be only effort after explanation in anything short of total explanation, and this yields us an Absolute having something like the mutual interpenetration of elements, compatible with a deep simplicity, which is described in certain mystical treatises and which is also expressed in Hegel's notion of 'totality'. It is indeed hard to say whether the mystics have here been inspired by logic or the logicians by mysticism. But we may re-emphasize that such a degree of close-knitness among the basic differentiations of an Absolute need not eliminate contingencies of existence on its fringes or in its interstices, nor yet contingencies and externalities in the mutual relations of such existences.

We next held with some reason that an Absolute must be placed in the supreme category of an ontology and not in some confessedly parasitic or subordinate position. Thus, in ontologies in which individuals count as the supreme category, all else being merely qualifications of, or otherwise dependent upon, individuals, such dependencies could not be counted as true Absolutes, even if in some contexts they were rightly denominated as 'absolute', e.g. absolute unselfishness, impartiality, etc. Only if Characters or Relations or Processes or Ends were promoted to our supreme category, and individuals and other entities correspondingly *demoted*, could we seek for our Absolute among the former. Entities placed in supreme categories are of course generally made to function as logical and linguistic subjects of assertions, and, although it would be possible, it would be unnatural not to put a confessed Absolute in this position.

We then stated the important theorem, by no means straight-forwardly justifiable, that an Absolute not only excludes the existence of other Absolutes external to itself, but also excludes the existence of *contingencies* external to itself. All contingencies must be *its* contingencies, ways in which our Absolute has mani-fested itself, not independent existences or circumstances cluster-ing about it or peopling its interstices. We have held it necessary for an Absolute to have contingent specifications: what we now add is that it is necessary for *all* contingent circumstances and existences to be involved in some manner in these specifications, so that there is nothing in high heaven or the nether depths that does not depend for its existence and character on that of the Absolute. There are difficulties involved in this omni-responsibility of an Absolute, especially for those who take an unnecessarily simple and direct view of its relation to finite contingents, but plainly the difficulties involved in denying this could be much more ruinous. There is something absurd in having an Absolute and then placing certain contingencies quite outside of it, so that as far as it is concerned they might not have existed at all; and this absurdity has led to the supersession of some sorts of Absolute by others more adequate. Thus an Absolute Space that merely happens to be occupied in certain ways, without in some sense *determining* its occupation, gets transformed into a Space whose deformations simply *are* its occupants and which is credited, further, with a tendency to 'generate' such deformations. The same holds of those Eastern Absolutes whose blank unity is surrounded by an unexplained cloud of delusion: they call for concepts, e.g. that of Shakti, which use and regularize such delusion. Obscurely we desire an Absolute to be an explanatory notion, one that reduces contingencies and internal loosenesses or at least gives them a rational place within itself, and we do not feel that the notion is being properly used if it is not used maximally, so that no contingency, and no possible contingency, eludes its explaining grasp. Otherwise we feel, using an Anselmian gambit, that it would then have fallen short in respect of Absoluteness and that another more embracing Absolute might have surpassed it. These comparative, alternative notions are, as we saw, inadmissible, and we must hold that partially explanatory notions (such as that of a natural law or persistent background of facts) do not even properly explain part of what requires to be explained, but only represent an *approach* to explanation. Only a complete explanation, we must say, really explains anything. Not only is it useless to push an explanatory regress back indefinitely, but the slightest injection of the inexplicable into an explanatory fabric must be held absolutely to rend and destroy the whole.

Great care and lucidity must, however, be taken here if we are not to confuse all-explanation with all-necessitation, the error characteristic of Spinozism. Some contingencies there are, and must be, which cannot be rendered noncontingent by any injection or addition. But these contingencies can still be explained by

something rather like an Aristotelian faculty of opposites, something that can educe a categorical outcome out of a radically
disjunctive situation, without, be it noted, the addition of some
further 'deciding' factor. It is usual, and Aristotelian, to connect
such a faculty with conscious, rational choice, but it is not necessary, for our present purposes, to limit it in this way; we need
not even confine it to matters that have a beginning in time.
What must be involved in the explanation of ultimate contingencies
must be the use of notions and modes of inference that yield
logical appeasement and raise no further questions, *whichever* of
a set of alternatives comes to be realized. We must be able to say
'Since we have an agent or situation of the sort X, we could have
had an outcome *either* of the sort A *or* of the sort B *or* of the sort
C, etc. and the fact that we *have* an outcome of the sort C is,
therefore, completely explained by the fact that we have an agent
or situation of the sort X, and requires no further explanation.'
There is a temptation at this point to introduce the concept of
chance and to say that, since there are no uniquely determining
conditions, what is the case must be the outcome of chance.
But chance is a case of an inexplicable conjunction of factors,
not a case of a single factor logically capable of alternative,
branching consequences. Logical systems of this branching sort
have not been normally developed: premises are not generally
thought of as issuing in alternative consequences, either but not
both of which, could be the case. But there is no reason why such
logical systems should not be developed, or why an issue of a
certain branching should not be further branchings, etc. and in a
logic of Absolutes such a branching system is not only admissible
but necessary. An Absolute must, in some not necessarily anthropomorphic manner, be in a position to *decide* among alternative
contingencies and to decide for there being further decisions or
powers of decision, for no other reason than that it is an Absolute
capable of giving itself a contingent content. We must of course
work towards notions that make such systems more than mere
marks on paper, and the notion of conscious arbitrariness, one
that chooses among alternatives without needing, though it may
of course have, further motivation, is here of use, whether or not
it is ever empirically exemplified. But it may be only by analogy
with such pure arbitrariness, if it exists, that the self-determination of an Absolute will have to be considered. It is, of course, open
to us to work out a scheme of necessary goals or values, intrinsic

to our Absolute, within which such quasi-arbitrariness will be exercised.

I shall now devote what little time remains to me to considering the claims of four candidates for absolute status, all of which seem to me to harbour deep logical defects. By criticizing them and making my own recommendations on their basis, I shall try to give flesh and blood to a discussion where one elaborates words without being sure what, if anything, one may be saying by them. I shall select for examination: (a) a cosmic or naturalistic Absolute; (b) a theistic Absolute; (c) a subsistential or Platonic Absolute; (d) an Absolute that is mentalistic or *geistig*. In each case I shall try to put the best face on the Absolute in question in terms of the requirements already sketched.

By a *cosmic Absolute* I mean an Absolute that develops to the limit of absoluteness that extremely nebulous, yet universally present and certainly unlearned notion that we call that of 'the world', a notion whose horizon-like, all-encompassing, *a priori* character has been well brought out both by Husserl and by Heidegger. Everything there is normally comes before us as being somewhere in the world, even though we may not know quite where it fits in, and our whole personal being is also in the world, even if more by engagement and intention than by mere position. To exclude some entertained content from the world is, in ordinary parlance, to declare it nothing at all, and it is never a wholly serious gambit in ordinary speech to suppose that there ever was or ever will be or ever could have been no world. Even if we *try* to be very serious in the elimination of all piebald contents, we still seem left with the gaunt skeletons of empty space and time, the limiting case, if one likes, of a world. The world, in short, or its space-time spectre, has all the features of a fully-fledged Absolute, going infinitely beyond what experience gives us or ever can give us; and one can only ponder in dumb amazement at all those naïve naturalists and materialists who quite fail to see the non-empirical immensity of what they so lightly assume, sometimes, like Russell, pretending to have a world which is the mere class of all there is, when the world plainly involves the immense, embracing continuity of space and time, which puts all things together and renders their interaction possible and also makes it possible and meaningful for us to talk of their reality or unreality. The world is to all intents and purposes a continuous background which could not be eliminated, which can be held to include the possibility and the actuality of all contingencies, which has arguably the highest degree of continuity and connection consistent with the necessary separateness of the instances of empirical contraries, and which belongs, in virtue of this connectedness, to the supreme category, that of the exhaustively determined thing, that a respectable ontology permits. World-absolutism is, in fact, a very defensible type of absolutism, to which we all adhere in unthinking moments and which can be made even more defensible by a few added nuances of the 'emergent' or the 'dialectical'. Make the world creative in respect of some of its contents, make it capable of focusing itself in organisms and mirroring itself in that focus, make it capable of organizing itself into societies or feeling the stress of 'values' or logical relations, and we are well on the way, as in Marxism, to making it do all an explanatory Absolute can do. The abiding defect of such a naturalistic Absolute lies, however, in the forced, empty, largely verbal glosses that must be put upon its immense disunities if it is to function as a satisfactory Absolute. For the world, considered by itself as an inclusive space-time system, and deeply pondered upon, shows itself, despite the shock of the revelation, as the most self-contradictory of beings. It has far too much unity, continuity, mutual accommodation, repetitive regularity, accessibility to knowledge and purpose and so forth, to achieve anything like the diremptive nullity of a Russellian class; yet it has also far too much looseness, unco-ordinated collocation, undisciplined variety, and harsh unamenability to knowledge and purpose to constitute anything like a self-explanatory, all-explanatory Absolute. It may be a shocking thing to say in modern America, but the world points ineluctably beyond itself: it not only is not, but also cannot be, all that there is.

Turning from the world to a transcendent Creator-God, we have an Absolute linked by free creativity (or by the abstention from such creativity) with all possible contingencies of existence, including the contingency of there being no world at all. We need not saddle the Creator with the actual properties of his creations, with their necessary one-sidedness, incompatibility, and lack of an upper limit: he may include them all in some higher fashion, in being capable of creating them all. The imperfect unity of the creation, evinced in the interconnections and cosmic continuities mentioned above, will reflect, in a necessarily imperfect, externalized fashion, the profound simplicity of its source. This absolute unity must not be conceived on the lines of a divisible, changeable, natural thing, nor yet on the lines of the changeable, developing, externally provoked intelligence that we share; it must surpass them all in some manner which itself surpasses expression and which at certain points dictates excursions into a new, unique, and not wholly understandable grammar. On the more orthodox view, which has both Greek and Jewish originals, the Creator's creativity is conceived as in some manner gratuitous, as making no difference to him, a view intended to heighten the dignity of the Absolute, but in effect lowering it, since it tends towards the disengagement, or half-disengagement, of the Absolute from such creaturely characters as brokenness, one-sidedness, and mutability, with all their pathos and their unique contributions to being and value. The faults of this orthodoxy are remedied by a more essentially Christian unorthodoxy, which sees in world-creation an activity essential to its Absolute, which can only be the surpassing, all-explanatory essence that it is, by continually putting itself forth in, alienating itself in, a world of imperfect creatures which it then leads back to and redeems in itself. These mystical Christian ideas, we may note, are the basis of Hegelianism. We may note further, however, as in the case of the cosmos, that when the Creator is thus forced into the role of an all-resuming Absolute, he loses his distinctive demiurgic, theistic features, and that he keeps these only by surrendering his claims to all-explanatory absoluteness. Christian experience always threatens to become nontheistic and mystical unless held in check by strong-minded, narrow-minded Popes, such as John xxii or Pius x. But these religious antinomies are much too fully documented to require further comment here.

From theistic Absolutes we turn to subsistential Absolutes, like the Form of the Good or of Unity in certain phases of Platonism. A supreme Form or Nature cannot in an individualist ontology be a true Absolute, since it is only as predicated of individuals or as otherwise dependent on them, that entities of other categories can be said to be. But in a Platonic ontology this state of affairs is inverted: there are not so much instances as instantiations of Forms and their whole being is parasitic upon the Form or Nature of which they are the instantiations. Subordinate Forms or Natures are merely how the supreme εἶδος is specified, rather than anything independently subsistent: only the supreme Form, we may say, holds in itself the whole range of what is and half-is. On a developed Platonic ontology, the language of generation and causation is not wanton; it expresses the parasitic dependence of subordinate species and individuals on the one supreme Pattern. They are *its* specifications and individualizations and no more, much as, in an individualist ontology, qualities, relationships, etc. are merely ways in which individuals are qualified, related, etc. It is, however, easy to point to the great weakness of such Platonic absolutism: it fails completely to bring the realm of changing instantial shadows into the explanatory embrace of the Forms and of their supreme source. It is not stated as a necessity that the timeless, perfect Form-realm should multiply itself in such shadows, or it is a necessity only in relation to some external, perturbing factor. The absoluteness, and complete explanatoriness of the Form-realm is thereby done away with, for, as we have seen, an incompletely explanatory Absolute is really no Absolute at all. Plato in later life seems to have given some attention to these difficulties, inasmuch as he gave Motion as well as Rest an indefeasible place in True Being and inasmuch as he admitted a restless, indefinite principle of quantity and multitude into the very citadel of the Forms and made it help in their generation. But if one thus embodies specification and instantiation in the very core of one's Absolute, as Hegel did in his doctrine of the self-specifying, self-individuating Notion, one's Absolute, though becoming more nearly adequate, certainly no longer wears a Platonic face.

I turn lastly to a form of spiritual absolutism such as some have attributed to Hegel, though not rightly in my opinion. Husserl in his phenomenology exemplifies it much more closely. On this absolutism the Absolute is categorized as mental, all that is not mental having being only in the sense that there are intentions, referential acts, directed upon it, such 'intentional inexistence' not involving that non-mental things are anything in their own right, or can walk out of their conscious frames and become independent subjects of true reference. They are 'transcendent' only in the sense that they are made or thought to transcend the thoughts in which they are constituted. But this mentalistic Absolute is also such as to individuate itself in a plurality of Egos or centres of intentions, to each of which the same round of natural appearances is presented and to each of which the inner existence and workings of other centres are 'appresented' in connection with the responses of living organisms. Nature enjoys intentional, noematic being in and for the minds of the system, but these minds are part of its absolute structure. This type of ever-recurrent absolutism has the merit of substituting for the maimed unity of the world, and for the splintered dust of Platonic subsistence, a sort of unity in which the most diverse content, even such as is imaginary and impossible, can be harmoniously assembled. But a spiritual unity that has gone beyond solipsism to a whole spiritual society, has also gone beyond intentionalism into realism, and might well bring matter into its purview. Conscious aliveness, further, when phenomenologically examined, seems of its essence to be 'angled' and developing: we can be aware of anything only in so far as we can see it in ever-changing 'lights', which then contribute to a developing picture. There seems no room here for an all-embracing Absolute.

What emerges from these hasty sketches is that some of the most thoughtfully constituted Absolutes have fallen far short of the requirements of Absolute-theory. And their internal flaws, if not remediable, bid fair to ruin the whole absolutist enterprise. The difficulty lies in the basic disparateness of the factors involved in absolutist construction—necessity and contingency, unity and dispersion, actuality and power, the good and the bad, the self, the others, the world, etc. etc.—and the need to integrate them all. It is arguable that no concept will do the logical work here involved but one that is inclusively teleological—a point all understand who feel that the world's absurdities and untowardnesses would be fully explained if a single, all-informing, self-justifying purpose could be found to lie behind them all. Only teleology, it seems, can blend necessity and unity of direction with variety and contingency of route and means, requires the ideal as much as the actual, and can, above all, display itself only on a soil involving the most immense untowardnesses and possibility of abuses as well as whatever we think of as well-rounded and well-fitting. Such teleology can, however, be successfully absolute only if it is 'infinite' in the Hegelian manner, if, like life, it aims at nothing beyond itself, and if it incorporates situations, means, routes, procedures and deviant possibilities in itself. What I would suggest is that some sort of such 'infinite' teleology, arguably passing at points into other-worldly, mystical dimensions which lend it a complete meaning, represents the one viable form of absolutism, if any form of absolutism is viable at all.

XIII

THE SYSTEMATIC UNITY OF VALUE[1]

This lecture is an attempt to carry on an exercise in which certain fairly recent German philosophers have believed strongly, in which some Anglo-Saxon philosophers have made half-hearted essays in the fairly recent past, though hardly any Anglo-Saxon philosopher now has anything to do with it, or would even seriously consider it, but in which I, who like isolated situations, believe profoundly, and on which I shall continue to write and lecture, though I am increasingly aware of the subtle intricacy and elusiveness of the ideas and argumentations that it involves. This venture is what Husserl called the constitution of a value-cosmos—a venture he mentioned but did not himself enter upon—the setting up of an ordered system of things ultimately desirable and undesirable, but in some such way that the whole constitution represents a work of reason, that it has something mandatory, non-arbitrary and, dare we say it, absolute about it, much as there are similar absolute constitutions in such fields as tense-theory, knowledge and belief-theory, the theory of syntax and meaning and so on. The setting up of such a value-cosmos proceeds on the basic assumption that in every sphere the arbitrary, the empirical, the contingent, necessarily nests in a comprehensive framework of what is absolute, of what must obtain, of what cannot be otherwise, of what holds whatever is the case or whatever we like to choose. The absolute in this sense involves the contingent and the arbitrary, and is precisely what will hold invariantly whatever the variable content of the contingent and the arbitrary may be: it *requires* the contingent and arbitrary, just as the latter in its turn requires it. For, on the view we are espousing, one can only raise questions or make decisions of a Yes-or-No type on a background of acceptances from which an alternative 'No' is excluded. We can only learn from experience in any field, provided we already non-empirically know, with some measure of clearness,

---

[1] The Lindley Lecture, given at the University of Kansas on February 22, 1968.

the constitution of that field, what sort of entities and arrangements it permits or does not permit, and empirical encounter can only fill in the blanks of the constitutional pattern thus laid before us. In the same way, we can only plan our lives, and counsel others to plan their lives, within the fixed constitutional pattern of a set of ends and counter-ends that we cannot evade, that are pre-accepted in every acceptance or rejection. This notion of an *a priori* background to everything that is subsequently discovered or chosen must not, however, be given a merely definitional meaning, that in effect turns it into something arbitrary and contingent: it must have a regional, contentful meaning, specified by the kind of territory or inquiry or enterprise we are undertaking or ranging over. And while there are ultimately *no* conceivable alternatives to the framework, the constitution that we, or rather it, is setting up, this is only so because at a more abstract level such alternatives are quite conceivable: specific necessities nest in others that are more generic, and from the standpoint of the latter the former are in a sense synthetic, mere matters of fact. It is in fact only by the deep attempt to conceive of them, to envisage certain alternatives clearly, as the mandates of a wider, more formal necessity seem to permit, that we become aware of their engaged, contentful incoherence, an incoherence in terms of which the *a priori* rules of our region or territory first define themselves.

To talk in general terms of a value-cosmos or an emotional-practical *a priori* is, however, extremely unsatisfactory unless you have some notion of the sort of scheme that this might entail. And I shall therefore briefly unroll before you the value-cosmos sketched by Nicolai Hartmann in his forty-year-old *Ethics*, a work which derived much of its inspiration from the earlier work of Max Scheler. My excuse for citing a work so old is that Hartmann's work is by no means as widely known and used as it ought to be. It has many faults of incoherence, unclearness, dogmatism and stylistic ebullience to explain its comparative neglect, but it does in some respects daringly show us what an accomplished value-cosmos would be like, and it is for this reason that I now make exemplary use of it. Also being the one systematic value-cosmology available in English, apart from my own poor efforts in *Values and Intentions*, I think it entirely justifiable to make use of it on the present occasion. Hartmann in his *Ethics* espouses the doctrine of a logic of the heart, a *logique du cœur*, a notion which had been previously put forward by Scheler and connected with certain passages in Pascal. The heart, apparently, is an organ that can range sensitively over the whole sphere of time and existence, of the possible and the impossible, and in all its rangings it can throb responsively in the presence of certain mysterious values and disvalues, quite different from the non-valuational 'materials' in which they are embedded, or the concrete 'bearers' which exemplify them, and belonging in fact to a different order altogether, a timeless, Platonic order of self-existent axiological entities. The heart in its ranging does not, according to Hartmann, often err or miss a beat, but it is curiously narrow in its sensitiveness, so that the opening up of each new territory of value tends to inhibit its responsiveness to others. Hence we have the constant shift of the valuational focus, and the revolutionary changes from Graeco-Roman to Christian axiology, from Christian axiology to Renaissance axiology, ending up with the trans-valued Nietzschean values, to which Hartmann, in company with many others, attributes an importance and a characteristic modernity that I find totally incomprehensible. Hartmann, however, does not think that any real transvaluations occur in these shifts: the heart merely opens itself to new ranges of value, and ceases to be sensitive to older ones. The old and the new are, however, alike *there* in their timeless Platonic home, and it is the special role of the philosophical heart, trained to beat more widely and strongly by a special course of Hartmannian *approfondisse-ment*, that can set the old alongside the new, and can effect a confrontation of pagan Greece with medieval Christianity, and of both with Nietzchean modernity.

Hartmann has many further original doctrines regarding the world of values and disvalues which the heart explores and maps: all such values have attaching to them an ideal ought-to-be-ness or *Seinsollen*, which becomes a positive ought-to-be-ness when the values in question are unrealized in the world of particular existence, an ought-to-be-ness which is experienced as a positive tension, an urge, to realize the value in the world of existence and becoming. Apparently men and their hearts and muscles are the one channel through which the world of values and disvalues influences the world of existence: Hartmann rejects any teleology of the 'good' operating over the unconscious field of nature, and speaks therefore of the 'demiurgic nature of man' as the one link between the 'irreal' world of values and the realm of reality.

Hartmann has further logical excitements connected with his doctrine of ought-to-be-ness, excitements that will not recommend him to modal logicians. In an ought, he maintains, we have a case of a must, a necessity which, by a logical miracle, has broken loose from its close connection with the actual and the possible, so that what ought to be, *must* be so, even if it is not so, and even if it is impossible that it should be so. It is here that we get Hartmann's extremely illuminating and acceptable doctrine of the antinomic character of the realm of value: there are values lying in opposed directions, e.g. those of innocence and sophistication, which are such that they cannot be combined, and yet it remains a mandatory requirement that they *should* be combined, that we should by some means become innocent sophisticates or sophisticated innocents. We are in fact involved in *guilt* whichever of the horns of the dilemma before us we may embrace. I find this doctrine extremely interesting, true to our value-experience and not at all logically incoherent. Our value-experience is that all choice and existence involve a sacrifice of some value or other, and yet that such a sacrifice is authentically regrettable, that it should not be. There is nothing self-contradictory in the eternal *requirement* of something whose full realization would involve self-contradiction, and contradictions therefore have a meaningful role in evaluative and also in religious discourse that they do not have in the discourse of science. The inimitable perfection of God, the absolute Good, lies arguably in the fact that He represents an ideal, a value-limit, that nothing creaturely, nothing instantial could *possibly* embody.

If we now turn from these general features of structure to the actual content of the heart's responses, Hartmann has much that is interesting to tell us. He believes in an axiological space in which there are several dimensions, so that not every value is comparable with every other in respect of height or preferability: aesthetic values, e.g. are neither higher nor lower than those of science or morality. He believes also in unfilled gaps or distances in the value continuum as remarkable and surprising as the gaps between the prime numbers. And he believes that certain values are built upon others as their presuppositions. Thus he propounds as a theorem the sensible doctrine that moral values always presuppose other lower classes of value, and that it is only by trying to realize something that is not a case of moral good, such as freedom from pain or from baseless inequality or insecurity, that one can be morally good. His most interesting articulations are, first, into a lowest order of what may be called logical or categorial values which are all antinomic: they occur in opposed pairs, and it is never possible fully to realize both members of each such pair, though compromises and adjustments among them are possible. There is a value of fixed necessity and a value of variable contingency, a value in the realization of values and a value in their permanent non-realization, a value in universal uniformity and a value in divergent individuality, a value in simplicity and a value in complexity, and so on. All this may seem banal, but its banality is not due to recognition by philosophers. From these categorial values Hartmann advances to values which represent as it were the foothills of moral value: the value of being alive, of being conscious, of being purposively active and efficient, of being able to withstand and suffer, of foresight, of having the opportunities for moral development represented by the situation, by language, by social intercourse, as well as by such Aristotelian goods as wealth, power, reputation, etc. Hartmann then proceeds to examine moral values, the values of the dedicated will, and here he sets the noble, the pure and the rich alongside of the merely good, and then takes us through a splendid gallery of the aretaics of Classical Greece, of Catholic Christianity and finally of modern Nietzscheanism. Throughout this wonderful and ingenious phenomenology one is amazed at the wealth and variety of valuational stances and questions, especially when one considers the hopeless poverty and emptiness of our recent ethics and meta-ethics: to go to Hartmann from the latter is like penetrating to the treasure-laden tomb of Tutankhamen after living in the impover-ished huts of Egyptian fellahin. One is also amazed at the general persuasiveness, or at least the deep discussability, of all the points put forth by Hartmann. It may not be easy to see *how* the heart-logic is operating, but that it does and can operate, and with its own genuine *rationale*, is what no one can think doubtful.

One feels, however, some reservations about admitting purely descriptive, intuitive work like Hartmann's *Ethics* into the highest reaches of philosophy. It too often merely tells us *that* something is so, it too seldom tries to show us *why* it is so. It does not, in other words, systematically consider the alternatives to each assertion that it makes, nor seek to exclude them on any definite principle. I shall not attempt to enumerate all the philosophical questions raised by a successful venture of the Hartmannian type, and particularly not those connected with the cognitive role assigned to feelings, nor those connected with the Platonic self-existence so lightly asserted, nor those connected with the unique demiurgic function ascribed to man, nor those connected with the strange transformation undergone by necessity in order to emerge as that new logical creature, the ought-to-be. But what I shall ask is how Hartmann can legitimate all the poignant and fascinating things he says about antinomies of value, hierarchies of value, many dimensions and orders of value and so on. We are often disposed to assent to what he says, but we as often wonder why we are so. And how do we counter the determined relativist, the true Nietzschean who is now becoming so abundant, or, worse still, the proponent and advocate of values of the abyss, of the utterly abominable and repugnant: the values attributed to meaningless arbitrariness occurring on a sorrowful background of equal meaninglessness, the values of surrender to a dark divinity who first demands the sacrifice of one's reason and one's morals, the value of gratuitous disturbance of social patterns which tends only to further disturbance, the value attached to cruelty and absurdity loved and cherished for their own sakes? Our age has exceeded all previous ages in the richness of its perversions, and without some principle that can sort out the valid from the deviant forms, it will not be possible to carry our value-constitution very far. We have therefore no alternative but to embark on something like a transcendental deduction of the realm of truly acceptable values, a deduction which will suffice to distinguish them from their many verminous and scrofulous imitators; this deduction will not be less valuable because both its first principles and its mode of developing them, or reasoning from them, has an element of the lax and the loose, and is not strictly and trivially deductive: the various 'deductions' which Kant offers us in his various Critiques are valuable and informative precisely on account of this element of the lax and the loose. I am now about to give you a savour of my own contribution to value-theory in *Values and Intentions*, an undertaking which my friend Karl Popper rightly described as an attempt to carry out a transcendental deduction, contentful and material and not merely formal, of the heads of value and disvalue.

I shall endeavour to construct the whole map of value and disvalue if you will grant me the ποῦ στῶ of a single assumption: that we are in the grip, and necessarily in the grip, of an aspiration towards what I shall call 'impersonality', and this I shall further describe as the aspiration, framed by a particular person having quite specific interests, to rise above the specificity of his interests and the particularity of his person, and to desire that, and only that, that he could and would consistently desire, whoever he conceived himself as being, and whatever he conceived himself as desiring as a concrete, first-order object of interest. Men, I am suggesting, may harbour a curious algebraic passion to substitute for everything that is definite and constant in the objects or subjects of their practical wishes, variables most utterly un-restricted, and then to be practically guided by whatever survives the removal of everything concrete and contentful and empirically definite in their practical endeavours. And I am further suggesting that if indeed men are subject to this algebraic passion, which is perhaps what is meant in calling them rational animals, then its long-term operation will not be simply an empty formalism or a killing annihilation of their primary interests in favour of nothing in particular, but the generation of a whole system of heads of worthwhileness and counter-worthwhileness which will have a necessary and authoritative and intrinsically justifiable position which no other substantially different aspiration or set of aspira-tions could conceivably generate. I am in short claiming not only that my aspiration will prove to have content, and not merely empty form, but that this content will be such as to generate a firm 'ought' from an 'is', and an 'ought' that not merely expresses a demand prescribed to someone by someone, but a demand pre-scribed by everyone to everyone, and that not merely in some matter-of-fact fashion but in a manner which combines necessity with normativity. The aspiration in question, I am attempting to argue, is really the dominant universal present in all the cases of value and disvalue that we can with some approvable colour regard as compelling, non-arbitrary, intersubjective or what not, and that it in fact defines what it is to be the sort of value or disvalue in question. There is, from the standpoint of the aspiration in question, no mystery in the compelling, non-arbitrary character of certain values and disvalues: they are the values and disvalues so framed and constituted as to have non-arbitrariness, inter-subjectivity written into their constitution, they are in fact no more than specific embodiments or applications of non-arbitrari-ness. It would be as absurd to regard them as merely arbitrary and personal as it would be to regard the values and disvalues which express ordinary personal choice and preference as mandatory and universal. That we are 'in the grip' of such as aspiration means further that its operation is not merely personal and variable and contingent, but that it is an aspiration that all men, in so far as they are men, inevitably must form, and which has in itself, further, the promise and the possibility of a growing strength, so that, whatever other tendencies may grow at its side, and be in no way derivative from or subject to it, they may none the less fulfil the role of the variable material, suitable or unsuitable, which exists in its framework or upon its background. For an aspiration which projected an impeccable set of values, and yet was itself a mere chance side-issue in human nature, would not quite do the logical work required in the constitution of a realm of values and disvalues. That anything will do all the logical work required seems, however, extraordinarily dubious and requires a great deal of argument.

Before I go on to such argument I shall, however, try to elucidate various points in the formulation that I have just put forward. I wish to advert, first of all, to the use of the words 'could' and 'would' in my formulation above: to aspire to be impersonal is to aspire to desire that, and only that, that a man could and would desire, whoever he conceived himself as being, etc. The 'would' of this formula is not an expression of logical necessity, for obviously there is nothing that everyone, whatever his primary interests, would desire in this sense: many persons desire only idiosyncratic personal objects varying from case to case. Nor is it a 'would' expressive of natural law, for, apart from the objection that there are no objects of desire demanded by the laws of nature, it would in this case have no absolute force at all, nothing that would generate a system of values holding for *all* practical beings. On the other hand if one defines the aspiration as the aspiration to pursue only what a man *could* desire, whoever he conceived himself as being, one is brought to a halt by the obscurity of the word 'could'. It must not be interpreted in an abstract formal sense, for obviously anything whatever, even stamp-collecting, *could* be pursued by everyone, and it is not clear that the laws of human nature or the structure of human society would rule out such a strange addiction. One's hesitation between 'would' and 'could' shows one, however, what one is looking for. It is the 'would' which one uses when one says that everyone who likes Michelangelo would like Tintoretto too, and that one is always willing to exchange for a 'could very well' or 'could as well' in such a context. One is not dealing with the analytic 'would' or 'must' of formal logic, nor with the empty 'could' of formal non-contradiction, but with what we may call a near-necessity of essence, something that is very likely to be the case, but on *a priori* rather than empirical grounds. It is as I say the sort of near-necessity that he who wills the end must or could very well will the means, or that he who likes this *A* could very well like something rather like this *A*. The realm of mind is honeycombed with these near-necessities in terms of which understanding of people and their attitudes is alone possible. And we may note that, almost invariably, this 'would' or 'could' of near-necessity passes over or paraphrases itself into an 'ought' or a 'should'. The near-necessity of essence is an unfulfilled 'ought' for the man who fails to carry it out to its natural limit.

Another point that it is important to stress is that my account of impersonality is not one that makes it inimical to primary interest, in the sense of the interest in empirical objects of various sorts, the interest which is essentially such that there is no intrinsic reason why more than one person should share it. The impersonal may be such as to espouse invariant rather than contingently variable objects of interest, but its invariants always permit and in fact require contingently variable interests, which it is in fact their function to organize, and in contrast with which they alone can *be* impersonal and can exercise their function of impersonality. This requirement of first-order interests is in fact part and parcel of the appeal to whoever and whatever that occurred in our formulation, for no one would find an intrinsic appeal in emptily universal ends that bore no relation to what he concretely wanted or that even ran athwart his primary interests. The desire to be moved *only* by what one might desire whoever one conceived of oneself as being, is not a desire to be *free* from primary interest, but to pursue its goals only as falling under, or at least not conflicting with, what one desires impersonally, and even this relative freedom is desired only *in so far* as one aspires to be impersonal, which does not preclude, and in fact requires, a rich growth of primary impulses, in the *other* segments of one's being. We may note here that even the desire to be free from all primary interests which has been so powerfully recommended by certain renunciatory philosophies and religions really presupposes primary interests: it bases itself on our first-order aversions from various concrete frustrations, and is itself nothing but a generalized aversion from frustration as such, which, rightly or wrongly, it believes to be the sole fruit of human endeavour.

It may be noted further that I have brought the word 'consistently' into my formulation, and that I have spoken of 'whoever he may conceive himself as being' rather than of 'whoever he may happen to be.' The point I am trying to make is that the impersonal goals are not the invariant ends that everyone would or could pursue, and that one consequently would or could pursue whoever one was, but that they are the ends which require that one should conceptually place oneself in every possible person's shoes, and should then frame ends that take account of and also rise above all that one might pursue in *all these conceived situations seen together*, and which would therefore have a certain ideal *collectivity* of attitude as well as the distributiveness which alone will not do the impersonal trick. The man who aspires to conduct himself impersonally, must not merely pursue ends that he might well desire whoever he was, for in this case victory over all others might be a very good candidate for impersonal honours: he must rather pursue such ends as he might pursue if he were everyone *at once*, or everyone *at the same time*, absurd as this may seem, if he entered into everyone else's predicament as intimately as his own. What we are saying is of course ordinarily phrased in the form that a man must be ready to pursue *for others* whatever he is ready to pursue for himself, but this brings into the arena a bedevilling surd which is only surmounted when the man abolishes the otherness of the other by treating the other as someone whom in some extraordinary sense he *might* be or might have been, or in other words by 'putting himself into his place.' What the individual wants impersonally therefore stands or falls with the strange procedure of disembarrassing oneself of one's own individuality, and deciding what one would desire not only whoever one was but even if one was everyone. What one here does may be meaningless or impossible from the standpoint of many philosophical theories of identity, but it is certainly involved in the commonplace talk of looking at things from everyone's point of view. And in terms of this strange procedure we can understand the harmless growth of an apparently formidable infinite series: that what a man desires impersonally he not only would desire whoever he conceived himself as being, but that he would also desire it for everyone else as much as for himself, and that he would desire everyone else to desire it for everyone else, and everyone else to desire everyone else to desire it for everyone else, and so on indefinitely. The strange gambit of putting oneself into everyone else's shoes involves, it seems, that *qua* everyone one again puts oneself into the sum total of available shoes, and that *qua* everyone one goes on repeating the same process indefinitely. Each added term of the series seems to complicate the old, but in reality only makes explicit what is already there. Only such ends as can consistently survive this whole process of shoe-exchanging can be the impersonal ends we are trying to sketch. It seems ambitious to hope that something clear and positive can emerge out of processes so murky.

What I must now attempt to do is to work out the main heads of a generally accepted value-cosmos from the aspiration that I have taken such trouble to state unclearly. Plainly, as has been assumed, none of the more concrete goals of human striving or liking, and none of the more specific doings or undergoings in which men take delight or from which they experience aversion, can be given any absolute value-status, no matter how important they may be to individuals. Tea-drinking, mountain-climbing, the reading of one's favourite philosopher, all fall under the ban which excludes from absolute value what some only may find interesting while others have to it a contrary attitude, or no attitude at all. They may of course re-enter the sphere of the absolutely valuable under another more general description, as special cases in certain circumstances of characters having a justifiable, mandatory appeal, but as what they are described they have no such privileges. Even the objects of universal human instincts occupy the same position: the objects and acts of sex, for instance, are objects in which we as a race for the most part happen to be interested, and interested in a primary fashion. They are not objects in which anyone would or could be interested no matter what his primary interests. There is an ἐποχή, a general suspension of acceptance of all such objects of contingent, primary interest: only under such headings as survive the ἐποχή can they make their re-entry into the field of absolute values. Are there such headings? And if so, what are they? Or have we, in the interests of an empty formalism expelled all positive content from the realm of value?

It is readily arguable that this is not the case at all. By a strange step into the second order, one can take satisfaction in the conformity of things to one's wants, one can, in other words, be satisfied with and want satisfaction or pleasure, as an object which *everyone* with some non-contingent naturalness must come to desire, whatever the actual content of his interests, and which we, who put ourselves into the shoes of all such interested parties, and who espouse only such ends as may be pursued by all and for all, also find interesting and satisfactory. To have what one wants, which is the basic presupposition of all pleasure and satisfaction, is no contingent object of desire or satisfaction like the tea-drinking or the mountain-climbing mentioned above; it is as it were what everyone *must* want as soon as he reflects calmly on the matter, and which, since he will want it into whoever's shoes he projects himself, he will likewise want for all and find satisfactory for all and will want all to want and find satisfactory for all, and so on indefinitely. If one wants to drink tea or climb mountains or to do other things, and does not want to be satisfied by these activities or to have any satisfaction whatsoever, plainly some special explanation is required for one's perverse and abnormal state. A man who has primary wants, but desires them all to be frustrated, is no logically impossible creature; such ascetic personalities have existed and always will exist. But the way their interests have developed is rightly considered twisted, difficult, improbable, illogical, something not natural in an *a priori* and not merely empirically inductive sense. We must at the same time avoid suggesting that there is something merely tautological, unprogressive in passing from an interest in primary empirical goals, to an interest in the satisfaction which such goals afford. It is, as Butler and others have stressed, the most immense of steps, and the one that makes man a rational agent, able to integrate and co-ordinate the most diverse concrete interests under the comprehensive rubrics of the satisfactory, the pleasant and the avoidance of their opposites. Beside this immense step the further step to being interested in the satisfactions that one might have in other people's shoes is entirely minor and inconsiderable. Egoism and altruism alike soar infinitely above the animal, and altruism is only intelligible as a transcendental, notional egoism that has shed the bonds of particularity. Problems of the adjustment of my own various and other people's interests will of course arise in the most numerous and vexatious forms, but they will not be intrinsically necessary as it would be if everyone sought to impose his particular goals and tastes upon all others. Satisfaction at least provides a currency, or set of currencies, vague no doubt in their precise exchange value, in which intra- and interpersonal practice may be adjusted. A similar intrinsic naturalness attends the interest in the process or activity of successfully progressing towards what one wants, and which is really one's goal in prospect, and not strictly separable from that goal. There would be something perverse, or very specially motivated, or supersubtle in saying that one did not care for success, or for the smoothly nearing prospect of the things one cherished and was bringing about. The will to power and the will to freedom are similarly directions of willing that are not on a par with ordinary contingent trends of personal desire: whatever one personally desires, one must tend to desire the power to achieve what one desires and the freedom from all that could hinder one in its realization. One must not, of course, ignore in one's survey the nigh-necessary second order aversion from frustration and pain: whatever anyone desires, one must impersonally desire anyone to be freed from these. I here leave aside the problem as to whether the pains of getting what one wants and the frustrations of not getting it are *ever* worth the countervailing satisfactions and pleasures: I make no pronouncement on what Buddhism calls its First Noble Truth. But even if it were a Noble Truth, it would be no more than an assessment of the overall values and disvalues of human existence: it would not make a difference to those values and disvalues themselves.

From the impersonal desire for satisfaction and freedom from frustration for everyone, one necessarily and naturally goes on, in avoiding internal discrepancy, to those ideals of justice and fairness, which involve no more than a viable accommodation of satisfactions and freedom from frustration for everyone, an accommodation which necessarily involves many arbitrary, conventional and institutional features. I shall not develop the *a priori* case for justice, nor dwell on the arbitrary element in its precise application. The demand for justice does not, however, become less of an absolute demand because the precise manner of its implementation is anything but absolute: for particular would-be just dispensations we may not care, but there is a plain absurdity in saying that one has no taste for justice as such. In so far as one considers and considers together, what one would feel whoever one was, one quite necessarily cares for it: it is precisely what shoe-changing both lives on and fosters. Last item of all in the present enumeration, an impersonal interest in the just accommodation of interest logically leads to an impersonal interest in the action and will of all persons concerned to implement such an accommodation, an action and will only abstractly separable from the accommodations that they effect. We have the interest in justice as a virtue, a virtue which, taken in a wide sense, as Aristotle says, comprehends all the moral virtues. You will pardon me if, in a condensed exposition, I go no further in the analysis of virtue or moral good. The whole system of varied objectives we have mentioned are all 'deducible', in a more or less cogent, if not formally necessary manner, from the aspiration towards impersonality understood as I have understood it.

We may, in parenthesis, briefly indicate the possibility of dealing with such values as those of dedicated love, the pursuit of truth, and the pursuit of the well-formed and successfully expressive which we also call the beautiful. In all these cases we have an analogue of the impersonality which rises above the specificity and particularity of personal interest, though here there is a rising above a specificity and a particularity which is not concerned with persons or their interests. In dedicated love there is a rising above *any* particularity and specificity which does not tend to the preservation and defence of what we dedicatedly love, and which, in its limited fashion, but with intensified strength, imitates absolute impersonality. In the love of truth we have impersonality directed to what is the case or to what may be the case, or to whatever is evidence for what may be the case, no matter what the content or source of one's evidence or information. In the interest in the beautiful one has an interest in doing justice to an object, in bringing out its character or its internal structure in the most poignant and vivid manner, no matter what the object may be and no matter what other interest it may arouse in anyone. The analogies between justice, equiprobability and aesthetic balance are not hard to point out, and love, truth and beauty certainly demand of us a detachment from primary interest which is fundamentally similar to the detachment which occurs in the pursuit of welfare, of justice and of moral good. Being fundamentally similar, this detachment receives and deserves the impersonal love which we all give it and desire all to share with us in giving it. Aesthetic, scientific and love-experience therefore enter the sphere of the absolutely valuable since they spring from a spirit akin to the spirit which projects and constitutes the whole sphere of the absolutely valuable. You will perhaps allow me the point without further argument, that there would be something absurd in using Stevensonian persuasion in the three cases in question. To say: 'I like love, truth, beauty: pray do so too': surely this represents the apogee of the grotesque and inappropriate.

We have therefore established, as well as we can hope to establish anything on an occasion like the present, that an aspiration towards impersonality is in a position to generate a whole order of impersonal goals, of heads of value and disvalue. If we seek only to desire what could be desired whoever we might conceive of ourselves as being, and we seek to do this with comprehensiveness, consistency and indifference to content, then we shall find ourselves forced to set up all the higher order goals of happiness, freedom from frustration, power, liberty, success, justice, moral zeal, dedicated love, scientific and aesthetic detachment, which are admittedly the worthwhile things in life, as their defects and contraries are admittedly its real blemishes. We have now, however, to ask whether there is anything like a necessary drift in the direction of impersonality, so that the realm of values may have power as well as dignity, and may with some colour be regarded as the irremovable background and necessary framework of practical life. It will be noted that I *do* regard it as an important matter whether the values I have set up do or do not guide the world, or at least help to guide human endeavour: values whose non-natural status is consistent with their guiding or influencing no one or nothing are to me totally unmeaning. There can be no meaningful ought which is not also to some extent an is, and which does not at least to some extent *tend* to be realized. Oughts and values express a criticism of what is, on a basis of what it is and what it tends to be, and a putative ought which bears no relation to the actual strivings and tendencies of a thing or a person is as unmeaning as it is, in the literal sense, impertinent.

Shall we say, however, that the strange passion for divesting ourselves of specificity and particularity and putting ourselves not only into every actual but also every possible pair of shoes represents an inevitable, natural and centrally powerful aspect of human nature? Must conscious, reflective beings tend more and more to do just this, and must they thus become more and more subject to the overarching influence of a firmament of impersonal values and disvalues? The answer to this query is, I think, curious and paradoxical: that the aspiration towards impersonality and the value-firmament that it generates have an *empirical* strength much greater than anything that we could have reason to expect on a not too penetrating, if *a priori* examination of human existence. It can certainly be argued, as I have argued in detail in my *Values and Intentions*, that the aspiration towards impersonality has deep roots in conscious experience as such, which can be said to be always in quest of an ever widening universality, whether in theory or practice, and which can likewise be said to be always in quest, whether in theory or practice, of an objectivity which sets a bound to personal variability, and to an intersubjectivity which makes communication and social co-operation possible. The things which generate the firmament of impersonal values are no *accidents* of human existence: they are inherent in the existence of objectively directed states of mind as such and in the existence of anything that can be regarded as an explorable, discussable real world. The search for the comprehensively universal, for the compulsively objective, for the communicably intersubjective: these are the basic *nisus* of our conscious subjectivity, and of the world that constitutes itself for our thought. I am not here putting forward an idealistic theory of the world, but only of the world as responded to and given to us. What we do not, however, have in all this *a priori* rootedness, is a firm guarantee that impersonality will be pressed very far, that it will not merely result in sympathies confined to a limited group, and in standards of worthwhileness and counterworthwhileness meant to hold only for this group. And this is what we do for the most part actually find in practice: that interests extending to anyone and everyone whatever they may desire are in general of little influence, and that there are even defences erected against them in the form of charges of emptiness, sentimentalism, exaggeration and disloyalty whenever they begin to show themselves in some strength. The whole process of divesting oneself of one's individuality and group-membership and becoming an algebraic entity concerned only with a total algebraization of interest is, moreover, so metaphysically mysterious as to arouse derision in philosophers as well as in ordinary persons, so that like Spinoza we begin to think it absurd to be concerned for the well-being of flies and other humble creatures. It would seem that all that we can predict with reliability are those tribally or racially limited values and disvalues whose great uniformity has astonished certain sociologists. What we do find, however, is the presence of a strange responsiveness in the most diverse classes of men to the total algebraizations I have mentioned and that even in the case of the childlike and unreflective. The monstrous inequity of treating even animals sometimes as they are treated in many slaughter-houses and in factory-farms is readily clear to many children, no matter how soon they may learn to dismiss it as weak sentimentality, and the moral devotion which refuses to see unpersons in blacks, lepers and other classes of the underprivileged and the unfortunate, and pursues them with burning, practical love, is another example of the same unexpected, astonishing responsiveness. Men certainly behave, with much greater frequency than is rationally predictable, as if there were something in them intrinsically and passionately transcendent of specificity and particularity, no matter how deeply and necessarily they may be immersed in either.

I may conclude this lecture by suggesting that the strange hauntingness of the impersonal value-firmament that I have sketched, and of the aspiration towards impersonality which projects it, points to an old shadow which meets us along many avenues of discourse and argument, no matter how little it may seem meaningful to modern thought. I refer to the notion of an ontological Absolute, the notion of something having that indiscerptible unity, that necessity of existence and necessary possession of essential properties, which goes together with and totally explains the existence of all that exists finitely, contingently, empirically and separately, which is one among others, which might not have been there, which seems to stand loose and separate and apart. Absolute-theory or the theory of what uniquely, necessarily and unitively is, and what is in some sense logically responsible for whatever contingently exists or is the case, is, I believe, an indispensable philosophical inquiry, and one that puts the logical keystone on to every other philosophical inquiry, and not least on to inquiries into the impersonal values and disvalues that we have been exploring. For an Absolute has precisely that transcendence of separate individuality and one-sided empirical content, while at the same time covering and organizing all such individuality and such content, which we have found to be essential to the realm of values. An Absolute is a very strange logical object, investigated if at all only by purely logical methods. For being the sort of thing that must exist necessarily if it exists at all, it is necessarily non-existent if there is even a doubt as to its possible non-existence, while on the other hand it can only be in any way thinkable and possible if it also exists certainly and of

P

necessity. This means that purely logical insight is the one tool through which Absolutes can be investigated, anything empirical, anything that we may or may not encounter, being rigorously excluded. It is only our deepening insight, our progressive exclusion of what seemed to be but are not genuinely alternatives, that can leave us at the last, if we are left, with a truly viable explanatory Absolute. If some think that this means that such an Absolute can be no more than an empty thing of thought, nothing can be wider of the mark. Absolutes by their indiscerptible unity and all pervasive responsibility are precisely the guarantors of those unitive, rational enterprises, whether in theory or practice, which, on assumptions of boundless logical pluralism and independence, are incapable even of an approach to justification. Absolutes and Absolute-theory are in fact justified by the justifying work that they do, and that radically empiricist and pluralist philosophies cannot possibly do. The logical impossibility and self-destroying meaninglessness of the latter are the only true proofs of an Absolute. And the difficult constitution of the realm of values and disvalues is of course above all a rational enterprise that requires such explanation and justification through an Absolute.

Absolutes can be, and have been, however, very variously conceived. For though there can be no alternatives to a true Absolute, there are always alternative Absolutes for us, and will be as long as we have a defective insight into the necessary and the possible and the existential and many other such categorial matters. For it is a wrong belief, and we must utterly reject it, that what is really possible or impossible or necessary or real can be settled by a mere linguistic convention, and not by an examination of the sorts of thing one has on hand, and of what being such sorts of things carries with it or does not carry with it. Absolutes have been conceived as self-diversifying media spread out in time and space, as transcendent godheads exercising unlimited optional creativity or non-creativity, as a mind or spirit scattered over a whole society of communicating intelligences, as an ideal Platonic world of forms deploying itself in a half-real world of instances, and so on. Part of the task of Absolute-theory is a discussion of all these alternatives, and of the degree to which they leave anything merely external or unmopped-up or unexplained. It is here that I shall simply affirm my belief in the superior merit of Hegelian-type Absolutes, Absolutes which can only be unitary in

THE SYSTEMATIC UNITY OF VALUE

so far as they go as far as possible in the direction of diremption and multiplicity and apparent mutual independence, and which reveal their deep unity, and are in fact one, only in the continuous *act* of breaking down and overcoming the diremption that they have at first seemingly introduced. The natural world in space and time represents such an Absolute in its nearest approach to utter dispersion and mutual externality, that essentially impossible condition which abstract formal logic often treats as the very paradigm of the possible. This dispersed natural world gives rise to the vastly closer unity of life and mind in order to demonstrate, as it were, the impossibility of such a merely dispersed, natural being. In life, and more so in mind, mutual interpenetration and dependence take over from dispersion and seeming independence, but there is still a higher independence seemingly maintained in the atomistic separateness of the conscious person, whose pathetic, logical incapacity for true sharing has been the theme of much of the modern thought of Wittgenstein and others. The various stars in the firmament of value represent, however, the Absolute asserting its unity over the seeming dispersion of persons: the Absolute shows itself in the utter impossibility of our living entirely unto ourselves, and in our necessary involvement with the life and inner feeling of even the most remote conscious being. It is, we may paradoxically say, because personal self-sufficiency and separateness are not and cannot be, because they are states approachable only because we can thereupon retreat from them, and utterly do away with them, that the various members of the realm of values have the firm status that they have, that they haunt us so persistently, and that they can at times overshadow the limited personal and social needs of our immediate being and environment. The sense of affirming an Absolute therefore lies, among other things, in the inexorability of the moral firmament, constructed as we have constructed it. The Absolute may not be a thing open to sensuous observation, but it remains like a grey eminence behind our otherwise incompletely intelligible postulations of absolute values. The Absolute is, however, something that we encounter along many avenues, and the avenue of values and disvalues is not necessarily the most important and most beautiful of its main vistas. It is, however, the only avenue that we have been concerned to explore this evening.

XIV

INTENTIONAL INEXISTENCE

This paper is an attempt to deal, with determined non-technicality and awareness of the shimmering mirages of the question, with the old issue of what Descartes and Spinoza called 'objective being', and what Brentano and the Schoolmen he derived from called 'intentional inexistence', and what might less perplexingly simply be called 'being for thought'. The reason why this question or notion is of such permanent interest is that, if given the slightest leeway, it is deeply and livingly self-contradictory: we cannot consider it without wanting passionately to maintain propositions that are not in any obvious manner reconcilable, which involve identities suddenly transforming themselves into utter diversities, continuities suddenly yawning to reveal unbridgeable abysses, and solidly palpable entities suddenly resolving themselves into thin air. Of course it is possible to regard all this magnificent dialectic as illusory, and it can readily be patched up or annealed in one or other of a number of dead ways. One can discover a fallacy or category-mistake somewhere in one's perplexities, show that one is being deceived by some plausible syntactical similarity, point to the fact that we experience no deep difficulty in using the concept in quite ordinary contexts, and make adjustments in our language which allay conflict and perplexity at the cost of depriving our notions of their uncanny suggestiveness and life. We can decide that it is thoroughly inexpedient to talk of objects of thought as if they were a special class of real entities, we can talk of senses and uses that are independent of actual references, and by using various incantatory phrases such as 'referential opacity', 'syn-semantic symbols', etc. we may contrive to sweep the queerness of our basic notions under the carpet, and go on in the firm confidence of some new-style empiricism, materialism, phenomenology or ontology. But in so doing so we shall almost certainly have silenced or ruled out of court one of the vital aspects of the notions we are trying to consider, and some essential aspect of human experience will have been scanted or suppressed. It may be human understanding that now limps misunderstood, it may be interior experience with its bewildering range of stuffs and stances, it may be truth or falsehood, it may even be the great real world itself. By quick-change artistry one may vary the mutilated vision, the bodiless lady yielding to the woman without a head and so on, but one does not thereby achieve that many-dimensioned grasp of what underlies these paradoxical transformations, what it is that really comes out and utters itself in them all. These questionable generalities of attitude and procedure may, however, be left to justify themselves as our argument proceeds.

Before I get into the heart of my problem I wish to set forth and put in the fullest light some axiomatic obviousnesses, *Selbstverständlichkeiten*, concerning the relation of what may be called referential experience to the realm of objects and ultimately to the real world, obviousnesses which I believe to be involved in our talk about either, but whose ignoring or distortion has none the less been frequently practised, and always with the most disastrous consequences for every sort of significant discourse. The first of the obviousnesses in which I am interested may be summed up in the phrase of the thoroughgoing correlativity and isomorphism of anything recognized in the world of objects, and in that privileged section of it that we call the real world, with the nuances and structures of our interior experiences: full-fledged talk of the former dictates full-fledged talk of the latter. This isomorphic situation is a two-sided isomorphism: not only is there nothing in the realm of objectivity that cannot be paralleled in the realm of subjectivity, but there is arguably nothing in the latter realm which cannot be paralleled in the former. This latter isomorphism is, however, far from obvious, and will be considered later; it is not very important for the purposes of the present paper. What we are, however, committed to is the principle that nothing whatever can be given tentative objective status, or referred confidently to the privileged sector of the 'real world', unless we are ready to postulate, with complete certainty, the existence of personal splinters of consciousness, or patterned wholes of such splinters, in which the objective matter in question is specifically 'constituted' for the mind, is set up in an appropriate category *for* it, is in some manner present *to* it.

This principle means that every naming or otherwise functioning expression in a language, has always a *twofold* use: it can be

used to refer to, or help refer to, or otherwise contribute to a
reference to, some object thinkably located in the world, or to
state some fact or some putative fact concerning it, but it can *also*
be used to throw light on the structure of the personal experiences,
the mental stances or patterns of reference or 'syntheses' in which
whatever is referred to is set before consciousness in the manner
in which it is referred to. Thus the name 'James' not only serves
to pick out a man in the world and perhaps credit him with certain
characters and relations: it also serves to express a highly personal,
only partially definite pattern of personal expectations, terminating in sensuous or imaged fulfilments which may or may not be
carried out, which pattern is *not only* a far-flung readiness to do or
say or imagine or perceive this or that, but which is also, at least
on some pregnant occasions, a single concentrated point of lived
experience, my sense of who or what the man is, what he altogether amounts to, at least as far as I am concerned. It is only
because there is, or can at times be, a stance of consciousness
which simply pinpoints James in so far as he is anything to me,
that he *is* anything to me, that his name is not just a meaningless
vocable tossed about on the eddies of the world-process. In the
same way the word 'teacher' not only serves to describe James or
someone else in terms of a certain complex social function having
a variety of aspects, but it also serves to express my own actual
seeing of him in the light of this function, with all that this involves in terms of a readiness for illustration and of the peculiar
terminal grasp of what it is to teach and be a teacher into which all
such illustration collapses, and from which it can again, if needed,
be restored to life. And if we turn to the utterance 'James is a
teacher', it not only purports to state a fact in the world, but it
also points to my possible inward grasp of this fact, with all its
synthesis of partial thought-items into a unified thought-whole,
and with all its location of that thought-whole in the yet more
embracing, all-encompassing thought-whole that we call the real
world. The same linguistic expressions which, seen in one light,
voice a commonplace fact, can be used also to bring out the far
from familiar way in which that fact is registered in our life of
understanding, in which it is made one with that inward grasp
which is one of the deep layers, if not the deepest layer, of ourselves. There is from this point of view no problem, apart from
that of a somewhat novel inversion, in knowing our own interior
life or that of others: to know or think anything whatever can be

to know it. To know what it is like for James to be a teacher, can be to know with crystal clarity what it is to understand James to be a teacher, and to know what it is like for *anyone* to understand James to be a teacher and not merely for ourselves to do so. And there is nothing communicable about the fact that James is a teacher that does not correspond to something wholly communicable in the interior understanding of the fact that James is a teacher, even if there may be *some* nuances of that interior understanding, which, owing to their use of personal symbols and pictures, are not so readily communicable. This is the reason why, for all but these subtler personal nuances, we require no special vocabulary or syntax for our thoughts. It is not, as some have thought, because thoughts are mere pictured analogues of words, fancifully introjected into the speaker, and given content and meaning by the words in which they might issue, that we use the same words 'James is a teacher' both to state a fact in the world and to register a man's thought regarding it, but because words are in fact two-edged in their implications. They function normally and primarily as object-indicators or describers or connectors or as fact-staters, etc. but they can also be made to function as expressors of possible thoughts behind them, and as expressors also of the fascinating structure of those thoughts, adjusted to and yet deeply unlike the objects thought of in them, in that what is unified and blended in objects is curiously dismembered in thought, while also contributing to an overall unity of personal awareness and felt grasp to which nothing need correspond in the object.

The whole way in which we have been talking is deeply repugnant to current conceptions, which would in fact see nothing in it but a mythology based on deep-set misunderstandings of language. On the sorts of view that would be flatly opposed to the intentional views we are espousing, there never are, behind the words we utter, any winged shafts of consciousness speeding on their way to actual or imagined targets: our words are given a sense by the way we employ them, by the situations, real or imagined, that they make us prepared for, by the modes of reaction we take up or are ready to take up to such situations, by the responses we expect from other auditors and spectators, and so on. When we locate a shaft of consciousness, or pattern of such shafts, behind a person's words, we are merely introjecting into his momentary state the long drawn out consequences that *could* be educed from it: we are imagining that in a sense bridges can be crossed before the actual crossing of them, that doings or sayings or confrontations can exist in a curious stored form before their actual employment, that there are meanings which exist before the meaningful use of words, etc. etc. To talk in this manner is indeed our normal use in talk of 'experience', but it must not be allowed to mislead us: we must not be led to believe in a queer interior school of archery. What really is there internally, in pure lived experience, are at best random feelings, sensations and floating pictures, all given a sense only by the complex real adjustments in which they find themselves.

It is this modern conception of a man's interior life as a rag-bag of irrelevances with which we must join issue, and that because it is utterly destructive, not only of the interior life it professes to sketch, but of the whole world in which it locates this life. For it is not enough that there should *be* such a world in which objects are located and mobile persons and animals encounter them and respond to them, and play language games in relation to them and with one another: it is also necessary that this world should be a world *for* those persons, that it should present itself to them in a shimmering and imperfect, but none the less not wholly piece-meal manner, in other words that they should understand, and see, and in some part be sure, what sort of a world it is. But no amount of confrontation, however privileged and complete, and no amount of response, however well adjusted, can conceivably go the least distance in making a situation objective to a person, in putting it there for him. Even if the response takes the form of a language-game played according to rules, this does nothing to ease the difficulty, since the whole game, and the situation in which it is played, and the parties with whom it is played, lie wholly in an unapparent realm unless the person *grasps* what sort of game is being played, and with whom and in what circumstances. And this grasp permits no analysis in terms of anything done or stationed out there in space, or performed or performable before or after a given point of time, since none of these things has any *locus standi* for a man unless he is himself cognizant of them, grasps that they are (or have been or will be) and what they are. Such a conscious grasp, with whatever imperfections it may be loaded, and whatever confirmation and deepening and supplementation it may crave from subsequent acts of grasping, necessarily exists whole and entire at every moment of its conscious enactment, and if it occupies time, as indeed it does and must, necessarily exists as the conscious grasp it is, *throughout* the time in which it is a lived reality, and whatever changeable shadings it may exhibit during that time. Consciousness is certainly successive in that it brings together what is experienced in moment after moment, but in the admission that it brings such items *together* we concede that it is never merely successive, but that it in a sense knows what it is doing and what it is handling at every point in the process.

We are in fact brought by these reflections to something like a new form of the Cartesian *Cogito*. If Descartes may be regarded as having really argued: The whole world is possibly not, but therefore certainly at least my thought of it is, we now likewise argue: The world of objects, men and language can significantly be said to be, therefore my conscious grasp of these certainly is. And, by a simple transposition, if one doubts whether such a conscious grasp exists, or, what is the same if one tries to reduce it to relations among the things in the world, or among thing-like items in a *soi-disant* mind, then the world and its contents dissolve in the same shambles as a man's interior life. The positions I am taking are strong, and I have no doubt that many will refuse to understand my key-phrases of being-there-for-me, etc. and will interpret them in some naturalistic sense that quite by-passes or blindly presupposes their essential sense. No one, however, who understands a proposition about the world, can really help understanding certain correlated propositions about his understanding of those propositions and can successfully avoid interpreting them in the manner I have gestured at, no matter how much his philosophical prejudices may prompt him to try to do so. I am of course not suggesting that we *always* understand situations in this truly grasping, seeing manner, and that there is not always a vast amount of mere readiness, or mere doing and confronting, surrounding our acts of grasp. What I am saying is that all this mechanical detritus can exist only in the interstices of authentic acts of grasp, and that only because it has this interstitial status can it be rated a part of our conscious life at all. We always glimpse a total scene, though much is not 'filled in' but only blindly reacted to: what is thus blindly reacted to can, however, be rated part of the total conscious scene because it *could* be brought into the living, conscious focus.

Having approached the problem of our intentional conscious

grasp from the standpoint of the realm of objects, I now wish briefly to reverse my approach and to say, though without arguing for it, that there can be nothing in the pointlike concentration of our conscious being, and so frequently counted as a 'feeling', a mere personal modality, that does not also permit of a spelling out, an unpacking, a writing large, in the arrangement and changes of objects, including our own phenomenally central bodies, or in *tendencies* towards such arrangements and changes. There may be much which seems unanalysably qualitative, merely sensational, merely affective, a mere colouring of our interior selfhood, but we adhere to the principle, by no means obvious in its statement, but clear in what we do and say, that each such seeming nuance of quality permits of a use, in a unique and peculiar sense of 'use', to add some shade of difference to the objective tapestry spread out before us and around us, and then also, by a sort of secondary indirection, to attract attention and direct difficult descriptive effort to its more mysterious self. There is, as Husserl expresses it, a *hyle*, a seemingly unformed element in our interior life, which, however, refutes its seeming formlessness by its perpetual use and using up of itself in various *Auffassungen*, or interpretative slants, which in an indirect way bring out all that it is. I am quite persuaded of the truth and the necessity of what I have just been saying, but I am not persuaded of its clarity or persuasiveness: if you wish to forget it, therefore, forget it. If you like to believe in mental 'contents' which in all cases only lend themselves to contingent, external employment as a mere sign or symbol, and are not in some manner intrinsically 'geared' as the wildest image or most nebulous conscious colouring seems geared, to some specific referential use (though capable also of an arbitrary use) you are welcome to believe this. I have enough for my purposes in the concession that whatever is before one as a reality, a fact or a possibility, or even as a non-reality, or a non-fact or an impossibility, points to specific and appropriate goings on in a correlated medium of personal interiority which precisely place whatever is thus intended before one, constitute it for consciousness, give it an apparent or intended status, or however one may wish to state what is thus utterly familiar.

What the purport of my argument has been is to justify the intentionalist view of mind, not as a high-grade quasi-empirical curiosity, discovered by *Wesensschau* rather than the senses, nor as an idle reflection of grammar, but as a difficult view transcendentally necessary to account for the fact that anything is sayable or knowable about the world. The elaborate hierarchy of acts built upon acts or boxed within acts which make Husserl such hard reading to many, are not the results of questionable exercises of extra-sensory perception: they are the underpinnings and bolster-ings necessary to make the world safe for our cognitive references, to make the sciences and, above all, logic and mathematics, possible. This is why Husserl's first two greatest works develop the problems of intentionality in connection with arithmetic and logic, and with the lowest, most commonplace applications of the same. Of course some minds at once smell a rat in all this: to explore a territory by argument seems to them automatically to forfeit any claim to be exploring it realistically. Reality is, on views which stem from Hume, essentially the unarguable, the non-necessary, what hits us in the face and confounds us: if ever it does not confound us, but seems to conform to reasoned expectations, this must be due to habit, linguistic convention or some other similar cause. I, however, believe Hegel's Doctrine of Essence to be a truer account of the world than the radical fac-ticity of certain philosophies, and this means that correlativity and mutual belongingness are part of nature and not merely cases of linguistic reduplication. Things may be expected to prefigure, register or reflect other things, though each in a characteristic medium and manner; there is, e.g. nothing absurd in locating the effect dispositionally in the cause, or the object intentionally in the thought.

Having established intentionality as fundamental and categorial, I now proceed to consider three aspects of it, that together define its peculiar mode of working. The first is that an intention is so little a mere reflection of what it intends or is 'of', that it may completely fail of its precise target, or indeed of any target, without thereby ceasing to be the peculiar sort of intention that it is, aimed and directed at the precise sort of object and situation at which it is directed. This aspect of intentionality has of course received the classical notice of Brentano, and is embodied in his doctrine that intentions are not relations but relationlike, since they do not presuppose the reality or being of their objects, but only at best of their personal subjects, whereas a relation can only be said to subsist when all its terms are given. One may very well doubt whether Brentano was right in placing all cases of this unilateral relationality in the realm of the mental: one would have thought that the causal dispositions we all attribute to natural objects involve a one-sided relation to what does not, and may never, exist, and that this one-sided relation is not to be explicated in terms of *our* subjective expectations: one would have thought, likewise, that the characteristic 'pasts' which objects trail after them, as a sort of ballast, involved a relation to what no longer is there, and which does not need to be explicated subjectively in the manner of Augustine. But, be that as it may, it is of the essence of the correlativity of conscious intentions with their objects, that, while it must be possible to conceive of something as being that of which they are, it is not necessary to conceive of anything *actual* which fits them, nor even of anything actual that *could* fit them. We must, in other words, always *be able* to specify the sort of thing or situation our mental grasp is of, without necessarily being able to take this sort of thing out of its object-position, its 'intentional brackets' and thereby make it a logical subject of predications. Intentional possibility is, if we may so phrase it, not the same as possibility *tout court*, the possibility of being or of being the case. Husserl here draws a distinction between *das eigentliche* and *das uneigentliche Denken* and does not thereby imply that *das uneigentliche Denken* is not *eigentlich* a case of *Denken*. It is *eigentlich* a case of *Denken*, of thinking, which is of its appropriate object, but it is also impossible, and not merely a matter of fact, that what it intends should function as a genuine logical subject, and have true or false predications made of it. There is not and cannot be any such thing as it intends, but one can none the less intend it. It is the privilege of mind, we may say, that it can raise, *as it were* or 'in brackets', a novel creation, that it can intend what cannot be taken out of such intentional brackets, what in fact is not or what perhaps cannot be. One may say, further, that this privilege is involved in all of our discourse. Thus the mystery of the verb 'to exist' lies in the fact that its basic force is doubly negative: it removes the intentional brackets which threaten to remove some object of simple intention from the field of our simple references, and so critically reinstates that object in this field with an added endorsement or certification. It is plain, likewise, that all negations, at least in their first inception, involve the bracketing of a positive reference, in the face of some situation that it fails to fit. And the notion of the impossible, which it is the whole aim of logic to fence off and hold apart from sanctioned discourse, involves precisely a privileged, *uneigentliche* ranging beyond the bounds of possibility, even if only in uncashed symbols, without which logic would have nothing to check. If logical truths, with their exclusion of impossibilities, are allowed a place in discourse, it is only because impossibilities have already preempted a similar place.

One's excitement over the possibility of intending the non-existent or the impossible, must not, however, be allowed to seduce one into the notion that it is impossible to intend anything else. For this is of course what is involved in all accounts which create a cleavage between intentional objects, objects of thought, and real objects, and make the one merely 'correspond' to the other, ignoring the fact that this is to turn intentional objects or objects of thought into a queer sub-species of real objects, and so to destroy the meaning of the word 'real' and its many equivalents. It is as possible, in general, that when I direct my thought to a so-and-so, or to the circumstance that a so-and-so should be such-and-such, what I intend should be the true target that in uncritical moments I necessarily take it to be, as that, when I thus direct my thought, its object should *not* be the true target that I take it for. And we may go further and say that it is part of the teleology involved in thinking, that the hitting of an authentic target should be no fortuitous, no abnormal occurrence, but the natural outcome of all intending. It is being off the mark that is abnormal: it is part of what we understand by the thinking upon objects that such thinking may progressively be corrected in a manner which suits the objects thought of, until in the end it is only by a confusion that we can draw a sceptical distinction between the object as it is given to us and the object as it truly or in itself is. *Selbstgegebenheit* is, as Husserl maintains, the necessary terminus of directed thought, without which it would not really have an object or a direction at all, and this is so even if in some fields such *Selbstgegebenheit* is rather an appearance on the horizon than anything actually reachable. The certitude which characterizes knowledge *par excellence* is not to be thought of in terms of some external certification which would require further certification without end: it lies rather in the steady vanishing of all grounds of doubt, until one really has the thing itself given as it itself is. Then the thing itself becomes the phenomenon, phenomenology becomes metaphysics, and the account of things as they are for consciousness becomes also the account of them as they without qualification are.

There is also a readily forgotten third aspect of intentionality: not only may there be intentions which hit their target or which fail to hit their target, but there may also be targets which intentions do not hit, and do not even perhaps try to hit. Not only error is contrary to knowledge and truth, but also ignorance. And intentions will differ according to the degree and content of their ignorance, or, what is the same thing otherwise put, the completeness and definiteness with which they envisage their object, and the precise angles or respects from which they envisage it. It is part of what we mean by the thought of an object that in it the object should only be intended in a more or less one-sided and incomplete manner, and there should be an infinity of other one-sided approaches through which such one-sidedness can be remedied and after a fashion eliminated.

Having enumerated these three *Selbstverständlichkeiten* of intentionality or mental reference to objects, I shall now go on to turn these very points of obviousness into points of difficulty; they are respects in which the self-evident is always ready to swing over into the incredible and the self-contradictory. I shall evoke this difficult, nigh-contradictory side of intentionality by considering three ways in which we may regard it, all of which seem to me part and parcel of its notion. We can consider it (in the first place) purely immanently, as it is for the person to whom it is a lived experience, or to those who enter with total sympathy into his condition. We can enter, as it were, into the brackets of a man's intentional cage, and see what there is to see from its vantage-point, without thinking of it *as* an intentional cage endowed with anything like a special, perhaps delusive point of view. To do this is to practise a partial ἐποχή or suspension of external criticism which removes any bracketing 'He thinks that . . .' from the total world as he sees it, though it does not, of course, remove any bracketings which occur *in* this total world: to remove these would be to arrive at an experience in which nothing was given as possibly delusive or erroneous, an experience remote from any we know, which would permit only of augmentation or supplementation but not of correction. We can, in the second place, consider it purely 'from the outside', in which case it will display many extraordinary aspects which though called 'phenomenological' in some treatments are yet infinitely far from anything immediately given or apparent. Husserl has developed much of this outside logic in his complex theory of mental acts, which

for most lovers of the appearances bristles with barbarous techni-
cality, and Frege, Church and many others have considered it
from the standpoint of linguistic expression, informing us, e.g.
that the phrase 'The concept Horse' does not express a concept.
We can in the third place stand hesitantly in the doorway of the
intentional cage, seeing the world as it appears from its vantage-
point and yet continuing to evaluate that vision from an outside
critical standpoint. It is this third half-and-half standpoint that
inspires most talk of intentional objects, and which erects them
into strange intermediates not unlike the Platonic objects of
δόξα, between objects proper and mere nothingness, at one time
fading out into and losing themselves in objects proper, while at
other times they maintain an obdurate, if phantasmal, identity.
It is this third way of conceiving intentionality that has all the
truth and the life, while also being ever fruitful of antinomy and
contradiction unless most carefully hedged about with restrictions.
For those who are not concerned to work out the implications of
notions in a finished deductive system, there may be a connection
between the antinomies and the contradictions, on the one hand,
and the truth and the life on the other.

Let us, however, develop the appearances that confront us
from each of our three standpoints. Let us suppose, first of all
that we genuinely try to enter what I have called someone's
intentional cage, that someone being either a real or a hypothetical
person, and being either ourselves in some past or future or
imagined phase, or some totally different person. In so doing, as
we have said, we must suspend all external criticism, though not
the internal criticism proper to the intentional cage we are entering. Entering, then, into any actual or hypothetical person's
intentional cage, and ignoring for the moment any objects that
he surrounds with critical brackets, either in full seriousness
or with some question, the remainder of his field of objects permits
no diremption into objects that are there for him and objects that
simply are there. Even if some of the objects and situations in
his field are, for a critical outside vision, quite delusive or mis-
takenly conceived, they are still for him completely on a level with
those members of his field which a critical outside judgement
would endorse: we have the standing paradox of the completely
solid-seeming, mundane character of the most insane, ill-founded,
even self-contradictory objects and situations. In this situation
the Anglo-Saxon mind longs to demand a certificate of critical

exemption for what is sensibly rather than cogitatively given, but it does not seem that even this exemption can be granted. What is sensibly given may, despite the shock this notion gives to empiricists, be logically unthinkable—it is arguable for instance that stereoscopic vision and many other types of sense-experience present the logically unthinkable—and yet it may be part of the solid world around us. From the standpoint of the uncritical segment of a man's intentional field there is therefore no problem of the status of intentional objects: they melt without distinction into the population of objects *simpliciter*, they do not inhabit a separate ethnic ghetto or territory.

Let us now take up the opposed stance and place ourselves completely outside of a man's intentional cage, not troubling to enter into his intentional references, but living entirely in our own. The uncriticized portion of our own intentional field will then appear as consisting of objects and situations *simpliciter*: it will in other words represent a somewhat redundantly styled 'reality'. There will, however, still have to be a representation of another man's intentionality in this critical, outside perspective, though it will not be one in which the status of intentional objects will need to trouble us. For if in the previous immanent presentation they were exalted to something like full-blooded being, they will now be demoted to complete nothingness. A man's references will have to be conceived 'existentially', i.e. entirely in terms of the resources and materials in the uncriticized segment of our own field, and it is plain that they will have to be conceived in terms of a manipulation or binding together of real elements of some sort, linked by identity or some intrinsic or extrinsic link with elements in the object or situation intended, and involving further the precarious and treacherous notion of the 'as-if', the elements being connected *as if* a certain immediate or remote object or situation existed or obtained, whether it does so or not. The elements in question may be of the most varied sort: they may be pictorial images tied by dispositional, associative links to certain unbracketed situations, they may be verbal signs or symbols similarly tied and occurring in overt or silent discourse, they may be neural excitations or reactivations of traces, they may be rudiments of muscular response causally linked to the appropriate objects or situations, or they may be the natural signs or intentional species of scholasticism or the more or less redundant 'contents' of Meinong and 'act-matters' of Husserl or the unvarnished particulars and dirempted universals of Russell's theory of judgement, recently reformulated and defended by Geach. It is plain, I think, that all these as-if devices banish the problems of intentionality and leave us with an aseptic world, in which there are many beings rather perversely acting and feeling as if there were many things in the world that are not really in it. The trouble with the treacherous notion of as-if is of course in the first place that it fails to do justice to the cemented integrity and real presence of what we intend: Othello was not disturbed by an as-if, thought-connection between his wife and Cassio, but by something indistinguishable from a real connection and of the precise sort that he found so damnable. And by the very nature of an as-if connection, it permits no certain inference from the elements which in their combination mediate intentionality and the objects intended by their means, the combination in question being as possible when these objects are and are not there. And as we have seen, if a man critically applies such an analysis to himself, and not merely to others, it destroys the world in which he and others and all objects are comprehended, since this world has to be there *for him* and not merely *simpliciter*, and this being there for him must now in consistency be reduced to assemblages of muscle-twitches, images, words, loose universals and what not. So that to remain resolutely outside of all intentional brackets, as counselled in certain forms of objective naturalism or metaphysics is in the end to liquidate the world and its contents.

What then is the remaining stance we may take which alone casts a difficult illumination on the scene before us? It is the alternative of constantly confounding and mixing categories, as they are in reality and experience livingly mixed; it is the alternative of constantly entering intentional cages and seeing things as they appear within them and yet constantly going outside of those cages and *comparing* what one has seen with a totally different outside vision, a comparison of things as indistinguishably like in one regard as they are categorially unlike in another. Antinomies and absurdities are ready to jump out at every step, and can only be coped with by very subtle formulae, yet it is only by continuing to face and cope with such antinomies that one can master the shimmering, ever reduplicated and multiply refracted structure of the world. Intentional objects must be in fact treated rather as phantoms are treated in ghost-stories, as things which are and are not, which have some but not all the defining features of fully real objects, which appear solidly where they should not be and vanish into thin air or simply lose themselves in ordinary objects when the occasion warrants, which have not merely to be dealt with but even talked of in a very propitiatory manner. An intentional object can be said to be, and in some sense to form part of the 'furniture of earth', yet we must always remember to add that it can only be there in the special sense in which to be is to be conceived: it cannot be said to be there *simpliciter*. An intentional object, an object as it is conceived, can undoubtedly be described, but we must always propitiate it or propitiate reality by adding that it is describable in a special sense of description, in which we say how it is conceived of as being, and not *simpliciter* what it is like. And as is well known the description ends abruptly after a number of steps: we cannot say what song the sirens sang or whether their tresses were golden or not. An intentional object can likewise be identified with a real object, it can stand in a relation of *Deckung*, of coincidence with the latter, for what is plainer than that the brother I am now thinking of is my real brother, and not some separated duplicate which exists only in my mind. Yet my identification of the two is not an identification in the sense in which London is identical with Londinium, since my brother *as* I think of him is not properly my brother. My brother as I think of him is in fact not properly an actual object and can be identical with no actual object except in an entirely special sense of identity, which has of course the special peculiarity of evading Leibniz's Law, so that only *some* of the things predicable of the real object can be predicated of the intentional object that is 'identified' with it. Thus there are countless things truly predicable of my brother as he exists in nature which cannot in the special sense of predication appropriate to intentional objects be predicated of my brother as he is for me, or indeed for any human being. An intentional object's being what it is, in the sense in which it can be anything, has likewise only *such* of the logical implications which the mind which entertained the intentional object would be capable of seeing it to have: it is not characterizable in the ways in which (perhaps *per impossibile*) a real object would have to be characterized. Thus a cube as thought of by most unschooled persons would not either 'have' or 'not have' twelve edges: as thought of by me, who have often used it as an example, it 'has' twelve edges. I can on occasion legitimately compare intentional with real objects, in a peculiar sense of 'comparison', as when I say that more people came to the party than the host expected, or that Napoleon was a more impressive person than Tolstoy pictured him as being in *War and Peace*, but I cannot push such 'comparisons' further than the intentional object itself permits: thus I cannot ask whether more women came to the party than the host expected since he may have formed no expectation as to the number of his women guests. And as to their location intentional objects are strangely ambiguous: they are, on the one hand, appropriately located at the time and place where the man who conceives them or conceives of real objects through them, is located, and perhaps bear evidences of this location, thus giving rise to the seeming problem as to how they can be separated from what is in a suitable sense identical with them, and they may with equal propriety be located where and when the real object with which they coincide is located, so that we then have the seeming problem as to how what we intend, which enters into the intimate description of our thoughts, can be so very far away from us. They are and are not what a man thinks of when he thinks: they are what he thinks of in the special sense that they are *as what* he thinks something as being, and it is not possible to think of anything if one does not think of it as something or other, but again they are not what he thinks of, inasmuch as the latter are thought of as being much more than and perhaps other than *as what* he thinks them or ever can think them. We have a position not unlike that of individuals in the Aristotelian metaphysic where *what* they essentially are is not the individuals themselves. It is plain that if one does not carefully mind what one says, one will slip into overt contradiction, and this is almost inevitable if one makes intentional objects subjects of predication, as has been done in the whole above treatment, instead of leaving them in the object-place in discourse which alone assorts with their condition.

It is then indeed possible, by a vast amount of poised tight-rope walking, as strained and unnatural as the abyss of nonsense which it avoids, to talk in a philosophically acceptable manner about intentional inexistence and intentional objects. And ordinary talk, which simply turns its back on uncomfortable self-contradictory implications, finds its both possible and natural to deal with them. The work of philosophy is not, however, done when one has avoided overt absurdity: it is only done when one has ceased to talk in a strained way about ordinary facts, or when, what is the same, one has reduced their immense improbability, and explained how, in Kant's phrase, they are 'possible'. The devices employed by philosophers to show how certain things are possible—how it is possible to know anything, how the mind can influence the body, how universals can be present in their instances and so on—may not always have reflected credit on their devisers, and para-mechanical, anthropomorphic, preformationist, *ad hoc* and *ex machina* and other like hypotheses may have suggested that many of such theories are at best only pseudo-solutions of pseudo-problems. But as long as this last solution itself fails to cure the questions it explains, and remains as obscure as they are, we shall continue to ask the questions in question. Intentionality certainly raises as many deep how-questions as any other of our fundamental concepts, but perhaps its central difficulty may be phrased in the question how, without really including an object, and without merely blindly tending towards it and without being at all like it, but in fact differing from it in category, and without being close to it in space or time or in other respects, a state of mind can none the less so unambiguously and intimately be *of* a certain object that it is impossible to describe it adequately without mentioning the object in question. It is always the things themselves that we mind, and this is an essential part of our mindedness, our *Zumute-sein*, and yet we mind them without needing to take them down from the high ontological shelves on which they are placed. How can mind be thus 'ecstatic', thus self-transcendent, we are inclined to ask, and it does not seem a sufficient answer at a sufficiently deep level of reflection to say that such ecstasy, such self-tran-scendence, is the very mark of the mental. There can be no doubt that these difficulties do not cease to haunt us even if the devices used to deal with them have been spurious and senseless. Inten-tional species, representative ideas, adjusted behaviour, inten-tional acts themselves, perhaps all these represent such spurious devices, which generate more difficulty than they remove. But we still feel the gnawing of a metaphysical gadfly which cannot be made to hold off by the bland assertion, unquestionable in its truth, that we are not even clear *what form* a truly appeasing solution would take. Perhaps we shall learn to look for a truly appeasing solution in the right manner when we recognize that it does not lie in any familiar, obvious direction, that it will have to be as strange and unique as the metaphysical anguish it appeases.

It is here that I shall bring into the picture something that I shall call 'unitive logic', which I believe to represent an essential technique in philosophy, though valuable only when it is used to round off and crown other philosophical methods. Such unitive logic may be vaguely characterized as directing our thought to an horizon where oppositions melt into coincidences, where identity prevails over difference, and where the 'moment' or aspect replaces the part or element. It appears in limited contexts in the thought of many, perhaps most, philosophers, but it is pervasively operative in the Logic of Hegel, and exaggeratedly present in what may be called the logic of mystical discourse. Acting alone, it can be merely a disruptive, confusing, self-contradictory force, but it is also capable of being a force which rounds off and makes intelligible rather than disrupts. It is in this latter light that I wish to present it on this occasion. For I am persuaded, to modify a metaphor used by William James, that the free water of unitive thought always surrounds the clear-cut pluralisms of our ordinary thought-procedures, and that the products of all these procedures are necessarily steeped and dyed in this free water. And I also believe that our endless philosophical puzzles bear no lamentable witness to linguistic abuse and confusion, but to our sense of the surrounding unity which our thought-procedures require although they often so desperately fight against it.

I shall present this unitive logic in the form in which it appears in Hegelianism, in which it is less controversially transcendent than it is in the out-and-out version of mysticism. Hegel thinks that the truth is the whole, and by this he does not mean, as many have thought that he means, that the elements of the real cohere in a single closely knit fabric, but rather that what is real has and can have no true elements, no sheerly diverse constituents, but that each so-called element we try to distinguish in it *is* the whole in one of its specially stressed phases, and that it includes all the other phases in a less stressed or implicit manner. As the morning star despite the time and place of its occurrence really *is* the evening star, so everything despite its far-flung dispersion always is and must be everything, and otherness, diversity, impenetrable atomicity and so forth are the limiting notions representing the sheerly impossible, the self-destroying nullity, which may be approached but which can be never reached. (Not that such notions have not a proper application in the sphere of the purely abstract.) Hegelian logic does not, however, wish to substitute an empty, blank identity for the sheer otherness it rates as absurd: it treats the former as being quite as absurd and self-contradictory as the latter. The ultimate unity of things can only be the unity it is, by both asserting itself in emphases which go as far as may be in the direction of disjoined independence, and then turning back on its tracks and breaking down this approach to disjoined independence, by making the as-it-were disjoined elements pass into one another and so refute their seeming separateness, or by making them all dissolve into a more explicit unity, which none the less only is the solvent unity it is in virtue of the quasi-separate elements that have entered into it. And this process of quasi-separateness passing over into solvent unity takes place both timelessly on the plane of pure notions, and also on the plane of existence in time. On the former plane we pass from descriptive and explanatory categories in which loose plurality and dualistic correlativity are prominent, to categories which embody more of many-sided, mindlike unity: on the latter plane we pass from dispersed individual existence in space and time to formations involving ever more concentrated unity and mutual inseparability of factors, until in the living organism Nature's half-hearted attempts at diremption all break down, to pass on to a still more complete break-down in the interpenetration and fusion of the life of mind. In such a logic, it is not an empirical accident that minds arise in the world: minds represent, we may say, the world's deep unity asserting itself over the world's attempted dispersion, an attempted dispersion as essential to the deep unity as the latter is essential to the former. And from this point of view the mysteries of intentionality cease to be mysterious: it is not at all remarkable that the special phases in which the world's unity is most emphatic should bring into one focus, in the guise of intentional inexistence, the whole gamut of phases in which the attempt at independent diversity has been most determined. This does not of course mean that there are not many contexts in which it is proper and expedient to say that we or anything are *not* everything, just as there are contexts in which it is important to separate Venus the Evening Star from Venus the Morning Star. But the sort of sheerly exclusive individuality which we try to reach when we speak of something and something *else*, is the one heroically interesting but also tragic casualty in the unitive logic we are studying. Intentionality is the truth, to copy a somewhat different phrase of Hegel's, that such exclusive individuality, whether of minds or objects, in relation to the others or among themselves, has no truth. But the lie must be asserted, must almost become the truth, in order that it may be conclusively denied.

After the stiff dose of unitive logic that I have been administering, some of you will cavil at the still stiffer dose of it that I am now going to administer. It consists in taking seriously the claims of various mystical writers, Neoplatonic, Vedantic, Mahayanist, and Contemplative-Christian, that there is and must be a whole spectrum of spiritual states varying from those of our normal waking earth-life to a state in which sensuous individuality is attenuated to vanishing point, in which the outsideness of time and space collapses into unity, in which personal separateness becomes a mere gesture, and in which the subject-object distinction becomes largely a matter of courtesy, the mind's notional grasp of something becoming only vacuously different from the varied self-display of the thing. These things are implicit in the residua of Platonism to be found in Aristotle's philosophy of passive and active mind, but their fullest, most gorgeous statement is to be found in the *Enneads* of Plotinus. 'Each thing holds all within itself, and again sees all in each other thing, so that everything is everywhere and all is all, and each all, and the glory infinite. One thing stands forth in each, though it also displays all.' It is this kind of vision which I believe to be, not the product of psychedelic confusion, but the necessary complement to the gulfs and diremptions and separatenesses of our ordinary experience, with their endless generation of philosophical puzzles. Our ordinary language and experience is not to be rejected—it is as necessary to the unitive vision as the latter is necessary to it. But it is not fully understandable except in the light of a language and an experience more explicitly unitive.

XV

TOWARDS A NEO-NEO-PLATONISM

The paper I am about to give requires some explanation: it does not propose to add to the mountain of scholarly comment on Platonism or Neo-Platonism, a mountain growing at every moment, in a manner as emptily threatening as the population of the world. Scholarly comment is excellent when directed to thought that is philosophically important by those capable of truly entering into it: it is idle and pernicious when directed to thought that is no longer a live option, or which is not capable of being made such by the philosophical commentator. Plato, if studied as a man monumentally mistaken, and taken in by verbal deceits from which he was only in later life partially recovering, and studied, moreover by methods and on assumptions of which he would not have had the faintest understanding, is a Plato not worth studying, nor do such studies of him deserve philosophical attention. Plotinus and Proclus, likewise, studied as mere elaborators and embroiderers of middle-period Platonism, who may have had a fortunate or unfortunate influence on Christian theology, are likewise no fit object of philosophical attention, except, perhaps, as part of a 'history of ideas'. My paper is based on a life-time study of Platonic and Neo-Platonic texts, and of Aristotle's writings on Platonism, read in the original, but whatever value it may have rests solely on its capacity to enter into what may be called the 'message' of these texts, and to make of this a 'live', and indeed a contemporary, option. With this goes an inevitable tendency to pass beyond them at certain points, or to practise a speculative 'filling-in' of them, a tendency never experienced by those to whom they are irrevocably dead.

I may say that in speaking of a 'Neo-neo-Platonism' I wish to imply both that Plotinus and Proclus understood Plato very deeply, far more deeply, in fact, than those who erect their own incapacity for system and their horror of mysticism and metaphysics into philosophical virtues. I wish to suggest that a profitable reading of Platonism is one that may criticize, but which will never fail to consider, their interpretations, which in my view erred, not so much by adding mystical touches to Platonism, as by an unmystical hardening and freezing of its outlines, so that Proclus's *Elements of Theology* reads like, and has even been admiringly compared to, a treatise on Set-theory. And my own attempts at a deepening reinterpretation of Platonism and Neo-platonism will take the form, not only of relaxing this hardness, but also of certain borrowings from Hegel, borrowings which are not so absurd when we reflect that Hegel professed to have found all the secrets of his dialectic in Plato's *Parmenides*, and that he devoted almost as much space to the Neoplatonists in his *Lectures on the History of Philosophy* as he did to Plato and Aristotle. Hegel as a thinker may have been born in the dark forests of German subjectivism, but by the turn of the century he had advanced, we may say, into Attic sunlight, the Idea, with its impersonal Hellenism, having taken over the functions of the Transcendental Ego or other forms of involuted Germanic interior self.

I may say, further, to conclude this introduction, that I shall not hesitate to be dogmatic and also to show prejudice. I shall be dogmatic because, while everything I say could be documented, such documentation would not persuade those who are determined to see only a reflection of their own nullity in the shining works of antiquity. And I shall be prejudiced, even to the extent of using abusive metaphors, since the best way to bring home the sense and worth of Platonism and Neoplatonism is to pit it against such inadequate types of thought as Aristotelian individualism, Germanic subjectivism, Semitic-Protestant theology, let alone extreme empiricism and certain forms of atomistic analysis. This is after all only what Plato himself did when he showed up Protagoras in the *Theaetetus*. But I am not really as prejudiced and as committed as I shall appear to be for the purposes of this paper. I hope by my efforts to put you into a metaphysical posture into which few genuinely enter, and by so doing to make clear what sort of thing such a metaphysical posture really is, and what profit and illumination we may hope to find by putting ourselves into it. By so doing I hope to make a worthwhile contribution to the theme of this conference.

I may say, first of all, that the sort of metaphysic I am interested in, for the purposes of this paper, is what has been called a *revisionary*, as opposed to a merely descriptive metaphysic, one that proposes to consider the pattern of categories and categorial commitments in terms of which the round of being *ought* to be envisaged, and can with most profit and illumination be envisaged, rather than that in terms of which it is actually envisaged, and which for some is embalmed in the most ordinary use of our words. I do not myself believe that there is any firm scheme of ultimate philosophical categories and principles to be discovered in what we unthinkingly say, or in the makeshift procedures by which we were taught the use of our terms. What we *really* think when we say things, and what was really put across when we were taught to say things, comes out only in our thinking, considered use of terms, when the stream of immediate idiom suffers an arrest, as it readily does even in the case of quite ordinary speakers, and when the hesitations and gropings latent in all our utterances and in all teaching are allowed to come to the surface. Ordinary usage suffices to pin concepts down and to put them on the table for scrutiny, but it is only when discomfort and puzzlement have done their modifying work, that anything like an acceptable system of categories or rules can emerge. That firm categories and commitments and 'criteria' can be found by examining unthinking usage is a view which unthinking usage itself disdains: it is a philosophical rather than an ordinary opinion, and its actual fruits, the multiplication rather than the removal of difficulties, have shown it up as misguided. And it is even more misguided from a point of view like our own which believes that only *very deeply* reflected on modes of speech and thought can claim 'correctness' in any truly significant sense, just as only deeply pondered and deliberated lines of action and decision can claim to be right or wrong. I shall not waste my time or yours pitting myself against a waning fashion: the categories and categorial commitments that we ought to accept are not those that we do, even after some thinking, accept, and much less are they those that are to be collected from an examination of surface-usage and of surface teaching-devices. They are such as have, when we try them out, a certain deep illumination, which is not only superior to that of surface-speech but also to that of many alternative forms of considered speech and conception. What the criteria of such deep illumination may be is of course a matter that can and should be considered, and it is one that I myself have fairly often written and spoken about from the standpoint of 'logical values'. I shall not, however, discuss this matter on this occasion, but rather consider a special case of illumination. I shall assume that we all know an illuminating conceptual realignment when we encounter it, even though we cannot always pin down the criteria for such illumination.

What then is the immense revisionary re-appraisal which distinguishes a Platonic categorization of the world from an ordinary one? We do not give the right answer if we say with Aristotle, who was probably excluded from the inner Platonic assemblies and who was certainly incapable of a full entry into Platonic thought, that it consists in setting up *beside* the things that we ordinarily acknowledge *another* set of supposedly explanatory or causative entities which merely add to the number of what we originally had, and do not make them more countable or otherwise easier to deal with. This is utterly wrong since the precise point of Platonism is that one does *not* leave undisturbed the ontological claim of the ordinary things of this world but dissolves it entirely, since it regards the so-called things in the world as things only in a qualified, derivative sense, while the only true things in the world, the only things that truly are or can be, are natures or characters such as being alive, being just, being equal, and so forth. To the ordinary or the Aristotelian mind these natures or characters are things parasitic upon the individual things that exemplify them or instantiate them, they exist *in* the latter or are descriptive *of* them, while the individual things have no such dependence upon these natures or characters, but simply include them as their appanages. To Platonism, however, this ordinary view of things is completely misguided: it is the things of ordinary experience which are in truth parasitic upon the true things or forms, and which are merely the multitudinous reflections or instantiations of these true things and nothing in themselves at all. We must learn a new talk in which 'being just' and 'the just itself' are the truly substantival locutions while expressions of instantiation here or there, or now or then, merely qualify or modify such substantival locutions. And we must learn a new self-predication of such truly substantival locutions which gives rise to no difficulties as long as it is not confused with the old predication which is merely the converse of instantiation. The inversion we are describing is abundantly spelled out in the *Republic*, *Timaeus* and elsewhere, but never really got through to Aristotle, though it sufficed to make him a tortured dualist, one who believes in ordinary individual things and *also* in species or natures which in a paradoxical manner tell us *what* these individuals are—one would have thought that the plain answer to the question what they are is that they are these or those individuals— and by buttressing his half-held individualism by rejecting at least the *generic* universals to which Plato had given the same status as the specific ones. And the *other* categories of quality, quantity, etc. are then all with satisfaction declared to be parasitic upon being in the primary sense, whether this last be that of the species or the individual. In this tortured ontology, which is rather a long worry than a definitive doctrine, we have strong indirect support for the basic positions of Platonism.

The basic strength of Platonism lies, however, in its appeal to our imagination, our understanding and our sense of values. It appeals to our imagination since it recalls us from the dull identification of objects and the dull recognition of them as being thus and thus circumstanced, to the more colourful, immersed entry into their character and situation, which is in a sense the background possibility that identification and factual determination presuppose. It is by the generic content of our references and assertions that they manage to hit targets, and such content is soon seen to be a more interesting and fundamental thing than the dull targets that it enables us to hit or the mere fact of hitting them. Nothing is more insignificant than who or what a thing or person is and whether or not it or he is really thus or thus circumstanced, though it is of the most immense concern to all but the grossest dullard *what it is* to be this or that sort of thing or to be thus or thus circumstanced. Our understanding likewise speedily moves to the insight that while we may be inclined to look in the direction of particular embodiment for a paradigm of what is, we soon find that we cannot successfully pin down such particularity in its purity, or identify *it* in varying contexts and occasions. All that is substantial, invariant in it is a pattern, a character, a set of suches which we hail and name on every occasion of their appearance. This character or pattern is all that we can grasp and handle in thought on many occasions, and introduce to and consider with others: the existence of an individual seems to be no more than the fact that certain identifiable, recognizable universals are instantiated and reinstantiated. The identity of such universals, so far from being a derivative, metaphorical sort of identity resting on resemblance or what not, reveals itself as in truth the paradigmatic sense of identity, to which all other senses of identity merely add complications or overtones. Only by practising the Platonic inversion can we justify science and scientific knowledge, which would be quite impossible if we had to plumb individuals exhaustively, or to make illegitimate extensions of what was true of them to other individuals similarly qualified. Our sense of values, moreover, as pervasively present in the intellectual as in any other sphere, makes us feel that what is standard, graspable, light-giving, directive, is not any and every mixed state or condition but only certain privileged sorts of state or condition, which stand out from others, and about which and between which other unprivileged states or conditions cluster and have their nearer or further place. The intelligible world is rendered intelligible by certain *prime* universals from which other universals *derive* their intelligibility. Equality as such is such a prime universal from which unlimited possibilities of greaterness and smallerness are divergent, being a whole number would be such a prime universal which further specifies itself in the countless precise numbers between which lie all the less savoury possibilities of fractional divisibility whether rational or irrational, and justice or right dealing is likewise such a prime universal from which the infinite forms of the devious, the inequitable, and the shifty make their departure. (Our examples are, of course, Platonizing rather than textually Platonic.) And the prime intelligible states are thinly distributed and of some specially marked out type as opposed to the unnumbered states which lie between them or which deviate from them, and over which they give us intellectual or moral mastery. There is good ground, then, for inverting the normal individualistic view and for making so-called individuals, with all their deviant specificity, into mere variations upon standard patterns, parasitic on standard patterns as the latter have wrongly been thought to be parasitic on them. They are the roughage, the barnacles that a Form accumulates in the process of instantiation. Forms in Platonism are then no more a luxurious duplication of being than individual substances are a luxurious duplication in the metaphysic of Aristotle. In the latter metaphysic qualities, relations, times, places, etc. have being only in the secondary sense of being how, towards what, when, where, etc. primary substance is: in the Platonic metaphysic so called individuals only have being as localized manifestations or near-manifestations of universals. The substance, the οὐσία, of the world, does not then lie in shadowy instantiations, but in the fixed, definite, changeless essences by which the shadows are cast, and of which they are merely the projections. That we give proper names to such projections does not make them into proper entities.

The ontology of Platonism is therefore an ontology of a thinly spread system of prime patterns, with a less confidently accepted set of interstitial patterns which deviate from these first and which are held in place by them. But to be a true ontology it must somehow include the half-being of the Forms' instantiations in the Forms' own being, and not merely place the latter alongside of and outside the former. They must depend on the Forms, be outlying appendages and offshoots of formal natures, they must in no sense be there independently or as of full right: to hold otherwise would be to Aristotelize both Forms and instances. We here see the meaning of a doctrine darkly obscure to Aristotle and to most modern commentators: the doctrine of the causality of the Forms. In an individualist ontology it is the merest confusion to ascribe some character of an individual to an independent, paradigmatic source: as Aristotle remarks, someone *like* Socrates could come into existence whether Socrates existed or not. But in a Platonist ontology instances of φ-ness are parasitic upon φ-ness itself, and it is only because there is a φ-ness itself that there can be localized sharings in it. It might be thought, and rightly thought, on Platonist principles, that this involves the being, in some sense of 'being', of a universal recipient of instantiation, a repertory of 'places', in which instantiations can take place, and be in a sense 'individuated'. Such a repertory is of course provided by the universal recipient, the enigmatically conceived Space of the *Timaeus*. But the *Timaeus* talks enigmatically about this recipient because it wishes to avoid giving full-scale ontological status to it: the recipient is even less real than the form-copies which flit in and out of it and which it seems to individuate. The recipient is in fact no more than a name for the multiple instantiability, the variously localized manifestability of the Forms, and this, it may be held, is of the Forms' essence, even if outlyingly so; it is a side, an aspect of the being of the Forms themselves. So much is this deeply accepted, that talk of Form-copies as entities distinct from Forms is comparatively rare in Plato: it is Proclus who first separates the unparticipated Form from its participated instance. Plato adheres in the main to a doctrine of 'real presence': it is the Form *itself* which is present in its participants, and which makes them what we recognize them to be. And we may hold that the first part of the brilliant argument of the *Parmenides* is nothing but a warning against treating the instantiations of Forms as truly separate entities which have it in their power to rend apart the Forms of which they are the dispersed 'presences'. Multiplicity of 'presence' and diversity of location of the same 'presence' are, we may say, part and parcel of what it is to be a Form, its extensional as opposed to its inner, intensional aspect: in neither case do we have to recognize genuine entities other than Forms. And a Form's genuine self-predication or being itself, while being in a sense the paradigmatic source of its connection with self in its instances, is none the less to be distinguished from the latter, and so will not give rise to an infinite regress. So much we may opine is to be understood by the doctrine of the Forms as causes: their instantiation is after a fashion an outlying phase of their being. And if it is still felt that there is something merely metaphorical about this doctrine, then we may remember that the Forms specify the Good, and that the Good is said, in more than one well-known passage, to lie behind the being and structure of the world of becoming, a doctrine also expounded, with much mythic detail, in the *Timaeus*. All this shows how seriously Plato took his formalist ontology, and how dynamic a role he gave to his Forms. If the Forms are the only things that there ultimately are, then whatever is done or undergone must in the last resort be done or undergone by *them*.

The Platonic ontology of course not only extends downwards from Forms to their instances: it also extends upwards from Forms to their supreme source. Distinct Forms are plainly specifications of Forms more generic, and generic Forms all specify a final transcendental Form of Unity of Goodness which is not so much a specific Form as Formality or the Formal Status as such. Plato does not consider all the complications which might stem from the fact that Forms, though in some sense all falling under one ultimate super-Form might none the less specify it in quite different *ways*, and so differ radically in category, and make differing contributions to the whole notional economy. Nor does he fully elucidate the 'dialectic' by means of which the architecture of the world of Forms must undoubtedly be established. It seems plain, however, that at a fairly early stage in his thought, this dialectic took the form of a preliminary mathematicization or Pythagoreanization of all the types and characters of things, and a subsequent properly dialectical attempt to show all these mathematical differentiations to be the deducible specifications of the principle of Unity or Goodness itself. The first phase was dianoetic or mathematical, and in some way involved the reduction of all qualitative distinctions, including those of psychology and ethics, to relations and proportions of numbers: the second stage, the properly dialectical, was to provide a complete *philosophy* of all these numbers and relations of numbers. As regards the first stage, it is by no means unintelligible to ourselves that being water, or earth, or air, or wood, or gold, or purple, or angry, or intelligent, or a man, or a dwarf-star, or an electron are all basically a matter of *specific proportions* or *quantitative measures*; this is the creed of modern science, for which we need not here argue. And that even the *values* of action, life and theory have a basis in number and measure is a view that many have found appealing. The *Republic*, the *Timaeus*, the *Philebus* and other writings make plain what Plato understood by the reduction of Forms to Numbers, no matter how little Aristotle was able to make of his doctrine. And the requisite numbers and numerical relations once arrived at, and consolidated as the 'hypotheses' of the sciences, it becomes the task of Dialectic Proper to show how they all 'proceed' from the basic form of Unity or Good.

The main lines of this procession are not in doubt: they involve the imposition of Unity or Limit on a 'recipient' characterized by a hydra-like multiplicity of dimensions and by an indefinite capacity for quantitative excess. Just as the world of instances presupposed a recipient which is in the end no more than a name for the multiple instantiability of the Forms, so the world of Forms presupposes a recipient which is no more than another name for the quantitative specifiability of the Super-Form beyond them. The two recipients are in fact one and the same,[1] as Aristotle engagingly tells us in Metaphysics 988a and as we can see from meditating on the *Philebus*: both are principles of indefinite quantity, variously specified as a many and few, a more and a less, a long and a short, a broad and a narrow, a deep and a shallow, a quick and a slow, a hot and a cold, an acute and a grave, and so on, a principle or principles which, in association with a principle of Unity or Limit, can 'generate' all cases of quantitative pattern, all the 'Forms' that there can be. This second, transcendental recipient principle is, however, as much parasitic upon

---

[1] It is perhaps wrong to identify the two recipients: the one instantiates and the other specifies, and they are analogous rather than the same.

the principle of Unity in the world of Forms as it was in the world of the senses. It is completely mastered and moulded by the latter. It can in fact be held to be no more than a name for the inherent specifiability of absolute unity, its necessary descent into an unending range of distinct quantitative patterns. All these doctrines, so mystifying to those who have never advanced beyond the notion of a set of disjoined, piece-meal universals, largely associated with Socratic virtues, and who have failed to see that Plato's whole endeavour was to *unify* the possibilities of being into one single, systematically ordered picture, assume comprehensibility when Plato's endeavour, with its Pythagorean background, becomes clear. This endeavour obviously lies behind the *Republic* as much as any later, reported teachings. And it may be argued that the second half of Plato's *Parmenides* is nothing but a semi-jocose, literary statement of this endeavour, in which the two transcendentals of Unity and Unbounded Quantity, play an elaborate game with one another, sometimes making interesting nonsense in their apartness, and sometimes joining in fecund union to generate the mathematical dimensions of being, sometimes revealing their categorial character by remaining indifferent to flat denials of their own being, sometimes by making use of such denials to pull the house of reason down. And the dialogue ends in a superb sentence which whatever else it may be is not meant to express a *reductio ad absurdum* but Plato's deepest sense of the meaning of the world: that Unity both lies apart from, and also is necessarily present in all the possible, incompatible variety that there can be in the world.

Plato's deepest intentions plainly also involved the development of a theory of mind which was no mere excrescence on the theory of Forms, but part and parcel of the latter. Even in the *Republic* the same specification of Goodness that generates the universe of Forms generates the possibility of states of mind that take cognizance of them, the two being in fact merely sides of one and the same process, while in the *Sophist* and also in the *Parmenides* and the *Philebus*[1] we have the recognition of a universal mindfulness and livingness, Zeus's kinglike life and mind, which in a sense pervades the whole realm of Forms, and expresses its living unity, its interconnections of relevance, its paradigmatic realization of Active Intelligence as such. This mindfulness and livingness is of course not to be confused with its instantiation in

[1] *Philebus*, 30d.

R

our soul or in any other soul: it is the pattern, the eternal Idea of the latter. But it is *present* in our souls and their activities as other universals are present in their instances, and such presence must, as in other cases, be part and parcel of its being. The intermediate, observer soul of the *Phaedo* must therefore plainly have its own representation in the formal world that it contemplates, and we therefore find in Plato a beginning of the distinction between the noetic and the noeric, between infinitely diversified objectivity and the subjectivity which is correlated with it, which was to be developed by Proclus, and perhaps carried still further by Husserl. In their doctrine of Νοῦς the Neoplatonists merely worked out what was plainly implied by Plato, and those who find their elaborations unnecessary are those who have not understood what Plato was basically intent on: not the construction of a set of isolated conceptual meanings, but of a whole map of the intelligible universe of possibilities seen from the standpoint of a paradigmatic intelligence that can compare and integrate them all. This living thought-map is also plainly conceived to be the source of such wisdom and insight as seeps down into our souls, and it certainly seeped down, in curiously coarsened form, in the Aristotelian doctrine of the Active Intelligence.

I have been very Neoplatonist in my interpretation of Plato and I can therefore be much more brief in my appraisal of the Neoplatonists. Plotinus, I consider, very strangely combined the capacity to work out the plain implications of Plato in endless scholastic detail, with an originality which some would connect with his mysticism, though I myself would connect it with a new line of logic. While I would criticize Plotinus for his scholasticism, which at many points gives undue fixity to the thoughts of Plato, I would admire him for his logical innovations. I shall try to make plain what I mean on both of these heads. As regards the first, it is characteristic of Plotinus that he accepts and canonizes a feature of Platonism in respect of which it is least strong, that he practically turns a difficulty and a weakness into a principle of explanation. This kind of inversion is a device of philosophers at all times, and often leads to an illuminating change of perspective, but in the case of Platonism it embalms and hardens its worst features. In Platonism there is plainly a certain necessity in the procession of 'lower' principles from 'higher' ones: there is a certain generosity in the higher genera, a freedom from 'envy', which ensures their communication to lower orders of half-being. There is, however, a pervasive suggestion that necessity does not amount to need, and there is a faint air of misfortune and discredit, even of guilt, in the descent into instantiation. The happiest and purest of philosophers may have to serve an apprenticeship in the cave, but the best state for them will be one where they are able to contemplate Forms shorn of all perturbing instances. In Plotinus necessity without need becomes a central principle of explanation, and it becomes a theorem that the *less* one requires anything beneath one or dependent on one, the *more* will one spawn such inferior dependents. One becomes like a tropical fish dropping infinite seed into the waters without concern or interest, or like a narcissistic woman coldly inspiring an infinity of unrequited passions, and the like. The conception is as strange as it is unedifying: it explains by non-explanation. It is as if one sought the cause of some great social movement in the fact that no one wanted it and that nothing led up to it.

There is, moreover, on reflection, nothing specially august, nothing σεμνόν, in the removal of instances: being a goat-stag is not of surpassing interest in that nothing fulfils such a description. While what is unexemplified, e.g. perfect circularity, *may* be of surpassing interest in view of the constant approximations to it, its lack of illustration none the less represents a poverty, a defect, and a life spent among uninstantiated universals, or in ignorance of their instantiation, would be as dull as a life spent in conversing in uninterpreted calculi. And what is true of instantiation is likewise true of specification: being numerous is interesting and exciting since such an infinity of specific numbers falls under it, being beautiful is august since it can be carried out with such typical variety, and so on. No one denies that there is an élan, a fascination, in steeping oneself in Number or Beauty as such. But despite the appeal of the Genus, and the dubious cogency of modern rejections of self-predication, it is *in* their instances and *in* their specifications that universals live, and the most profound immersion in an essence as such involves a sidelong awareness of *possible* species or instances.

None the less it is precisely such a shearing of the generic from the specific which Plotinus systematically practises, and what is for many a sign of his admirable remoteness from 'pantheism'. Unity Itself is simply Unity Itself, of which nothing whatever can be properly predicated: we are back in the half-truth of the first hypothesis of the *Parmenides*, regarding which the

Platonic interlocutor remarks that he does not think it can be true. We proceed thereupon to the infinitely rich field of the specifications of Unity Itself, the Forms or cases of Being, of which the Shepherd, to use a Heideggerian phrase, is Intelligence or Mind as such, the omnipresent, eternal possibility of thinking which at all points matches the variety of what can be thought. But this noetic-noeric realm derives its richness, not so much from the Unity lying above it, as from *its own* attempts at a hermeneutic applied to that inscrutable Unity. It is, moreover, a realm given over to 'eternity', which means, despite protests as to its livingness, that all in it is frozen into lifelessness. An unchanging, perfect intellectuality confronts a perfect round of unchanging intelligibles. The lesson has not been learnt that the preciousness of the eternal lies in its revelation through, and in contrast with, the changing. And while Plato showed some disposition to find an interstitial place in his Form-world for the ignoble, the botched and the deviant, Plotinus admits none but Forms of prime lineage, so that his noetic assemblies become rather like the star-studded gatherings of some hostesses, wholly dazzling, quite without contrast and not a little dull. If the descent to what is individual has a reflection yonder, there is nothing that reflects a descent to the ignoble. Beneath this realm we of course have the realm of Soul, where living thought and action occurs, and where there is also a stimulating decline towards the sensory. The realm of Soul is, however, responsible for its own fun, even if its fun may be an attempt to mirror in the servants' hall the frozen aristocratic relationships above. And below Soul lies Nature, creative without caring to create, lost in admiration of a life of thought which in its turn cares nothing for it. I shall go no further. I have deliberately exaggerated the curious unilateralism of Plotinian concepts, so as to bring out their deep perversity. They satisfy certain instincts of self-prostration, but they do so at the cost of systematically affronting our understanding.

At once, however, we come to another side of the Plotinian coin: its profound and living logic. In the system of Plotinus there is literally no work for the ordinary notion of diversity to do. Things are in a sense *other* than one another, but such otherness never excludes a deeper identity. The realm of pure intellection does not merely lie outside of the Supreme Unity: it aspires towards it and is in a sense always in touch with it. And the objects of intellection and the intellect which contemplates them are not mutually exclusive: each is in a sense the total intellectual system, even if with some special emphasis. The logic of systematic interpenetration has never been more sublimely stated than in some of the Plotinian accounts of the intelligible world. And the realm of Soul with its changeful temporality, does not merely lie outside of the realm of intellect, but aspires towards it and enters into it: eternity becomes fully significant through its pervasion of time. In the same way Nature in its blind creativity is in its own fashion practising the contemplation practised yonder by Soul and by Mind. Not only in the realm yonder is 'each all, and all all, and the glory infinite', but 'everything yonder is also here'. There is nothing remote and alien even about the Supreme Unity: He is what we find when we enter most deeply into ourselves. In this magnificent denial of diversity as understood in formal logic—which of course some will not find magnificent at all—Plotinus removes the disadvantages of his system: the scholastic hedges melt away, and the lifelines to the Absolute become open. We have achieved the thought that is characteristic of philosophy as opposed to that of the dianoetic sciences. If we turn from Plotinus to Proclus, the other great διάδοχος of Plato, much the same is true. The scholasticism is at times almost more preposterous in its rigidity, but there is also a great overriding of the firm distinctions drawn. There is a stress on the immense *power* or *might* of the higher hypostases, a might proportional to their approach to simplicity, and on the manner in which this might is outpoured as a sort of providential care over the lower reaches of creation. We are moving into a region where Aquinas will afterwards construct his theology, where the infinite variety of mind and body will exist 'as if conflated' (to quote Dante) in the simplicity of God.

All that we have said does not, however, affect the fact that there is something unsatisfactory about this whole Neoplatonic restatement of Plato: there is an imperfect fusion between its structure of unilateral dependence and the deep identity which pervades all its hierarchically ordered members. It has no real, no understandable procession comparable to the moment of return which is so emphatic in it. To continue the Platonic succession further one must move over the centuries to early nineteenth-century Germany where Hegel, newly emancipated from the subjectivism of Kant and Fichte and from the darkly neutralistic

Spinozism of Schelling, suddenly took up the Greek thread and became Plato's greatest διάδοχος. Greek thought had, we may say, a renaissance on that remote German soil, in the Walpurgis midnight of German romanticism, much as Greek aesthetic sensibility had reflowered in the *Iphigeneia* of Goethe and the poems of Hölderlin. Hegel's following of Plato is evinced in his choice of the *Begriff*, the Notion, as his categorial Absolute, of which the Idea is the mature phase: the former being a principle of Universality which also declares itself in Specificity and Individuality, while the latter further embodies the Livingness and the Mindedness in which Universality declares itself supremely. In this new Germanic Platonism the defects of the old Platonism and Neoplatonism were cunningly removed: the Kantian interest in the empirical, and the Fichtean interest in the concretely moral, and the Schellingian interest in the natural, had all made their precious contribution. Individualization, instantiability is a 'moment' of the *Begriff* to be set beside its Universality and its Specifiability as something organically part of it and without which it would not make sense. And the *Begriff* has, further, all the causative, dynamic quality which Plato only half-heartedly attributed to his Forms: objects in the world develop and behave according to the *Begriffe* which are instantiated in them. In the Idea, further, the mature form of the *Begriff*, all the patterning of conscious experience which had been excogitated by Kant, Fichte and Schelling, becomes part and parcel of the *Begriff*. The *Begriff* essentially divides into a subjective and an objective phase: it involves, on the one hand, interior subjectivity, ready to impose universals on, or to extract them from, a pre-existent objective order, and, on the other hand, an objectivity, ready to have such universals imposed upon it, or extracted from it. And what emerges is the necessary accommodation of the one to the other: the Idea is not merely Intellection as such, or Intelligible Objectivity as such, but Intellection finding itself in Intelligible Objectivity, the Idea of a thinkingness which both involves and overcomes objective otherness. What Plotinus had worked out in his account of the intelligible world, and what went back to Plato's account for the Form of Good as a source both of knowable universals and of their knowability to minds, thus receive a final working out, and not, be it noted, as some external reflection upon it, but as something demanded by and developed out of its structure.

We may further see in the Hegelian *Entaüsserung* or self-alienation of the Idea in Nature and finite Spirit, a mature form of the Neoplatonic emanation, and of the Platonic metaphors from which this was derived. The Absolute Idea releases its moment of *Besonderheit* or Specificity, which is also its moment of intuitive sensuousness, in the spatio-temporal order of Nature, much as the Demiurge, the Ideas conceived as agency, is responsible for projecting images of the Forms into the impassive medium of Space. The *Entaüsserung* of Hegel has, however, this great superiority over the emanation of Plato and Plotinus, that it is *needed* as well as necessary: without a descent into instantiation, an embodiment in actual instances, whether natural or spiritual, the Idea would die from very need, like the God of Angelus Silesius. Hegel sees that it is only by being exemplified in specific and individual forms that the Idea can be the unifying peak and centre of the whole system, and that it can return to itself, not in empty ecstasy, but in the positively mystical experiences of artistic creation, religious worship and philosophical illumination. The two systems have the same teleological structure, but in Hegel the teleology works both ways: not only does Nature aim at Soul, and Soul at Intellect, and Intellect at the supra-intellectual Unity, but the Hegelian Idea fulfils itself in the total logical system of concepts and categories, and the latter fulfils itself in the conscious experiences of spiritual beings, and these last require the natural, corporeal order in which they can embody themselves and out of which they can gradually develop their interior life. And not only does Hegelianism incorporate the Other in the most intimate being of the Idea, as Plato also does in his conception of the Great and Small, the indefinite materiality which is part of the being of the Forms, but it also incorporates the whole hierarchical arrangement and *movement* of the system in its supreme Category. The Hegelian Idea gathers up in itself the whole ideal dialectic of the logical categories, and the whole real dialectic of Nature and History: in all that issues from it we have only itself.

We suggest accordingly that it is in Hegelianism that Platonism finds its highest fulfilment: in an Idea developed into an ideal world of specific conceptions, arranged in an order, not merely of generality, but of inclusiveness and surmounting of opposition, and terminating in the idea of a subjectivity which truly meets itself in and through a matching objectivity, such an Idea being, moreover, inseparable from an actual carrying out in the ordered array of natural forms and the living, developing, historical consciousness of men. I do not, however, wish to suggest that the fulfilment is all on one side, and that the Germanic Platonism absorbed and resumed all that had been excogitated at Athens and Alexandria and in the Roman Campagna. For the Germanic Platonism suffers from a deep fault which the passing years have made all too evident: it is too entirely this-worldly, too tied down to place and to period, too deeply reliant on actual arrangements in which we can no longer trust. It rightly sees in Nature and History the eternal strategy of the Idea, but it is misguided in thinking that the whole of this strategy can be dug out here, and that, moreover, in the trivial span of centuries that we call 'world-history'. We live, moreover, in a period full of menace, not merely of the relatively supportable menace of the destruction of Spirit by Nature, but of the intolerable menace of the destruction of Spirit by Spirit, which accords ill with the optimistic teleology projected both by the Platonic Form of the Good and the Hegelian Idea. It is not a question of interstitial evil, parasitic upon goodness, and bound to wither away through its own inner contradictoriness, but of evil so mighty that it seems likely to destroy all in destroying itself. It is here, I think, that we should take seriously, and not as a mere myth, the otherworldly prospects offered us by Platonism and Neoplatonism, the prospect of a spectrum of states leading from sensuousness and corporeality and this-world immersion to an increasing attenuation of these things, until we end in the pure enjoyment of the total gist and sense of the world, and of the supreme Unity in which that gist culminates. Even if the noetic order is as much dependent on instantial existence as the latter is dependent on it, it may still represent a genuine and specific type of experience and being, characterized by interpenetration rather than diremption, which mystics experience from time to time without always fully understanding its peculiar logic, but which we hope to experience more perfectly when we lose our present bodies. What I shall now do is to talk a little of what I shall call the 'cortical predicament', a predicament which I regard as the source of most that is most darkly miserable, but also of much that is most radiantly glorious in the human condition.

The Orphics who inspired the Pythagoreans who inspired Plato saw the source of man's problems in the body: σῶμα σῆμα— the body is a tomb. I do not myself believe that there is anything wrong about having a body; I should be very sorry not to have one. A body enables one to express oneself palpably, to be there for one's friends, to illustrate meanings in a manner in default of which they would not be meanings at all. Our misfortune is not in having a body, but in having the sort of body we do have, incorporation in which is the very essence of cave-life, of existence 'down here'. For the bodies we have are not tenanted solely by ourselves: they are dense with a population of other tenants and a noisy and scrofulous batch of tenantry at that. Sometimes it is really remarkable that we can hear ourselves speak. There are the innumerable cells and organs, doing their work consciously or unconsciously, but certainly not by any grace of *our* direction, and there are the lower-grade atoms and molecules, no doubt grumbling at being subordinated by organic order at all, and having their grim revenge in the final triumph of death. I my-self—for I am a hylozoist and an animist—believe that all these beings have their own life and consciousness. I believe, further, that this conscious life is in some ways superior to our own. They are less cut off from environing objects which have not the distanced character for them that they have for us: they are less cut off from one another. Solipsism and scepticism about matter are not possible at their level, since the diremptions that make these kinds of theory possible do not exist there. And I believe that they enjoy undoctored sensations in a manner that some philosophers have thought that we ought to or once did: the sensational life of the retina, for instance, must be positively famous. We, how-ever, like a lot of fainéant aristocrats fallen on evil times, live in a true ivory garret in the grey matter beneath the skull-bones. Here ready-made views of things are handed up to us, with inter-pretative slants put upon them by our minions and not at all by ourselves. Our minions likewise manage to filter that living past that we always carry about with us, and decide what we shall, in our ivory garret, be able or unable to bring to mind. In some inscrutable fashion, the revival and use of our past has become bound up with certain cortical excitations, much as a lecturer's power to give a lecture may be bound up with certain often silly, ill-set-down notes. These minions have the power, after a fashion, to separate us from ourselves, and in old age effectively do just this. Who has not witnessed the pathos of some elderly friend or parent groping for words and meanings, which the decay of a cerebral transcript has rendered inaccessible? Worst of all, these grey minions, who as intelligences grasp little, and as grey cells grasp nothing whatever, have managed to corrupt philosophers into believing that it is *they* who do all our referring and inferring and understanding and abstracting and remembering and deciding and loving and hating and so on, and that our categories and norms are built into *their* structure. Whereas all these beliefs are not merely false, but categorially absurd: if the grey cells are considered merely as grey cells, no one can attach even the slightest sense to such beliefs, and they merely create an asylum of ignorance and pseudo-explanation worse than any believed in the heyday of the soul. To be crucified in the cortex is, among other things, to be subject to all the problems of philosophy, for cortical life means precisely that we can never fully document or authenticate or explicate all that we know and remember and understand. If the cortex thus makes philosophy and all the other great rational enterprises possible, it remains arguable that the perfection of these enterprises will lead us beyond the cortex. We shall then have bodies, as long as we want them, but they will be our own bodies, pejoratively called shades, that will express our every whim and stirring, we shall have a concentrated, gistful grasp of things remote and complex that will not need to be spelled out in laborious inferences or explorations, and we shall be able to share one another's feelings at will in a manner which will make solipsism a laughable superstition. All this has been described in some of the most unforgettably gorgeous passages in Plotinus, and it is all much too good not to be true. And it makes it possible to believe in an ultimate, overall coincidence of Goodness and Being, and so lends credibility to the Platonic-Hegelian metaphysic that we have been considering. That this is the best metaphysic may be a matter of inherent logic, but will none the less be best seen in connection with the facts, and the totality of facts, that it orders, and many of these facts will not be accessible till the cortex and its deceits have been laid aside. If anyone wishes to pursue these topics further, I shall refer him to the sixth chapter of my *Transcendence of the Cave* which deals with 'Otherworldly Geography'. This chapter contains the whole message of my Gifford Lectures on Cave-life, but it is inconspicuously placed in an obscure part of the volume, as I feared that it would otherwise prove a grave source of intellectual scandal. It has in fact been misunderstood, and I wish here to say that it is based neither on speculation nor clairvoyance, but purely on philosophical argument. If you are interested in that argument, I must refer you to the peccant chapter.

I wish, in conclusion, to say something about the religious value of the metaphysic I have been elaborating, a question important for me since I regard religion as the most embracing of the rational enterprises, one that engages the heart and the will as well as the mind. I give it as the verdict of my feeling that only a Form, something basically universal, though uttering itself in the individual and the specific, can be truly adorable, can in any way deserve the name of 'God'. One cannot rationally worship this or that excellent thing or person, however eminent and august: only Goodness Itself, Beauty Itself, Truth Itself, and so on are rationally venerable, and to bow one's knee to an instance is to commit idolatry. And whatever philosophers may say of the fallacy of self-predication, it remains plain that τὸ αὐτοεκαστόν, or each thing itself, is what it is more ultimately and absolutely than the instances which exemplify it: it is in fact the inexhaustible source from which instantiations flow and of which they necessarily fall short. And the various prime αὐτοεκαστά all cohere together and form a single rounded ideal as is not possible in their instances. All this is something which the Jews, with their fine sense of idolatry but imperfect theology, only dimly perceived, but which was always perfectly plain to Plato, who may therefore be hailed as the father of all rational theology. And we may be glad that the deceit of a Syrian monk enabled this wisdom to fertilize the West, which could take from a bogus Areopagite what it would never have taken from Proclus. Of the deceit of this monk one may say: *O felix culpa quae tantam ac talem nobis tradidit theologiam.* It was this Platonic theology which is responsible for the note of deep rational liberalism that one repeatedly encounters in Aquinas. And perhaps it even influenced John XXIII, when he said that the Russians, however much they might deny God, could never free themselves from the values and the influence which were from God, i.e. were God Himself. Without this Platonic infusion we should all be foundering in the semi-darkness of such as Kierkegaard. It will be plain that I am a prejudiced person, and that I do not admire many things that many others admire. But I remain spiritually in orbit about quite a number of very different luminaries, even if my central sun remains Platonic.

INDEX